Revisioning Aging

ERUPTIONS
New Thinking across the Disciplines

Erica McWilliam
General Editor

Vol. 4

PETER LANG
New York • Washington, D.C./Baltimore • Boston • Bern
Frankfurt am Main • Berlin • Brussels • Vienna • Canterbury

Revisioning Aging

Empowerment
of Older Women

Edited by
Jenny Onyx, Rosemary Leonard,
and Rosslyn Reed

PETER LANG
New York • Washington, D.C./Baltimore • Boston • Bern
Frankfurt am Main • Berlin • Brussels • Vienna • Canterbury

Library of Congress Cataloging-in-Publication Data

Revisioning aging: empowerment of older women / edited by
Jenny Onyx, Rosemary Leonard, and Rosslyn Reed.
p. cm. — (Eruptions; v. 4)
Includes bibliographical references and index.
1. Aged women. 2. Middle aged women. 3. Aging—Social aspects.
4. Feminist theory. I. Onyx, Jenny. II. Leonard, Rosemary.
III. Reed, Rosslyn. IV. Series: Eruptions; vol. 4.
HQ1061.R455   305.26—dc21   98-26794
ISBN 0-8204-4131-7
ISSN 1091-8590

Die Deutsche Bibliothek-CIP-Einheitsaufnahme

Revisioning aging: empowerment of older women / ed. by Jenny Onyx…
–New York; Washington, D.C./Baltimore; Boston; Bern;
Frankfurt am Main; Berlin; Brussels;Vienna; Canterbury; Lang.
(Eruptions; Vol. 4)
ISBN 0-8204-4131-7

Cover design by Nona Reuter

The paper in this book meets the guidelines for permanence and durability
of the Committee on Production Guidelines for Book Longevity
of the Council of Library Resources.

© 1999 Peter Lang Publishing, Inc., New York

Printed in the United States of America

Dedication

This book is dedicated to the memory of Chris Wieneke and Pam Benton, our friends and colleagues who were part of our Women and Aging Research Network and integral to the creation of this book. They were neither very old nor very young but died before the task of this book was complete.

Acknowledgments

We acknowledge the contributions of our respective institutions in providing resources to complete this book, in particular the University of Western Sydney, the University of Technology, Sydney and the Older Women's Network.

Our thanks go to Helen Leonard for her inspiring photographs of older women.

We also wish to acknowledge Glenda Browne from the Australian Society of Indexers for the creation of the index. and Womanspeak for allowing us to republish Noeleen O'Beirne's poem *Ode to the Older Woman*.

We thank Beverley McNicoll, Janice Allbutt, and Lyn L'Estrange, the staff who helped with the painstaking work of compiling the book, collating the bibliography, and preparing the camera-ready copy.

Most of all we would like to thank the hundreds of women who gave their time to our various studies and whose voices are reflected in this book.

Contents

Section Three: Revisioning Aging

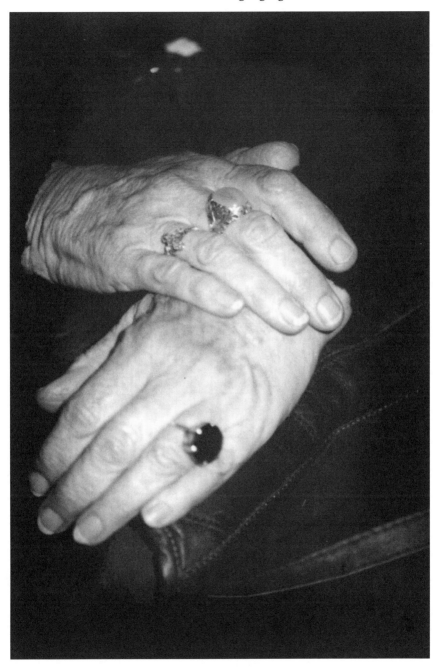

HANDS by Helen Leonard

SECTION ONE

Contextualizing Aging

Prologue

We are older women. Some of us are old by society's standards, some of us are not yet as old as that. But we have all experienced what it means to be considered "too old". Too old for what? Too old to be in a beauty contest? Too old to attract a young male lover? Too old to bear children? Too old to do a competent job?

Too old to be silenced by the fear of speaking out!

We are also academic women. All of us are teaching and learning in universities. We know how to play the "academic game" of learned discourse. We *are* experts in our fields, we know the literature, we are all engaged in empirical research, we know the rules of detached reasoning. We bring to this book our skills and knowledge as academics. We speak about older women. But, unlike other texts, we position ourselves with older women; we speak about ourselves, as older women and as we engage with older women. We speak with anger and passion about the agism and sexism that come together in our society to oppress. We speak about the loss of dignity and quality of life that result. It does not have to be that way. We have an alternative vision of what is possible, the contribution that older women do make and could make; of what women can make for themselves. To that end, we end this book with a celebration of older women.

In this book, we speak as and for the universalized older women of much of the literature—what is assumed to be the common experience of much of the population of those older women living in English speaking Organisation of Economic Cooperation and Development (OECD) countries. We argue that the experience of growing older in a modern postindustrial society has similar dimensions for those living in the U.K. or in Canada, in the U.S., or in Australia. We share similar living standards and lifestyles, similar histories and oppressions. The feminist movement of the 1970s has strongly influenced our shared perceptions of life, and a shared commitment to social change. We, as social scientists, draw heavily on each other's literature of theory and research. Certainly in this book we locate our own empirical and theoretical work within the larger body of international literature and find more parallels than discrepancies.

At another level, however, we speak much more specifically, as older, white, relatively privileged women living in urban Australia. We recognize that our experience is vastly different from that of older women in non OECD countries, or even of our Australian Aboriginal sisters. We cannot pretend to deal adequately with the issues and exclusions these other women face. Yet even here there are commonalities. For example, in common with women in many south east Asian countries, we share a recent history of colonial domination and the emergence of nationhood that has helped shape our sense of citizenship (we also recognize that we and others continue to be colonized by transnational corporations). We are beginning to form regional and international ties with older women of other cultures and conditions. These emerging networks sharpen our awareness of difference, but also our awareness of the conditions of oppression that we all face.

Nonetheless, we cannot speak about them, because to do so ascribes them the status of "other" and lays claim to a superior knowledge. Most labels carry connotations, not only of difference but of inferiority. The "other" is subtly made responsible for their condition (they are mad, bad, or stupid) or else rendered as objects of pity, and ultimately, of contempt. All disadvantaged groups are thus further marginalized. We know that to be true of terms used to identify older women: terms like hag and witch and old crone, but even the more subtle labels like "seniors," "the aged," and "the elderly." We talk of people in "third world" or "undeveloped countries," or "developing countries." It is hard to avoid the patronizing overtones embedded in these terms. We speak of "migrants" and "the disabled." The labels used vary from country to country, within the English speaking world. Even in our attempts to identify value neutral terms, we find ourselves nonetheless reconstituting "the other" as lesser. Better then to limit our analysis to ourselves. We are "older women"; we would like to reclaim the title of "crone" as women of age, power, and wisdom (Walker 1985). Like others, we sometimes have one or more disabilities, but reject that our disabilities define who we are. Some of us may be immigrants; we are all daughters or descendants of those who once migrated.

We speak of empowerment. We think it important to reclaim that concept for ourselves to reflect what it originally intended: the reclaiming of power for ourselves. The concept, like so many others has been co-opted to serve the political interests of others. Government programs often claim to empower, but always, and only, within the constraints of their own control. Empowerment from this perspective presupposes an agent of empowerment and a notion of power as property, that is, some person or group who has this property gives some of it away to others. But to the extent that the agents keep some of it, then they maintain a position of superiority and a position as a potential oppressor, or at least they have power over the other's dependency (Gore 1993). We reject such a concept. But we *do* claim our own power, that which we have always had and that which others would usurp. We empower ourselves through our writing, our resistance, and our capacity to organize.

One of the things that we realized in writing this book was that being old and enjoying the opportunities that aging offers entails a recognition of death. We cannot speak about living without speaking about death. Death is, of course, the final silence. But the closer it comes, the more vital the awareness of living. The colors of life are all the more vibrant when set against the backdrop of darkness. The urgency of speaking out becomes more imperative when faced with the impending silence. We learned that when one of our number died suddenly and unexpectedly while we were writing this book. Death is always unexpected, even when we expect it. Chris was not yet old. She was not yet 50. She died before she could finish speaking out. We remember her and her wisdom and courage. She is very much a part of the writing of this book. So is Pam, who battled with cancer through much of the writing of this book, and who died before it came to fruition. We dedicate the book to them.

The Process of Writing

We write as feminists. We do not necessarily identify ourselves as second wave feminists; we suspect that every age has spawned its own cohort of women of power and vision. But certainly we who have been influenced by the women's movement of the late twentieth century, in particular, are forming a critical mass as we now come of age.

As older feminists we intend two things. First we intend to re examine the world of older women as seen from our position of women growing older. We are engaged in the process of challenging and reconstructing reality so that it better reflects our experience, our interests, and our values. Second we intend to adopt methodologies that are consistent with our intent. We do not adopt a positivist approach. As Margaret elaborates in chapter three, we adopt a social constructivist feminist epistemology, one located between modernism and postmodernism. In tune with a political economy perspective, we agree that we are dealing with some entrenched social structures of power and oppression. But, following Foucault's lead, we seek to identify the discourses that support those structures, to locate the cracks or fissures in the web of power relations, and working within those gaps, to weave a pattern of resistance to the hegemonic practices.

Most chapters are written by an individual, or in some cases by two. Each of us is drawing on our own discipline, our own preferred methodology, our own style of expression. These vary with our diversity. However, we agreed to rules.

1. While we draw heavily on our empirical research, this is not a collection of research papers. We wish to speak much more broadly than a narrowly conceived empirical study could allow. We therefore each locate our own empirical work within the larger context of the literature and our lived experience. Methodological details are left to other reports and published accounts.

2. The language is, we hope, accessible to a broad range of interested people, and particularly to informed older women. We specifically avoid the language of social gerontology.

3. We work as a network and not as a collective. Nonetheless, much of the process bears the hallmarks of the best of collectivity. We address each other's writing in dialogue. We reference each other within the book by given name because that is how we have worked (in referencing previously published work we maintain the convention of referencing by surname only). We have, over the months and years, provided various forms of personal and intellectual support to each other. We have critiqued each other's work. Decisions about the content and structure of the book unfolded as we proceeded and were made by all of us together. Several of us, and Pam in particular, have taken on the role of copyeditor.

4. The approach is self-reflexive. We locate ourselves within the text. Our experiences as, and with, older women, inform our analysis. Our feelings and lived experience are central to our intellectual analysis, and we are aware that we break some of the rules of conventional academic, malestream discourse. Nonetheless, the oppression we expose will not be changed until older women demand it. We try to ensure throughout the book that the dominant voice is the voice of older women. The goal of voice is political, being the empowerment of older women.

The Structure of the Book

The book is organized into three sections. Section one puts aging into context. Section two deconstructs aging, and section three provides a new vision of aging.

Section one provides the context. Here we explore the prevailing discourses of and about older women. Noeleen examines some of the cultural images and expectations, their contradictions, and their impact on the experience of being an older woman. Jenny sets out the demographic and social indicator "facts," the population projections, the employment and retirement history of women, and the statistical summary of morbidity rates and accommodation options. It already becomes clear that the existing "facts" are invariably portrayed to emphasize "the burden of the aged," to emphasize dependency and not independence, illness and not wellness, economic burden and not contribution. The "facts" disguise and do not illuminate the potential for a fulfilling old age. Margaret examines in greater detail the way in which the cultural images and social expectations and the perceptions of burden and dependency have created, and in turn, been created by gerontological discourses and practices. We reject the medicalization of aging and the effects of professional control of our lives.

Section two offers a more detailed critique of three functional areas of our lives: work, health, and housing. They cannot really remain separate considerations because each affects the others, all are a part of our whole lives. But for analytic purposes we focus on each in turn. We see at once that women work all their lives, and this does not artificially stop at retirement. Rosslyn explores how our life course is marked by discontinuous paid employment, and casual, intermittent careers. Rosemary highlights the fact that much of our work before and after "retirement" is the unpaid work of caring and of voluntary work in the community. But, as Jenny and Pam argue, because so little work is paid, we often face old age with few financial resources. Nonetheless, we struggle to maintain health and independence, where possible continuing an independent life in the community. We, are for the most part, healthy, despite the various handicaps of age. However, as Noeleen argues, our aging bodies become useful targets of a mammoth medical industry; we are placed under increasingly intrusive medical surveillance that may render us passive and dependent before the need. Ultimately, as both Sharyn and Rhonda argue, we may become the victim of the "benevolent oppression" of the nursing home. Still, we are blamed for creating the financial burden of care. The alternative may be a life of independence but isolation. As Chris, Aileen, Lyn, and Diane point out, living independently in the community is preferable, but requires connections and support.

Section three introduces a change of pace. We are not victims, but survivors. More and more of us can expect an enriched, even exciting old age, as we shed the old limiting social demands and discover our freedom. Most of us are healthy for most of the time, at least until the final encounter with death. Most of us can enjoy good social connections and find a thousand ways to empower ourselves and contribute to society. We are beginning to work together, informally and through formal organizations of our making, to find solutions to our problems. Margaret explores ways of living together for mutual support, sharing resources, and maintaining independence. Rosemary explores ways of forming effective political lobbies and gradually influencing social attitudes with our own public education programs. Above all we are rediscovering a sense of fun, of adventure in aging. We conclude the book with a celebration of aging.

Chapter One

Growing Older, Getting Better: Than What?
Noeleen O'Beirne

You can't sit around all day playing tiddly-winks with your valium and trying to remember the bonk you had on VE day (Diana Trent, Waiting for God, BBC TV).

This chapter will present a series of cameos that depict what it is to be an older woman in contemporary society. It aims to highlight the tension that exists between the older woman's perspective on aging that was gained through her lived experiences and the dominant images of the older woman. Arber and Ginn state that

Stereotypical images do not accurately describe social reality, but are in tension with it, reflecting the values, beliefs, and power relations of a particular society. Stereotypes therefore function as propaganda creating and reinforcing negative attitudes towards a group. More than this, the ideological message of the stereotype tends to be learned [internalized] by the oppressed group, contributing to the social control of its members (1991:35).

Representations will reflect views of, and from, older women, with the intention of bypassing many of the currently held stereotypes of older women. The diversity of older women is such that to present an encyclopaedic description of her is beyond the scope of this chapter. It is hoped, however, to stimulate the reader's critical faculty with a soupcon rather than a flood of images and a recognition of difference and the influence it has on older women.

To further the question, I have started with a quotation from a character in a TV show, Diana Trent, a crusty old virago living in a retirement home, who while she is presented as "a bit of a character," conforms through her stubbornness and irascibility to the image of the "bad" old lady. It is a quotation that encapsulates in a humorous way some of the more stereotypical expectations of older women as being drug dependent and asexual. Diana eschews this role and erupts on the screen through her forceful personality as a liberated, sexual, independent, and mentally active older woman vitally engaged in the process of living.

Contextualizing Aging

An increased lifespan in the late twentieth century has led to the problematizing of the aged amongst health professionals, social welfare workers, economists, and the media. On the economic front, the aged are seen as a burden on a population where the social welfare bill is burgeoning. They are marginalized together with the single mother and the unemployed. Culturally, age is depicted as a dreaded and undesirable state. This is due to a number of factors— a youth oriented culture a society that is given over to the "administration of life" and so pathologizes age as a time of physical decline and ultimately death, the gender factor, and the perceived burden of an aging population, with its increased use of the monies allocated to health and social welfare. It is for this reason, according to Arber (1995), that aging research is mainly quantitative with policy for, and adjustment to, the aging process as the objective.

Tensions arise between the vision of aging projected by the health, media, and economic lobbies and that of the government instrumentalities charged with the administration of aged services. These services actively promote a positive view of aging. It would appear that attitudes toward aging in Western society are indicative of an era of culturally induced "schizophrenia"— denial and dread on the one hand and positive aging on the other.

One example of the existing tensions is the designation of aging as a deficiency disease that is characterized by a gradual enfeeblement of mind and body. Although this vision of the older person appears firmly embedded amongst health professionals, other government instrumentalities are bombarding the broader community with positive messages of aging that are designed to offset the negative stereotypes. Slogans such as "Age Adds Value", "Growing Older Getting Better", "Positive Aging", "It Gets Better", and "Older and Bolder" are meant to project age as a time of fullfilment. The older person is entitled to be confused, with very good reason, for we are aged in a society where the norm is considered to be young; retired in a society where identity is heavily invested in occupation; where quality of lifestyle is equated with the ability to consume; and where negative terms like "has been," "over the hill," "past it", "down hill", are commonly used when referring to older people.

Adding to this confusion is the exercise of community consultation and participation by older people when decisions are made that affect them. It is difficult to determine whether this is just a cynical exercise but when the needs of the client, who has run the labelling gauntlet from "case" to "customer," are weighed against the needs of the bureaucrat and the instrumentality that she or he represents, the decision as to whose needs are to be met is a political one. However, this is not to say that the opinions expressed by the customer/client representatives do not have a leavening effect on policy. Many older people, however, comment that while their opinions are canvassed, it is often mere tokenism (for a cited case of tokenism in community consultation see Onyx, Bradfield and Benton, 1992).

Bengston suggests that the function of discourse surrounding the concept of "normal aging" inducts "vulnerable older people into a role of social and intellectual incompetence" and that

> once begun, this loop initiates a cycle of self-fulfilling prophecies that is buttressed by mythologies and stereo-types surrounding socially held views of "normal aging" (Cited in Friedan,1994: 65).

The Aging Agenda—A Societal View

How are older women positioned in today's society? Older women today are characterized by a greater heterogeneity than has ever existed. They come from different cultural backgrounds; may have had the personal and financial independence of careers; may have a home and family with their lives centered around husband and family; or may never have entered the workforce, been married, or had children. Some may have been politically active, financially independent, or born overseas. There are older women who have always been single, who are childless, who are wealthy or pensioners, or have different sexual orientations. The heterogeneity engendered by older women's lived experience is ignored by policymakers and service-providers. When she is depicted, the older woman is white, middle-class, and hetero-sexual. The investment in ignoring the plurality of these women is cultural, political, and economic. Their invisibility, on the one hand, leads to marginalization and normalization, while on the positive side it has allowed them temporarily to escape surveillance and legislation.

Against this generalized background of alterity of the aged is the otherness of aged women, who are longer-lived, experience a greater morbidity, are poorer, less mobile, and more likely to be isolated and alone than their male counterparts. In the ninety-plus years of the twentieth century, women's life expectancy has increased from an average fifty-two years to eighty-one years (ABS,1994:13). Women make up two thirds of those aged seventy-five and over.

Although it is we who are experiencing the aging process, older women's experiences have been invalidated and our opinions have been devalued. It is the professionals in the field who are the designated experts (Anike and Ariel 1987; Greer 1991; Davis, Cole, and Rothblum 1993; Friedan1994), and it is an expertise that is gender blind with most research until recently being concentrated on older men and generalized to older women. Anike and Ariel state

> that "we are unable to find studies and writings which deal fully with the social realities and experience of older women" (1987:8).

It is only recently that older women have been given a voice but again it is a well-regulated voice, an organizational voice, heard through the ventriloquism of the peak bodies that "represent" them. It is a class-modulated voice often expressing the needs and aspirations of an articulate middle-class. It acts as a sounding board for policymakers and provides a feedback loop before the introduction of new policies. To illustrate my point, homeless bag-ladies do not attend policy consultation and community forums, but neither do isolated, housebound, non organizational older women who are rarely accessed and are certainly not canvassed for their opinions. The point I wish to make is, that even when given a voice, the overwhelming majority of older women still remain dis-enfranchised.

Theory has already indicated the series of exclusions that are necessary if one is to present a unified identity for the older woman. Although I will persist with these exclusions based on race, class, and sexual orientation, it is because I do not wish to participate in that which I am criticizing, the colonization, or the patronage of these groups, by assuming that I know what their experience of aging is and that I have the right to define or describe this experience for them. In those countries which have had significant numbers of immigrants, the issues of older migrant women need specific attention. Older migrant women are often less socially integrated than male counterparts due often to poor language skills, loss of secondary language proficiency, or the opportunity to even learn the language. The paucity of information on older women of varied ethnic backgrounds needs to be addressed because they will become an ever-increasing proportion of the population.

The issues of indigenous women also need separate attention. In Australia, Aboriginal women have a low life-expectancy due to living conditions which often replicate those of the poorest countries. Older Aboriginal women who have often been relocated and separated both from their families and children, experience alienation from the land because of no sense of belonging, and a state of exile exacerbated by poor health and housing due to low socioeconomic standards.

Some of the following cameos will be indicative of the diversity of older women while others, in contrast, will provide illustrations that adhere to popular assumptions regarding older women. In reflection, the reader may find some answers to what is invested in negative portrayals of older women or, on the other hand, merely further questions. At times theory and experience will be intertwined as it is my belief that they are inseparable.

The Bag Lady

Returning each afternoon from an international conference on research into aging, I saw an elderly "bag lady" sitting outside a service station, all of her worldly possessions contained in a shopping trolley. The incongruity of the situation was striking. I was returning from the five star venue that housed the conference. I questioned how relevant the conference was to this older woman? Were her needs being addressed or even considered? Were they even considered worthy to be considered? Comforting as the liberal-humanist thought was that she had the right to make choices and this was her chosen lifestyle, or that her position should not be judged in the light of middle-class views, it struck me that these considerations presumed that, as a homeless person, she was impervious to the privations of Melbourne's often inclement weather. Also overlooked was the possibility that the choice may not have been hers, but a bureaucratic one of deinstitutionalization. Without an address and proof of identity, how would she open a bank account, register with Social Security, or collect a pension?

On a More Positive Note—Older Women with Attitude

I was present at a meeting of older women where a heated discussion arose. This discussion illustrated the socially constructed identity of older women in two instances. The first instance was a discussion of the assumption that older women were particularly vulnerable to psychiatric illness due to low income, mourning, and social isolation. In the discussion, a positive acknowledgment was made of older women's skills, abilities and wisdom in coping. Although it was not denied that social causes were often at the root of psychiatric disorders, it was acknowledged that these factors affected all age groups, many of whom, particularly the young, were more vulnerable than older women, as shown in the high rate of youth suicide. Indeed there were indications that older women, with their life experience, were less likely to fall prey to psychiatric illness and had better coping skills. Another point raised was whether stress could be termed a psychiatric illness. Rather it was deemed that stress and the resulting depression were normal reactions to negative social factors that affected quality of lifestyle. The apparent acceptance of the cultural stereotype of older women as prone to mental deterioration was also of concern.

The second issue was even more hotly contested. It was the portrayal of older women in a popular, politically correct soap opera, *G.P.*, which had a well-deserved reputation for dealing with controversial issues in a socially responsible and sensitive manner. This fact lent more weight to the negative portrayal of older women in a particular episode. They were depicted as helpless and dependent. The one positive portrayal of an older woman as strong, independent, and in control of her life was negated by the murder of that particular character. That the scriptwriters, producers, and director of that episode were well-intentioned and wished to convey a socially responsible message (the vulnerability of older women) was accepted, but good intentions did not satisfy these women. None of the women present accepted or identified with the TV portrayal of older women and were proactive in their resolve to inform the broadcaster of their concerns.

We have, in these instances, examples of well-intentioned but misinformed views that provide a feedback loop via the media for the legitimizing of cultural stereotypes. These views were based on medical and psychological models of the older woman. Older women were being cast as powerless. The media message was reinforced, as has been remarked, in that the older woman who was independent and in control of her life was murdered. Not only was this a message of powerlessness and vulnerability but inadvertently, one of control. It provides a definition of the identity that is "safe" for the older woman; a sanction and a warning for those who step outside the boundary to challenge the stereotype.

Society attempts to impose a static and unified identity on older women. Those who depart from it are considered exceptional or eccentric. There is a type of social determinism that envelopes older women in a blanket identity. What informs this construction? Is it that the older woman subverts historical representations of woman? Here, in the person of the older woman, is a living deconstruction of the feminine body as dictated by the regimes of beauty and sexuality. Here is a site of resistance to the control of the female body. If a woman is deemed of value by her usefulness to man as reproductive, productive, or desirable, the cultural portrayal of the older woman signals her devaluation as no longer representative of the feminine. The object of desire has metamorphosed into the object of disdain. The older woman's body demonstrates that femininity is fleeting, that it evaporates with time, and that adherence to beauty regimes and reconstructive or cosmetic surgery will not halt the inexorable passage of time. The social construction of the feminine body has its nemesis in the body of the older woman.

The person of the older woman is not the acceptable face of womanhood, hence her invisibility. Authority "hides dimensions of human reality that disorient and disturb" (Jones 1994:122) so she is excluded from occupations where she is in view of the general public—such as model, TV hostess, TV presenter, receptionist. The older woman is an anomaly in a youth-obsessed society.

The Print Media

Flipping through the pages of *Playboy*, it is impossible to find an older woman featured as Playgirl of the month or indeed featured anywhere in the magazine. With the exception of high profile older women, advertisements use younger women, not only in the general run of women's magazines but also including those purportedly aimed at the older woman. The attitude of sponsors is cited as a rationale for this.

Children's literature plays a significant role in the creation and reinforcement of stereotypes of older women. Think of older women in children's literature and the dominant image is that of the wicked witch—an old woman who lives on her own, with supernatural powers to trap children—for example, the old woman in *Hansel and Gretel* who is depicted as a cannibal who feeds on children. Stories such as these inculcate fear of old women in children, especially of those older women who live alone. However, even more modern stories influence children's beliefs about older people. In an analysis of two books on grandmothers, Gibson (1995) noted the judgmental comments about older women who departed from models of behavior deemed appropriate for their age. Gibson demonstrates the molding of children's attitudes toward older women in the stories. The acceptable line for grandmothers is demonstrated in one story, *Kevin's Grandma*, by comparing and contrasting two grandmothers. The first passage denotes acceptable grandmotherly behavior:

> My grandmother belongs to a bridge club and a garden club and a music club. Last winter her music club put on a Christmas program for the children in hospital. (Williams 1975, cited in Gibson 1995)

In contrast to this:

> Kevin's grandma belongs to a karate club and a scuba-divers' club and a mountain climbing club. Last winter her mountain-climbing club spent Christmas on the top of the Grand Tetons. (Williams 1975, cited in Gibson 1995: 5)

Although the second grandma seems much more fun, doubt is cast that Kevin's grandma could engage in such activities. It is suggested that her activities are the result of Kevin's fertile imagination in the coda:

> I'm not sure I believe everything about Kevin's grandma. (Williams 1975, cited in Gibson 1995)

Again, the tension between children's internalized expectations of older women and the reality is contained in the following passage from *Foxspell*.

> Weren't old women meant to be quiet and gentle with soft, creaky voices? And they were meant to live in retirement homes away from everyone else, and smell of lavender water and blue rinses. Grandma dressed like a man in old moleskin trousers and workboots. (Rubenstein 1994, cited in Gibson 1995: 5)

It would appear then, that from a very early age we are given quite definite pictures of how grandmothers "should" behave.

Those who are not grandmothers have the worse fate of being demonized as wicked witches.

Visual Representation

From the seemingly invariable image of the older woman as grandmother in children's literature we proceed to her portrayal in the media. When she does appear in TV advertisments, the older woman will be baking cakes in preparation for the family's arrival or bursting into tears at a phone call from an absent family member or gazing at her husband as he talks about *his* retirement plans and superannuation. Again we have the acceptable face of the older woman who is married or widowed with a family. Single, childless, or lesbian older women suffer a further exclusion.

Although some films have contributed to positive portraits of strong willed, independent older women, such as *Driving Miss Daisy* and *Fried Green Tomatoes at the Whistlestop Cafe*, there are many films and shows on TV that do nothing for the image of older women.

Monty Python's Flying Circus has an episode that presents older women as delinquent, bag-snatching thugs who roar away on motorbikes with the legend *Hell's Grannies* on their leather jackets. The humor of the episode is contained in the role reversal of older women engaged in behavior judged antisocial in teenagers and younger adults. It is so atypical of representations of older women as to be a subject of amusement.

Mother and Son is a long-running Australian show with high ratings. Maggie Beare in Mother and Son is portrayed as frail, dependent, forgetful and manipulative, stubborn and strong-willed. She is able to manipulate others into complying with her wishes, particularly the son with whom she lives. Ruth Cracknell, an excellent actress who plays this role, makes the observation that: "People just relate to the relationship . . . the slight power struggle." Henry Szeps, who plays the manipulative, ingratiating, selfish, greedy son whom she favors, was intrigued as to why Maggie Beare appealed to children and adolescents. He remarks: "I thought it was about how we mistreat our parents and don't deal with them adequately. But of course, it's that she is the dependent." "I'll take it a step further," Cracknell replies, " She's a child." "That element," Szeps picks up, "the fact that she is dependent, the child, and wins, is one of the reasons the whole thing works."

Its faithful replication of the stereotype of older women influences its success, as it portrays older women in conformity with the model that is familiar to people. Maggie conforms to the stereotype that infantilizes older women, depicting them as childish, dependent, and manipulative (as discussed in Hockey and James 1993). The provision of a model facilitates a range of behaviors described by Featherstone and Hepworth as the "mask of aging," which refers to a strategy adopted by older people of "concealing or masking inner feelings, motives, attitudes or beliefs" (1993: 378) in order to conform with cultural expectations. A second facet of Maggie's characterization shows that by adopting this position, she can actually exercise a modicum of control over her own life and power over others. I am merely commenting on, not recommending, this strategy, even though I believe some older women have found that it works.

Challenging the Maggie Beare stereotype is the character Diana Trent, played by Stephanie Cole in *Waiting for God*. She is strong, assertive, independent to the point of aggressive, mentally alert, proactive, sensual, and an actively sexual being who does not suffer fools gladly. In a battle of wits with Harvey Baines, the manager of the Bayview Retirement Home, she is invariably the victor, thanks to the collaboration of her friend and lover, Tom Ballard. The BBC has found it an unexpectedly popular series. Stephanie Cole's portrayal is of an older woman in control of her life despite being physically disabled and suffering from late onset diabetes, which allows for a realistic rather than idealistic portrayal of an older woman.

Diana's investment in her identity provides returns in her having the satisfaction of being able to change circumstances that she finds irritating and unsatisfactory. This results in a better lifestyle and the love and companionship of Tom Ballard. The downside for Diana is dislike and disapproval by the management, who regard her as a troublemaker because she asserts her rights and those of the residents of Bayview Retirement Home. She departs radically from the common representations of older women, although American television has produced shows such as the *Golden Girls* that also contribute to alternate images. Perhaps society is ready to take on board a more realistic picture of older women and a realization that contemporary older women are healthier, more mobile, better educated, assertive, and politically active.

Active Older Women

The stereotype of older women as being "at a loose end," as having nothing worthwhile to do, or as being at the "beck and call" of family members, was reinforced in interviews from a fitness project for older women conducted in 1995 (Leonard and O'Bierne 1995). When asked for reasons for nonattendance at gym sessions, the responses were all connected with caring, either for a sick family member or, in the majority of cases, for grandchildren. Family members and the women themselves all considered that older women "had to lend a hand," even at the expense of women who were engaged in an activity that was enjoyable and beneficial for them. It was an example where dependency was located not in the older women participants but in their families.

The mention of the fitness project leads into images of active older women who work out at a gym. This was an initiative of a women's health center, a government department, and university gym instructors who undertook to design and implement a gym program for older women. At the beginning of the project, the women saw themselves as physically active and they engaged in a variety of activities such as walking, golf, gardening, swimming, and yoga, but were concerned about fitness levels. Yet others indicated they were also involved in tai chi, belly-dancing, and line dancing (Boot Scootin'), while two of the women were interested in building up strength as a matter of safety. They found the experience of working out at a gym beneficial and many enrolled to continue on at the gym after the program finished.

These women are not atypical but representative of older women who engage in activities such as orienteering, bushwalking, and master's sports such as swimming, kayaking, cycling, and running, in addition to many of the activities already mentioned. It is a far cry from society's image of the frail, physically declining older woman. Four women in their seventies were the first swimmers to break a world record (Master's Sports) at the Homebush Aquatic Center, which was built for the Sydney 2000 Olympic Games. However, they did not receive the sponsorship money, which was to be awarded to the first to break a world record in the pool, because these older women did not reflect the image or glamour that this event was meant to convey. Achievement ran second to image.

Cultural Framework

The media plays an influential role in framing and reflecting representations of older women, who comprise the majority of the aged. However, in the attempt to produce a normative model of the older woman, tensions and contradictions appear in the discourses that seek to define her. Multiple agencies compete to construct the older woman. As well as media advertising, which portrays dependency on husbands and children, there are biomedical models of aging proposed by geriatricians, gerontologists, social workers, and community workers from government instrumentalities.

Although the marginalization of older women can be attributed to both sexism and agism, the primary factor in their inferior status is that of gender, for while both sexes are subject to agism, an older man is regarded more favorably by our culture, reflecting the privileging of the male throughout the lifespan. He is usually healthier though shorter lived, more mobile, financially more secure, and more likely to have a partner (Russell 1987). In a society that emphasizes sexuality and reproductive powers, he is, unlike the older woman, considered a sexually potent being. He is also considered to have carried out a socially useful role in that he has "worked," whereas the women whose lives have centered around childrearing and housekeeping are considered never to have "worked" or to have been "kept." Women who have been in the workforce have had their contribution to the finances considered adjunctive to their family duties. Again the old adage, "a woman's place is in the home," has contributed to the belief that for a woman there is no problem with the transition to the retirement years. Until recently, most research on the aged was centered on men's adjustment to retirement and loss of work role. Friedan remarked that "most of the policies and programs and research on age had been designed by and about and for men" (Friedan,1994: xvi).

The marginalization that has rendered older women almost invisible and characterized society's attitudes to older women has also had a positive effect in that the lack of visibility meant that there was freedom from scrutiny.

Meeting the Challenges

Increasingly older women are objecting to their marginalization and challenging the media's stereotypical depictions of them as frail, dependent, manipulative, feeble-minded, prone to disease, and "over the hill." The second wave of feminism has seen the maturing of the feminists of the seventies, who are now in the forefront of this challenge, and who have directed attention to the fact that the discrimination and devaluation of older women is the culmination of a lifetime of attempted subordination of women.

Better Than What?

The negative presentation of the model older woman renders invisible the discourses controlling gender and helps to produce the "docile-useful body" of woman as a reaction to this negative image. Why else do so many women fear becoming old? Why do young female executives wish to know how they can avoid menopause (Daly 1993)? Why is there such an over-investment in "keeping young and beautiful"? Surely, a blatant description/prescription has been provided as to what constitutes the desirable body; one that engenders a constant self-reflection and dissatisfaction: am I overweight, do the wrinkles show, can you see the grey in my hair, am I still attractive? It masks the regulation of the woman's sexuality and her bodily appearance. So the deconstruction of the beauty myth, embodied in the aging body of the older woman, is utilized by society to produce greater regulation of the woman's body in the form of dieting, exercising, beauty routines, and foundation garments to produce the fashionable shape. In other words, a use has been found for the older woman's body to coerce her into an excess of consumption (cosmetics and other beauty aids), self-surveillance (weighing, checking in the mirror to see that make-up is on straight), and self-regulation or self-discipline (beauty routines) to avoid looking old. In the desire to have the "look," physical well-being and pain are often ignored by women who have internalized these values.

Older women's specificity is not acknowledged. Older women are considered an amorphous, homogeneous group relegated to a powerless, subordinate position in society. But it is this very excess of misrecognition that is the incitement for their growing resistance. Within this discourse, ruptures are appearing. Both here and overseas, older women are mobilizing, subverting, and resisting the discourses. They have formed networks and coalitions that challenge the stereotypes that give legitimacy to oppressive practices relating to older women. By using current models such as the Older Women's League in the United States or the Older Women's Network in Australia, the processes and effectiveness of this resistance will lead older women themselves to dismantle the mythical norm of the "regular old woman" through challenging the stereotypes surrounding her and expressing her everchanging diversity.

Older women have the opportunity to form networks and coalitions through such organizations that were formed by groups of disaffected older women who challenged the stereotypes, the lack of consultation, and their exclusion from the decision making processes that affected them. The Older Women's Network (OWN) is an organization that is now statewide, nationwide, and worldwide, with an OWN in Europe and accreditation with the United Nations. Surely this resistance is much better than the beliefs and attitudes conjured up and imposed by an agist society.

The diversity provided by older women of color, working class women, women of different sexual orientation, and childless older women has, until recently, been ignored. The myth of singularity and the corresponding recognition of difference owes much, particularly as it affects women, to the dialogue that resulted out of tensions within the feminist movement.

Arber (1995) summarized the freedom of being an older woman: "Aging potentially liberates older women from the restrictions placed upon them by their family and conventional gender roles"1995: 5).

She ended with a quotation that acknowledged and emphasized the growing importance of older women.

> Three sets of factors intertwine to make the role of the older woman increasingly important in the future. First is our growing numerical strength with its potential political power. Second is the struggles experienced by many older women against poverty, institutionalization, and the combined effects of agism and sexism. Third is the gender-structured positions held by women in our society which teach us to care and connect with others in both perception and action. (McDaniel 1988, cited in Arber 1995:9)

It is these very characteristics of caring and connection with others, as well as the strength derived from the experience of struggle against agism and sexism, which will make older women as a force in the twenty-first century.

Chapter Two

Preliminary Overview: "The Facts"
Jenny Onyx

Aging is often regarded, unproblematically, as a fixed and invariant process that is totally determined by the biological processes of decline and decay leading to death. The "problem of aging" then becomes an issue of dependency and care. The concepts that are used to define aging, and the way in which statistics are presented, all reflect and support this ideologically conservative construction of aging.

We, the authors of this book, totally reject this perception of aging. We argue that nothing about the experience of aging is invariant. The experience of aging varies tremendously, from one cultural context to another, from one historical period to another, from one class or gender or race to another (Fennell, Philipson, and Evers 1988). Aging is "a problem" in our society because we have made it so. It does not need to be that way.

We hope to construct a new and positive vision of the experience of aging, drawing on what we know to be possible. However, before beginning that task, we need to deconstruct, to critique existing practices and perceptions of aging. The first step in that process is to examine "the facts" as we currently know them. We already find a problem in doing so. "The facts", as presented, are already value laden. For example, the data on "health" is not about health at all, but about illness, with an almost exclusive preoccupation with mortality and morbidity rates. Although this information is useful for some purposes, it does not in fact tell us a great deal about women's health, except to imply that we haven't got much! It is necessary to search hard to discover that, up to the age of 74 at least, 60 to 70 percent of women report good or excellent health.

Similarly, it is difficult to distinguish how data is categorized, between women who chose to "live alone" but with an intact network, women who live in isolation and alone, and women who "live without a partner" but not necessarily alone. The categories are not synonymous, but in a society that defines "family" as man and wife and children, an older woman living without a partner is assumed to be also alone, and one living alone assumed to be also isolated. In this chapter we reexamine the available data for our own purposes in an attempt to develop a more accurate picture of the position of older women. We believe that this alternative picture begins to show a different story. Far from "the problem of aging," we see evidence for "the triumph of aging."

Our data deals almost entirely with statistical data drawn from the U.S., Canada, U.K., and Australia. We look most closely at U.S. and Australian information and policy. Where appropriate these are positioned with reference to situations elsewhere, and particularly in relation to other OECD countries. There are some interesting differences between these countries but, by and large, the picture is a consistent one. We believe the situation to be quite different for older women in developing countries, but a close examination of those "facts" lies beyond the scope of this book.

The Demographic Panic

Almost all discussions of aging start with a discussion of the demographic trends, which indicate rapidly increasing numbers of old, and particularly "old old" people, both in absolute numbers and as a proportion of the total population into the twentyfirst century (e.g., Clare and Tulpule 1994; Rowland 1991; Sax 1993). This increase in the aged population is expected to lead to an increase in the dependency ratio (the proportion of the dependent population to the active workforce) and greatly increased demand for services. This will create a burden that few nations consider they will be able to support. For example, the NSW State Government Office of Aging stated:

> The number of older people in Australia will almost double over the next 30 years. The rate of increase should far exceed that for the population as a whole. . . In the OECD region as a whole, there is currently one older person for every five working age persons. However, it is estimated that by the year 2024 this ratio will be two to one. . . . The aging population will have a significant impact on the Australian economy.

There will be a growing proportion of dependent older people supported by a diminishing proportion of active workers (Kendig 1989: 3).

Embedded in this statement of "fact" there are a number of assumptions. Chief among these are that aging means inevitable dependency and that older people cannot financially support themselves, but instead must be supported by younger people currently in the workforce (Sax 1993). It is further assumed that older people cannot care for themselves or each other, but must be cared for by younger people, and that the consequent weight of this burden will prove intolerable to younger people. Added to the direct cost of economic support and care is the expected blow-out in medical expenses, to be borne by an already stretched public health system. Let's take a closer look at these assumptions.

It is certainly true that more people are living longer throughout the world. The United Nations has nominated 1999 as the International Year of Older Persons, in preparation for which it has issued the following statement:

Without doubt, longevity is one of the great achievements of the twentieth century. Between 1950 and 2000, the situation created by the decline in fertility and in mortality rates will have added 20 years to the average life span. But the aging of the world's population is producing unprecedented challenges to citizens and policymakers— particularly regarding the protection of the economic and social security of older persons. (United Nations 1996).

Within all OECD countries, the projected increase of the "old old," that is those over age 85, is predicted to increase at an even faster rate. In the U.S., Hobbs and Damon (1996) note:

According to Census Bureau middle series projections, the population aged 85 and over will more than double, from 3 million in 1990 to 7 million in 2020. This group will again double by 2040. . . By 2050, the oldest old would be nearly 5 percent of the total population, compared to just over 1 percent in 1994 (Hobbs and Damon 1996: 2–9).

Other OECD countries report similar trends. Within Australia, the proportion of those over 80 is expected to increase from 2.2 percent of the population in 1990 to 7.7 percent of the population in 2050 (Clare and Tulpule, 1994). Table 1 sets out the projected proportion of the population over 65, for selected OECD Countries.

Table 1.
Projected Percentage of Population 65 Years of Age and Over
from Selected O.E.C.D. Countries

Country	Year 1990 %	2010 %	2030 %	2050 %
Australia	11.2	13.3	19.1	20.4
Canada	11.2	14.0	21.6	21.0
France	13.8	15.6	21.5	22.0
Germany	15.5	20.0	25.0	24.4
Italy	14.0	17.0	21.0	22.0
Japan	11.2	17.2	19.5	22.0
New Zealand	10.8	11.8	18.4	21.8
Norway	16.0	15.0	20.2	22.0
Sweden	17.8	17.0	19.2	21.8
Switzerland	15.0	20.0	27.0	26.2
United Kingdom	15.0	14.2	18.8	18.5
USA	12.2	12.2	19.2	19.2

Source. Clare and Tulpule 1994.

Among those over 65 years, in all OECD countries, women outnumber men. In Australia, women make up 56 percent of those over 65. The proportion of women increases with age. In the U.K., for instance, in 1995 almost two-thirds of people aged 75 and over and almost three-fourths of those aged 85 and over were women (Age Concern, England, 1997). Similarly, in the U.S., women outnumber men by six to five at ages 56 to 69, but they outnumber men by five to two for those aged 85 years and over.

However, these figures are misleading bevause they assume a homogeneity of older women. For example, in 1981, in Australia, 75 percent of all those over 60 years of age were Australian born, while 11 percent were of non-English speaking background. By the year 2001, the proportion of Australian born people over 60 will have dropped to 64 percent, with an increase to 22 percent of people of non-English speaking background. In 1981, little more than 7,000 Aboriginal people over 60 years of age were counted, representing a minute proportion of all Aboriginal people (Kendig and McCallum 1986). In 1991, only 1 percent of Aboriginal and Torres Strait Islander females were aged over 75, compared to 5 percent of all Australian females (ABS, 1993, Cat. No.4113). As Kendig and McCallum note:

Life expectancy at birth remains fully 25 years less than for the total
population . . . in several important respects one could say that
Aboriginals become old at a much younger age than other Australians
(Kendig and McCallum 1986:17).

These figures point to the increased burden of support for the
aged population. How this is read depends partly on the
traditional support base for aged services. In countries such as
theU.K. and Australia, where the state has traditionally taken
the main role, this increase is viewed with particular alarm. As
Sax (1995) points out, "communities may accept the costs of
programs for younger people comparatively easily in view of their
value as a form of investment. Expenditures in favor of elderly
people are less acceptable, particularly when they draw on
already overstrained national budgets" (Sax 1995:20). The
dependency ratio is commonly taken as the index of potential
levels of dependency; this is calculated as the proportion of those
over 65 relative to those of working age (15–65). This age
dependency ratio for Australia is expected to increase from 13
per 100 in 1971 to 35 per 100 in the year 2041 (Borowski and
Hugo 1997; Clare and Tulpule 1994). Similarly, in the U.S. the
ratio of elderly persons to those of working age is expected to
nearly double from 1990 to 2050. In the U.S. concern is also
directed toward the increasing familial support ratios (Hobbs
and Damon 1996) as a measure of the need for family support
over time. The assumption is made that the burden of care for the
aged is accepted by their middle-aged children, or in the case of
those over 85, by their "young old" children (i.e. those between
65 and 69). The "sandwich generation" may be simultaneously
caring for their aged parents and paying for higher education for
their dependent children.

In all cases, the assumption is that older people in general are
unproductive, nonparticipating members of society who will
remain entirely dependent on younger, productive members. This
use of the dependency ratio is extremely misleading and can be
criticized on numerous grounds. It assumes that all people
between the ages of 15 and 64 are productive, an assumption
that ignores those out of work, dependent disabled adults, and
those engaged in full-time education. The dependency ratio
focuses on the more visible costs of care of state provided
services for old people, who are seen as more expensive than
dependent children, and ignores the enormous, but private and,

therefore, invisible cost of raising children. Most importantly, the formula assumes that no persons over 65 are in productive work, have access to private income, or are able to live independently of community support (Sax 1993).

In 1991 in Australia, slightly over half of those of pensionable age received the age pension (75 percent of women). This proportion falls to some extent as more women remain in the workforce longer, and as more workers, including women, participate in superannuation schemes. Forecasters have failed to note that the better health that older people now enjoy, and women's increasing participation in the workforce and higher rates of pay, will reduce our dependence in old age (Sargent 1994). Nor has any account been made of the enormous unpaid contribution that older people make to the care of other older people, to the care of the young, as well as to the community at large.

Employment and Income

Labor force participation rates in OECD countries are typically low at about 16 percent for older workers. Table 2 sets out the labor force participation rates, by age and sex, for selected OECD countries.

Table 2.
Percentage of the Population Participating in the Labor Force by Age and Sex for Selected OECD Countries

	U.S.	Canada	U.K.	Japan	Australia
Male					
15-24	70.3	65.2	76.0	48.0	70.7
25-54	91.7	92.4	93.4	97.5	91.4
55-64	65.5	60.3	64.3	85.0	60.7
65 and over	16.8	11.0	7.4	37.6	9.0
Female					
15-24	62.5	60.6	66.0	47.1	65.9
25-54	75.3	75.7	73.8	65.3	67.4
55-64	48.9	37.4	39.7	48.1	26.5
65 and over	9.2	3.5	3.5	15.9	2.3

Source: OECD Labor force Statistics, 1995

As evident from Table 2, labor force participation rates decline rapidly after the age of 55 for both genders, with participation rates for women declining at a faster rate than those for men. Although this is true of all OECD countries, there are important national differences. For example, participation rates remain much higher for a longer period of time in Japan and the U.S. than they do in other countries with different approaches to welfare state provisions.

Participation rates disguise several other significant facts. First, participation rates include both those actually employed and those who are looking for work but are unemployed. In at least one documented case, for the U.S. most of the growth in participation rates from 1991–1992 included the long term unemployed (AARP 1993). This suggests that older people are attempting to return to the labor market to augment their income but are unable to secure employment. Second, participation rates do not distinguish between full-time and part-time employment. Women over the age of 25 are far more likely than men to work part-time and older workers, both men and women, are more likely to work part-time. For example, in Australia (NSW) in 1994, 41percent of all employed women aged 45 years and over worked part-time, compared with only 9 percent of employed men of that age (Social Policy Directorate of NSW 1995).

Third, the snapshot picture obscures historical developments. In fact, the distribution of labor force participation has changed dramatically over recent years in most OECD countries. In the U.S., participation in the labor force for older men (over 55 years) has decreased from 69 percent in 1950 to 38 percent in 1993. Over the same period, women's participation rates for those aged 50–54 increased from 31 percent in 1950 to 70 percent in 1993 and for those aged 55–59 participation rates increased from 26 percent to 57 percent. There has, however, been no such increase for those over 60. In Australia, participation of males aged 55–59 has declined from 90 percent in 1966 to 74 percent in 1995. On the other hand, participation of women in this age group has dramatically increased from 26 percent to 40 percent, while participation for those over 60 has declined slightly. Although women still have a lower participation rate than that for men in both U.S. and Australia, the age/gender employment gap appears to be closing. This pattern is repeated in other OECD countries; however, in most OECD countries labor force participation rates rapidly decrease to less than 25 percent by age 65 and less than 10 percent by age 70, with women participating at half the male rate.

There are contradictory pressures on older people's employment. With the aging of the population comes greater pressure for older people to remain employed. This trend has recently been supported in Australia when in New South Wales anti-discrimination age legislation made it unlawful for employers to impose a compulsory retirement age. On the other hand there is an increasing rate of "voluntary" early retirement associated with company restructuring, retrenchments, and "downsizing." The evidence suggests that employers continue to hold a negative attitude toward older workers (usually defined as over 45 years), and that older workers are more likely to be unemployed, to remain unemployed longer, and to be overrepresented among the ranks of discouraged job seekers (ABS 1995 Cat 6203; AARP 1993). Participation rates for older women have historically been very low. However, increasing numbers of older women are now entering the labor force and are remaining longer.

There is considerable similarity in women's working life patterns across western industrialized countries (Reed 1996). Women have interrupted careers, earn less than men, are employed in a narrower range of occupations, and are more likely to be employed part-time. There are also crossnational differences, which are reflected in women's workforce experiences and rewards in later years. Germany has a lower workforce participation rate for older women than France, while Sweden has the highest rate, being approximately 62percent for women aged between 55 and 64 (Katz and Monk 1993). In the United States, participation rates are somewhat higher than Australia, but research shows the gender wage gap for the 40–50 age group is greater than at earlier ages, irrespective of education, qualifications, and broken or unbroken employment (Hollenshead 1982; Nuccio 1989). In Britain, education provides some protection to the earnings of women with broken careers (Crompton, Hantrais and Walters 1990). In Australia there are higher levels of gender segregation in occupational fields but centralized wage fixing has narrowed the gender wage gap. Here, men's rather than women's earnings decline with age (Kalish and Williams 1983).

From the evidence of Table 2 above, it is difficult to determine if higher participation rates in some countries reflect improved or poorer economic support. On the one hand, employment should guarantee an adequate standard of living. On the other hand, if employer-based pensions/superannuation or the provision of government pensions is adequate, there should be no need for those over the age of 65 to seek employment. There is some evidence from U.S. data that many older women do not have access to government pensions or social security benefits and are forced to work for very low wages that keep them below the poverty line.

The levels of poverty experienced by older people in the U.S. varies greatly by population subgroup. In 1959, more than 35 percent of people aged 65 and over were poor, compared to 12 percent who were similarly poor in 1990 (Kassner, 1992). However, the 12 percent is not a uniform figure. The rate of poverty is lowest for those men who are less than 65 years of age and who are white and married (the rate is about 5 percent). Poverty rates are highest for those women who are older than 85 and who are black and live alone (over 67 percent). Class, race, gender, and age intersect in producing these patterns of disadvantage (Hobbs and Damon 1996). Although those who worked for some period in the past year were rarely poor, older women workers were disproportionately likely to be among the ranks of the working poor. Those most likely to find themselves in this position are women who have worked all their lives, raised children, were either out of the labor force for long periods or worked for low wages, often as single parents (Morgan 1991). Those who divorced within ten years of marriage could not claim social security from their ex-husband's earnings. Those on low wages could contribute little to social security. It is hard to believe that so many older women, having worked all their lives, should find themselves in poverty, in the wealthiest nation on earth!

The situation, however, is not very different in other OECD countries. In Canada, the percentage of "unattached senior women" below the poverty line is 38 percent (26 percent for men) (National Advisory Council on Aging 1993). In the U.K. in 1995, over 50 percent of pensioner households depended on state benefits for at least 75 percent of their income, while 15 percent received all their income from state benefits, well below the minimum standard of living (Age Concern, England, 1997). However, as Johnson and Falkingham (1992) point out, it is fallacious to regard older persons as homogeneous with regard to income. In the U.K., those in the top quintile of earnings receive incomes five times as high as those in the bottom quintile, with income derived from a variety of sources. Those in the top group are more likely to be male, under 75, married, and in the middle to upper social classes.

Older people in Australia are very unlikely to have income below the poverty line, as comprehensive government pensions are available to all those women over age 62 (men over 65) who meet the income test. The poverty line is a fairly austere measure and likely to understate the adequacy of pension income. Given the uncertain employment history for the majority of older women, income in retirement is likely to be uncertain and heavily dependent on government pensions. Those unable to acquire assets such as a home are particularly vulnerable. The main sources of income of retired people in Australia are outlined in Table 3 (ABS, 1995 Cat. No 4102). It shows sources of income at retirement and at October 1992. The October 1992 measure is more current than that at retirement. With the October 1992 measure, however, the amount of time after retirement can vary from a day to many years.

Table 3.
Main Sources of Income for Retired People: Proportion of income from each source.

| Main sources of income | At retirement | | In October 1992 | |
| | males | females | males | females |
	%	%	%	%
Government benefits	50	36	64	62
Retirement schemes/ investments/ savings	39	18	28	14
Someone else's income	3	36	2	15
Rent/ farm/ business/ property	3	2	3	2
Part-time work	4	6	3	6
Other	2	1	1	1

Source: ABS, 1995, cat. No. 4102

The major source of income for both men and women is a government pension or benefit (Table 3); the dependence on this source of income increases with time since retirement, as indicated in the shift from "at retirement" to "October 1992". About a third of older women depended on their spouse's income at retirement, but less than half this figure could continue to do so. Men, far more than women, had access to private pension/superannuation schemes or similar investment income.

In 1992 the Australian government introduced compulsory superannuation and the superannuation guarantee charge (SGC) with the aim of eventually making retired people independent of the age pension. As a result of this and other market forces, the superannuation coverage of the adult population has increased from 34 percent to 51 percent, while the increase for employed people went from 51 percent to 80 percent (ABS, 1995, Cat. No 4102). However, to provide an adequate income in retirement, it is recommended that workers contribute some 15 percent of their income in addition to the 3 percent contributed by employers under the SGC legislation, and to do so over an extended period of some 30–40 years continuous employment. For the majority of women who experience interrupted careers, casual or part-time employment, and low income it is unlikely that superannuation as it currently operates will ever provide sufficient retirement income (Clare and Tulpule 1994; Rosenman and Warburton 1997).

The above figures refer to paid employment only. The available evidence suggests that older people, and older women in particular, contribute considerable unpaid labor. Older women do enormous amounts of unpaid work in a wide variety of contexts that are of major social and economic benefit. The estimated contribution to the gross domestic product of unpaid work in Australia, if it were included, is 34 percent to 38 percent, or roughly 150 thousand million dollars per year. Of this, women contribute two thirds of the value of domestic and childcare activities and half of the value of community and volunteer work (ABS, 1993). In particular, older women make a significant contribution. Over 30 percent of women over 65 years participate in voluntary activities.

Much of the unpaid work of men in their youth relates to sport and emergency services (e.g. bush fire brigade). In later life, they take a greater share of the caring, mainly for frail wives. However, most of the unpaid work of older women falls into the area of health and welfare, in terms of both informal caring (not identified in these statistics) and the more formal volunteer community work. The 1992 NSW time use survey (Social Policy Directorate 1995) found that nearly two-thirds of all people who helped sick or disabled adults were aged 55 years and over, the majority of these being women. Similarly, Kendig (1986) found that 25 percent of the older people in that sample were doing unpaid work, mainly in women's traditional roles in health and welfare. This trend is consistent with that found elsewhere. Arber and Ginn (1990) report that older people in the U.K. give more personal care services than they receive. The greatest source of care for frail old people is other older persons, usually a spouse or daughter. Fit older people also provide personal care to the very young and the young sick or disabled. In addition, many older women are involved in the care of grandchildren.

Health Status
    There are two salient, but apparently contradictory "facts"about the health status of older people in Australia. The first is that the vast majority of older people, including women, report good or very good health most of the time. The other salient fact is that the incidence of disability and chronic illness increases among the old, and particularly among the "old old," with concomitant increases in health expenditure.
    Table 4 sets out the overall self-reported health status by age within Australia in 1989–90 (ABS, 1990, Cat. 4366; ABS 1994, Cat. 4365). As that table makes clear, while the proportion of men and women reporting poor health increases with age, that proportion never exceeds 15 percent. Up to the age of 74, 60 percent of women report good or excellent health.

Table 4.
Self Assessed Health Status in Australia in 1989–90 by Age and Gender.

Health Status	Age							
	25-44years		45-64years		65-74years		75+years	
	female	male	female	male	female	male	female	male
	%	%	%	%	%	%	%	%
excellent	36	36	24	23	15	14	14	13
good	51	52	48	49	45	43	39	44
fair	11	10	21	20	30	31	34	29
poor	2	2	6	7	10	13	13	15

Source. ABS,1990, Cat. No. 4366; 1994, Cat. No. 4365

This overall picture of good health among older women needs to be highlighted. It is invariably and inappropriately overshadowed by the detailed reporting of disability, disease, and death among the aged, thus giving a misleading general picture of disease and decay instead of the more realistic and common picture of high energy and good health, until "the terminal drop." Nor is Australia unique in this. In the U.S. 74 percent of non-institutionalized persons aged 65 to 74 consider their health to be good, very good, or excellent compared with others their age; as do 67 percent of persons aged 75 and over (Hobbs and Damon 1996). Furthermore, those who considered themselves in good health experienced longer life expectancy, regardless of actual disability (Rogers 1995, cited in Hobbs and Damon 1996). In Canada, in 1994, about three quarters of older persons living at home rated their health as good, very good or excellent (Statistics Canada 1997).

The Australian National Health Survey, 1989–90, from which the above figures are drawn, also reported the relative incidence of long term health conditions. The most common long term health conditions among older people (aged 45 and over) were eyesight disorders (affecting 70 percent of women) followed by arthritis, which affected 37 percent. Approximately 30 percent were affected by hypertension (ABS, 1994, Cat. No. 4365). In the 1993 Survey of Disability in NSW, approximately half the population of people aged 60 years and over reported having some sort of disability.

Disability increased with age. It is not appropriate, however, to focus on the disabilities of older people. While about half reported some disability, in terms of daily functioning less than a quarter had a disability that could not be overcome with minimal aid (Social Policy Directorate, 1995).

For females of all ages in NSW in 1993, cancer was one leading cause of death, accounting for 24.5 percent of all female deaths. Breast cancer was the most common kind of cancer, followed by lung cancer. However, marginally more women died of ischemic heart disease (24.6 percent) than cancer. Another 13.5 percent died of strokes, and 6.6 percent died of respiratory disease (Social Policy Directorate 1995). The picture in the U.S. is similar, with highest death rates for men and women from diseases of the heart, cancer, or stroke accounting for three-fourths of all elderly deaths (Hobbs and Damon, 1996)

In the U.S., 88 percent of persons aged 65 years or more visited a physician during 1991. This figure may represent both the increased need for care and an increase in regular preventative care (Hobbs and Damon 1996). In 1986 in Australia, persons aged 70 years and over accounted for a third of all bed days in hospital (Kendig 1989). Half of all prescriptions to women were for anti-depressants. Ironically, the drugs prescribed to deal with psychosocial problems such as depression, anxiety, and insomnia may create mental and physical conditions that are a major factor in the hospitalization of older women for adverse drug effects (Russell 1987; Homburg 1991), thereby causing rather than alleviating ill-health.

The increased dependency of older people results in greatly increased expenditure for health and welfare. For example, it is estimated that around 40 percent of total hospital and community service expenditure in the U.K. is on people aged 65 or over (Age concern England 1997). In Australia, education expenditure comprises the greatest national expenditure up to age 30, while both welfare and health expenditure rapidly increase for those aged 60 years and over (Clare and Tulpule 1994; McCallum 1997). Furthermore, the proportion of health expenditure received by older age groups is projected to increase further in the next 50 years, as Table 5 illustrates. It is this kind of projection that raises concerns about the financial "burden of the aged."

Table 5.
Proportion of Health Budget by Age Group in Australia.

Year	Age 0–14 %	15–64 %	65 and over %
1990	10.4	56.1	33.5
2001	9.3	54.2	36.5
2011	8.4	53.5	38.2
2021	7.5	49.2	43.3
2031	6.8	44.3	48.9
2041	6.5	41.6	51.9

Source. Clare and Tulpule 1994.

On the other hand, there is also considerable evidence that the medical and support needs of older women in particular have been socially and politically constructed to fuel burgeoning aged services, as well as medical and pharmaceutical industries (Sargent 1994; Townsend 1981). For example, Germaine Greer (1991) refers to geriatric care as the "menopause industry" because of the increasing pressure for older women to subject themselves to costly hormone replacement therapy, repeated breast cancer screening, unnecessary and inappropriate drug prescriptions, particularly tranquillizers, and other forms of intrusive medical intervention (see also Noeleen's chapter 7). There is some evidence, for example, that the admission of older women to the hospital may be necessitated by adverse reactions to medically prescribed drugs in as many as 25 percent of admissions (Sargent 1994). There is also evidence to suggest that by far the largest proportion of health expenditure is used in the last six months of life, regardless of the age of the patient. Clare and Tulpule (1994) note that half of all medical expenditures occur for the 13 percent who will die in the next two years, sixteen times the population average. This suggests that we are really talking about the financial "burden of the dying" rather than of the aged. Presumably it costs as much or more for the young to die.

Housing

In most OECD countries there is a high rate of home ownership among older people. In the U.S., 76 percent of those over 60 years of age own their own home. This drops from 80 percent for the 60–64 year olds, to 63 percent for the over 85 year olds (Administration on Aging 1990). In Canada, 80 percent of "elder families," but only 41 percent of "unattached seniors" owned their own home. Among women over 80 years of age, 48 percent rent their dwelling (compared with 29 percent for all older people). In NSW (Australia) in 1991, 80 per cent of people aged 65 years and over lived in homes that they owned outright or were purchasing (Social Policy Directorate 1995). Most of the remainder were living in private rental (7 percent) or government rental property (6 percent). More men than women own their own homes. However, in the U.K. only 52 percent of "elderly only" households were owner-occupied in 1988, while 39 percent were in public rental housing (Johnson and Falkingham, 1992). Many of those over 65 in the U.S. and Australia are relatively "asset rich", regardless of their income. However, the fact of home ownership does not necessarily suggest a high standard of accommodation. Older properties may be sub-standard, with poor lighting and access, and in need of maintenance that older owners are unable to afford (Sax 1993; Johnson and Falkington 1992). There may be serious impediments to realizing equity assets. On the other hand, the majority of older Australians in private rental spend on average 35 percent of their income on housing (Sax 1993). In the Australian context, home ownership is a major factor in keeping older people from sliding into poverty.

There is a strong preference for older people in most OECD countries to "age in place," that is to remain living in the community independently, for as long as possible, and for as long as community support services are available (Hobbs and Damon

1996; National Canadian Advisory Council on Aging 1993; Sax 1993). As a consequence of this, and given the greater life expectancy of women over men, and the older age of husbands than wives, an increasing proportion of older women live without partners. In 1994, in Australia, just 5 percent of women aged 25–34 years were living alone, compared with 39 percent of women aged 65 years and over, and 17 percent of men of that age. The figures for the U.S. are almost identical, with 41 percent of women over 65 years of age, compared with 16 percent of men, living alone in 1993. The proportion of women living alone increases from 32 percent for those aged 65 to 74 to 57 percent for those over 85 years (Hobbs and Damon 1006). In the U.K. in 1995, 36 percent of women aged 65 to 74 lived alone, compared with 62 percent of those aged 75 and over (Age Concern England 1997).

One of the consequences of the high proportion of older women who live alone is that older women have been defined out of the family. By 1993, the Australian Bureau of Statistics defined the family household as consisting of two generations: parent(s) and children (or couples without children). An older person living alone was not regarded as being a member of any family (Sargent 1994). Consequently, while the pressure remains for older women to adopt grandparenting childcare responsibilities, those who choose to live independently are identified as not belonging to a family in theory, and may be increasingly socially isolated.

The stereotype and fear of many older women is of being left to die in a nursing home. In fact the data for several OECD countries suggests that relatively few older people ever stay in an institutional setting, although the likelihood increases for those over 85. In the U.S., in 1990, 1.4 percent of those aged 65 to 74 years lived in nursing homes, compared with 6 percent of those aged 75 to 84, and 24 percent of those aged 85 years and over (Hobbs and Damon 1996). Similarly, in Australia, 4 percent of those aged 65 to 79 lived in an institutional setting, but 23 percent of those over 80 years of age did so (Social Policy Directorate NSW 1995)

We may now summarize this introductory overview of "the facts." The current focus of much of the reported statistics is on the problems of an aging population and the huge burden of care and medical support this will impose on the "productive young" who are in the labor force. The assumption is one of care and dependency. However, a closer look at the "facts" suggests a different interpretation. Contrary to expectations and prevailing stereotypes, the vast majority of older women experience good health until at least our late seventies, with minimal handicap. The majority live independently in the community. We live an active and full life and continue to make a valuable contribution to the economic and social life of the community, despite our often impoverished financial condition.

In the chapters that follow we will discuss some of the implications of the prevailing stereotypes of older women, the messages suggested in the way the "facts" are presented, and the contradictions that ensue. In particular we will focus on the medicalization of our bodies which is manifested in programs that can operate against our own interests. We examine the contradictions around employment and retirement, and our paid and unpaid labor. We also explore our housing options. Throughout, the evidence will suggest a picture of our struggles to maintain and enhance our independence, often against seemingly overwhelming forces that are conspiring to perpetuate an unwanted and unnecessary state of dependency.

Chapter Three

Not Gerontology, but—
Margaret Sargent

The first beginning. We, the authors of this book, have a variety of approaches to our material, which are influenced by our perspectives on theory, especially feminist theory, and are grounded in our own experience. At the same time there is a unity among us that stems, partly at least, from our overall rejection of some of the basic assumptions behind much gerontological work. Within the interdisciplinary malestream approaches of gerontology (the study of aging) there is also variety, and recently broader and more subtle methods and analysis are developing.

The second beginning. From the above paragraph you can see how I initially planned this chapter. But when I came to revise it months later, I asked myself "how can theory (and some experience) be enough to account for the authors' feelings of unity and commonality as we created this book? And then, how is it that we all feel such an antipathy to gerontology"? Thinking this way, it seemed at first surprising that many members of the Older Women's Network, nonacademics, felt exactly the same way.

Then I realized that older women believed that the work of gerontology had affected them as individuals and as a group. These effects include the devaluation of older women in the general social discourse and in government social policy toward women, the sexist and age related attitudes that accompany discriminatory behavior, and the idea that there is something abnormal about being old that legitimizes a medical takeover of our lives and the medicalization of aging itself. Older women had been objectivised by the medical gaze and transformed into geriatrics. Most important of all, we authors had positioned ourselves, primarily, not as writers and students of aging, but as older women on the receiving end of the effects of gerontology. This way of positioning ourselves is wholly supported by feminist theory. We are not detached observers, but participants in the damage. We are women with first-hand experience of what we are writing about.

At the same time I think we are ready to admit that the above account exaggerates a little and displaces onto gerontology some of the blame for damage due to other social factors.

To continue. To clarify our shared position, I offer in this chapter a "map of the field"—sketching in those approaches we are most skeptical about, those where we have "radical doubt," and those feminist approaches where we locate ourselves and what we are doing. First, I will present a brief critique of what we are most dubious about, namely gerontology's usual claims to be like science—scientific, objective, and certain. Second, political economy approaches are praised on some grounds and criticized on others, especially for neglect of feminist perspectives. Last, I shall describe alternative methods of studying and theorizing about aging that are available through feminism, methods that we ourselves have used and found appropriate to our positioning of ourselves as older women.

Scientific, Objective, and Certain[1]

The context within which gerontology began was science, seen as the source of all knowledge about the natural world, and expected to produce solutions to all the major practical problems of human kind. These expectations are still held by functionalist theorists in the social sciences. It is still often considered, especially in psychology, that we are daily adding to a body of certainly known, scientific factual knowledge. This is the philosophy usually called *positivism*, which makes two major assumptions: (1) that knowledge is based on sensory experience, and is related to a reality that is directly known by the observer through the senses of sight, touch, hearing, etc.; and (2) that no observations we make of the external world could be affected by value judgements because those observations are scientific, certain, and verifiable. Since sociology was considered value neutral or value free, it was not thought to carry any implications for practical policy. Scholars following Weber believed that while *policy* refers to values, a "science of society" dealt only in *facts* and could offer no guidance concerning everyday life.

As regards the scientific method, the experts have never quite agreed on a standard procedure, but in general it was taken to include formulating a hypothesis on the basis of theories and what is already known; deducing predictions that are empirically testable; and carrying out experiments or observations, thus verifying or disproving the predictions. Research was thought to consist in the discovery of hard facts.

A thorough critique of the assumptions behind science cannot be undertaken here. Briefly, there are many possible theoretical frameworks (or paradigms) within science, and these must be regarded as ideologies that change from time to time. From the study of phenomenology, it seems that truth or knowledge could never directly correspond with the material world, but can only be coherent within itself.

Irigaray emphasized that all "knowledges" are produced by individuals who are situated in particular positions in society. It is this positioning that substantially influences the nature of those knowledges. So knowledge produced by men reflects their (ideal) characteristics and interests (Irigaray 1985). Science provides men with guarantees about the stability of the world as they see it.

What we discover in science is not directly observed data. We find only our indirect perceptions that we inevitably shape to fit in with our previous knowledge, attitudes, and opinions. Scientific method cannot yield certain knowledge about the material world because science incorporates from the start the values and assumptions that form part of our particular culture.

Feminist critique has exposed the impossibility of the scientist-observer standing outside the objects of research. There are still, however, some feminists who retain the principle of value free, objective research—perhaps more for career reasons than scholarship (for example, Cynthia Fuchs Epstein cited in Reinharz 1992 and Elizabeth Ettorre cited in Reinharz 1992). Research has largely been conducted by and on behalf of those with dominant interests and resources in society. Therefore, scientific method and knowledge have mainly promoted the interests of men and perpetuated the subordination of women.

Like some scientists, many gerontologists have been prevented by their positivist philosophy from seeing their work as ideological. They have not necessarily understood that their "scientific" activity has supported the status quo and the present distribution of power in the world. They have made moral, ethical, and political decisions without acknowledging them.

We continue discussing the areas of the authors' greatest skepticism and reach the medical model.

Medical Model

The medical model has been a major source of devaluation of older people, especially women, both in theory and practice. The term "medical model," is sometimes used in a broad way, but more narrowly it focuses mainly on disease and treatment for individuals. There is a need to link the personal with the political sides of the medical model, which was perceived and accomplished in Sharon's innovative chapter (chapter 8). In most forms the medical model has the following characteristics.

- It removes the individual's responsibility since she or he is expected to passively assume a sick role and undergo the doctor's treatment without question;
- It focuses on illness and intervention rather than on prevention, education and social change;
- It takes conventional medicine to be the only appropriate profession to take responsibility for health problems;
- It maintains the status of the medical profession against the different but vital expertise of nurses, social workers, osteopaths, etc.;
- It results in a patient being treated as only a diseased kidney, or one eye, rather than a whole person;
- It denies the political implications of policies that neglect the basic health needs of indigenous people, and the unique needs of special groups such as women.

The authors of this book, being only too aware of these characteristics, avoid the use of the medical model except as an element in the social construction of aging. Its political uses in practice are many, one of the most notable being the legitimization of the nursing home industry, enabling government and unscrupulous nursing home owners to profit at the expense of the rights and quality of life of the residents (Rhonda's chapter 9).

Medical Dominance

> This. . . is the key feature of the production of health care in Australian society and the central analytical focus in explaining the social structure and organization of health care (Willis 1989).

The medicalization of women's normal functions is prevalent in older women's experience. It is not only menopausal conditions, incontinence, depression, and dementia—it is *aging itself* that has been medicalized. Zola pointed out in the 1970s how the professions went beyond their technical expertise, resulting in the medicalization of social problems. Medicine, because it medicalized day-to-day well-being, was called a "disabling profession." This medical dominance has been effected through the health system, the profession of medicine, and by means of "knowledge." Like other professions, medicine has substantially contributed to the control of individuals through the process of "labelling" and "prescribing" the appropriate treatment of marginalized social categories. Women have been among the foremost subjects (or perhaps "objects" is a more correct term!) of medical dominance.

Willis considered that this dominance "prevents the most effective utilization of health resources in society . . . [especially] the skills of other health workers." For example, there is medical opposition to the establishment of better training facilities for other health workers, to their professional registration, to their practicing without medical supervision, and to their obtaining research funding. Medicine has dominated the division of labor of health occupations economically, politically, socially, and intellectually.

The health workforce is structured hierarchically by sex and by occupation. About three-fourths of the practitioners are women, but males predominate in medicine, chiropractics, optometry, dentistry, and administration, and are in the upper ranks of every health occupation. Because of their autonomy, Willis considered the four professions named above to be part of the "new middle class." He described all the others as "subordinated" occupations located in the working class. The incomes of health practitioners differ markedly according to occupation and sex. The survey conducted by the Australian Bureau of Statistics in 1995 found that for every $7 earned by men, only $5 was received by women in the same occupations (ABS 1996).

The "territory" of the various health occupations has resulted from historical struggles of the classes and the sexes. The relative positions of the occupations has been explained by their amount of control over technology, or alternatively by the degree of the medical profession's control over them.

Because of changes in training during the 1980s, most Australian nurses and other health workers now have university degrees or diplomas, and several professions consider themselves autonomous. Nurses' status in relation to doctors has changed and improved. Yet doctors still have authority in many areas of health. They still have by law, for example, the exclusive right to penetrate the female body physically by surgery or chemically by drugs.

Through the Australian Medical Association (AMA) and similar medical "clubs" in other comparable western countries, the most highly trained doctors have acted as jealous gatekeepers for their elite status and territory. (Exceptions to most of these generalizations are found in alternative professional associations of medical practitioners such as the Doctors' Reform Society in Australia.) Many immigrant doctors have been excluded from practice.

In medicine, women are narrowly confined to certain areas: there is a smaller percentage of female than male specialists of any kind, and a smaller percentage of female consultant physicians and diagnostic specialists (Palmer and Short 1989). The gender imbalance is most marked in the specialty of surgery, among whom there are very few female heart or brain surgeons. Almost all women specialists are gynecologists, pediatricians, or plastic surgeons—areas of medicine of comparatively low status and evidently regarded as "women's work."

Largely through the influence of the AMA, medical practitioners were not permitted to associate in their practice with chiropractors or other alternative ("natural") medical practitioners because of official licensing requirements. The AMA even disputed the right of chiropractors to be paid! Nevertheless, alternative medicine is proliferating. Women, in particular, find alternative medicine attractive. Its low-key, gentle atmosphere, home remedies and dieting, different modes of massage, movement, and exercise, its informality and absence of high-tech—all these have appeal for women. Doctors should take note of these women's preferences.

Mystification Through "Knowledge"

Advice given by "experts" to consumers is often assumed to flow from knowledge which is certain. Yet it may be based, for example, on studies of very few subjects who were not necessarily human, conducted in an artificial environment such as a laboratory, without using control groups, and producing results that cannot be evaluated or replicated, and unacknowledged assumptions. Yet in practice the medical profession makes use of the high reputation of science, with its dubious positivist assumptions and claims that medical "knowledge" is scientific and certain. In reality its knowledge is legitimized by the high status and income of the medical profession, by its lengthy specialized training, by the positions of authority in the health system, and by its social origins in the "cream" of society. A consumer, mystified and often feeling powerless to influence matters, frequently feels forced to leave her or his health problem to the "experts."

Such "knowledge" is advertised as truth by well meaning but sometimes uncritical health promotion workers. Sets of beliefs are propagated, which may appear to justify a particular policy. But they may actually be adopted mainly to further powerful interests. To further these policies, educational campaigns are undertaken that ostensibly protect health but which—without adequate factual basis—instigate social practices that impose controls and risks on certain groups, and women in particular.

Doctors are still widely regarded as the institutionalized experts on all matters related to health and, indeed, to almost any aspect of our lives. Many areas generally regarded as within the medical ambit are basically *social* problems that may have social, political, and economic solutions—for example, aging, drug abuse, and mental illness. Yet doctors have rarely been known to make a disclaimer to knowledge about a given topic, no matter how far from their experience in medical training and practice.

In certain circumstances doctors have control over the life and death of their clients. This apparently gives them authority and expertise to pronounce on topics such as the legalization of euthanasia, which should surely be seen as involving the human right to choose or reject, to give or withhold consent. If the medical profession is involved, it is because of the potential for abuse of individual rights, and involves profound consideration of the ethics of the medical profession.

Professionalization

Both the medical and the legal professions have upper-middle- class origins, and this social positioning is associated with their dominant group interests and beliefs. Law and medicine share very high occupational status in western countries.

The attitudes of most members of these professions could also be expected to be like those of members of the dominant groups. Education at medical schools mostly reinforces such attitudes, and adds professionalization, whether instituted by the curriculum, textbooks, educators or peers.

Like science, professional work is usually claimed to be objective, value free, an have judgements that are detached and impartial. There is no recognition of the operation of any ideological framework, nor that theirs is essentially a viewpoint biased toward masculine middle-class interests. The mystique of professionalization maintains that the expert has skills, "knowledge," and training that will enable her or him, in contrast to the ordinary citizen, to solve problems. The loyalty of professionals is to the system, the profession, or the employing agency rather than to the consumer.

Above I have discussed the approaches that the authors are most skeptical about. Our "map of the field" now brings us to an area with which we have some sympathy, but also doubt, political economy.

Political economy

The political economy approach is based primarily on the analysis of state relations both within and between countries, and includes relations of states with transnational corporations. Such an analysis reveals the economic differences between people's lives in the OECD group of countries, which we talk about in this book, and conditions of life in most of the rest of the world. The interdisciplinary background and broad macro level approach of political economy can enhance our understanding of aging through examining the "big picture," and seeing "how economic, political and socio-cultural factors interact to shape and determine the meaning and experience of old age" (Minkler 1991: 1).

There is some support among the authors of this book for the approach of political economy as expounded by Minkler and Estes. In particular, we agree with Estes' criticism of "other gerontological perspectives" for taking for granted existing structural arrangements and the importance of the market in distributing rewards in society. We also value political economy's critique of gerontology's conventional explanation of the "dependency" of some older people as the result of their individual life course choices in their work and behavior (Estes 1991: 21).

But we do not find acceptable either the priority given to state and class in Estes' analysis, or the accompanying neglect of the *gendered processes* that play a vital part in structuring aging. Feminist analyzes in this area have been late in coming, but now they seem to be superseding approaches based primarily on class. For example, the malestream political economy analysis has typically failed to remark that the lives of many women, especially indigenous women the world over, have been grossly affected by globalization and has neglected also to examine how inequalities of race and age have been exacerbated. The enthusiasm of many political economists for "freeing the market" has been based on increased profits made by banks and other corporations, ignoring the deteriorating conditions and poverty in developing countries and elsewhere. Jan Pettman (1996: 171), however, taking a feminist approach, points out that "Women's different but related location within a global political economy both links and divides the women of the world." Partly as a result of this, the authors of this book are very conscious of the differences in our oppression and that of older women in less fortunate countries and groups. Consequently, as Jenny states in the prologue these differences make us unable to position ourselves with women in poorer countries or validly represent their conditions.

We appreciate the fact that political economy has also enabled continuous exposure of the exploitative role of transnational corporations in industries related to aging—such as pharmaceutical firms. Similarly, it has helped reveal the economic motivation involved in medicine as profession and practice, especially in its relations with government, the health sciences, and with nonorthodox medicine. However, the political economy approach regards people as passive products of social structures: "The structure and operations of major social institutions shape the subjective experience and objective conditions of older persons" (Estes 1991: 23).

We, in our turn, view ourselves as older women and consumers who *actively* shape our lives and influence the structures. The interaction is an important source of social change that is influenced by the rise of a new spirit in older people. It involves a determination to be healthier and more active than people of their age in previous years. This spirit of embracing aging is pragmatically based in the continually increasing longevity and well being of older people: in a survey of 1,050 people of 60 years and over in Sydney, Australia, most people described themselves as healthy and unaffected by sickness and disability (Gibson 1983). Such a spirit does not jibe with the way gerontology has tended to equate aging with chronological age and with biological decline and illness. It throws doubt on assumptions about an "aging process," for political economy does not always take account of the diversity of the older population, nor the complexity of social and psychological factors in aging, nor the variety of environmental and cultural influences.

Aging, we find, is better seen as a social construct—like disability or suicide—and not an objectively existing state or process. To summarise the authors' view of political economy, we share some of its basic perspectives, while having radical doubts about others.

Theories Affect Policy

Social policy rarely rests on theory. But policymakers interact with the "experts" and the consumers so everyone participates in creating the prevalent discourse, with all its underlying assumptions about appropriate roles, who is to blame, who is deserving of help, and so on. So it is legitimate to ask how much of the discourse's devaluation of older people is to be found in gerontology. In this area, theories have, in fact, remained rather static and unhelpful in the formulation of policy—that is, unhelpful from an older woman's point of view.

Devaluation occurs, for example, in the analysis of older women as the cause of a crisis in welfare provision. As Rosslyn points out, this crisis ideology has been adopted by gerontological perspectives not only in western countries, but in Japan, India, and elsewhere (chapter 4). The approach has been discredited by the use of ethnographic research and by deconstruction techniques (Cohen, 1992). A second example is found in *disengagement theory*, which asserts that there is a process of gradual withdrawal from society. This idea is based in functionalism, and the disengagement is taken to be natural, inevitable, and beneficial. Thus, for the frail aged confined to a nursing home, it has been thought natural to withdraw from the present into a state of reminiscence about the past, leading to further social isolation. It must be argued that withdrawal and isolation may well be forced on some older people by society's devaluation of them and policy toward them. For example, rural neglect of older people and lack of public transport increase isolation.

The reverse of disengagement theory is *activity theory*, and this provides another source of devaluation. It holds that continued activity is characteristic of older people and beneficial to them. This inspires judgmental exhortations to "successful aging," a concept that has been taken as proven correct because older women have been found to learn to "cope" (another judgmental concept) on below-poverty line income or by means of entrepreneurial ventures taken up in later life. This implies that those who do not manage "successful aging" have failed in some way to respond to the benefits that policy is seen as offering. The "failure" is taken to indicate that older people, not social policy, are to blame.

There is still, unfortunately, a continuous orientation toward the older age groups as a problem population—it can be seen in the use of terms such as "management," "dependency," "problems of the elderly," in misconceived calculations of the "dependency ratio", (Jenny's chapter 2), and even in "the burden on the baby boomers."

The influence of the medical model on policy is profound. It narrows the desirable focus on the promotion of healthy aging for all to concentrate on catering to individual older womens' medical problems. This is a retreat that affects policy fundamentally. Some older people themselves, as well as policymakers, are convinced that aging is a pathological condition, requiring doctoring and health services galore, stoical endurance of the sick role, multiple medications, spending on hospitals rather than preservation of well being, and nursing homes. What an industry is created!

The result is that policy toward aging reinforces the present state of power relations and assigns a powerless, dependent role to older women, especially those who are also close to living in poverty. Fortunately there also exist encouragements to refuse this role and embrace human rights and a feminist philosophy.

Feminist Critique of Science and Gerontology

> Being able to generate, validate and control our own knowledge about ourselves and society is then of critical importance to women (Spender, 1983).

There have been feminist critiques along three separate lines.

1. Scientific thinking and method are seen as masculine and patriarchal, resulting in "systematic biases and inadequacies in malestream theories," thinking, and methods (Bleier and Bleier 1996);
2. Science has been used to establish and perpetuate the oppression of subordinate groups, including women. It has enabled other humans to dominate the world and to use,

destroy, and exterminate its resources and creatures. Similarly, gerontology has perpetuated the subordination of older people.

3. As mentioned, women have been largely excluded from scientific occupations, especially from crucial policy positions high in relevant occupational hierarchies.

I shall concentrate on critiquing the first of these, scientific thinking and research method, and reaching an affirming statement about feminisms and feminist approaches to research.

Of course there are many perspectives on feminism, from the most conservative, "liberal feminism" (which has affinity with functionalist theory and right-wing politics), to "socialist feminism" (which recognizes that class, gender, race, age, etc., all play a part in oppression) and "marxist feminism" (which gives priority to workers' oppression over women's oppression), to "radical feminism" (which holds that the oppression of women is the most fundamental kind of oppression), and "post-modern feminism" (which insists that deconstructive techniques must be applied to critique feminist theory)(Tong 1989). None of these feminisms present distinct viewpoints. I would not find it easy to fit any individual (not even myself) into one of these boxes even if I had the right to do so. Most of us have elements of more than one kind of feminism and change from time to time. A feminist can be defined as such only by herself.

However, let's hope my fellow authors will forgive me if I try to characterize our feminisms a little. Jenny has already positioned us in various ways (prologue), and this will give the reader a little more understanding of where we are. On the whole we seem to have a leaning toward radical feminism. For some of us have a background (now largely left behind) in socialist feminism, with a varying amount of influence of post-modernist feminism. All of us have been involved in the women's movement and for some there is also the influence of lesbian experience.

Male theorists have for too long justified speaking for women as well as men by claiming that their theory is universal and ungendered, and applies to all human beings. While it is still mainly men who have the power and resources to create, represent, and convey "truth," women have *different* and varying experiences, needs, preferences, and solutions to problems. In this book we are claiming "space" for discourse and theory about our gendered experience, and reconstructing their meanings.

Both sexes have pointed out the contrast between the approaches of men and of women.

The attributes of science are the attributes of males; . . . science is cold, hard, impersonal, "objective"; women, by contrast, are warm, soft, emotional, "subjective." (Elizabeth Fee 1983).

Yet feminist theorists criticize the abstract categories used by male social scientists and the oversimplification in their two-fold divisions that have served to legitimize and conceal women's oppression—such as male/female, pure/applied science, mind/body, public/private, culture/nature, cognitive/affective, and left/right brain.

At this point there is a general divergence of view between feminist socialists and radical feminists, though there is no very clearcut difference. In the main the socialist (and liberal) feminists' standpoint is that science and social science could be *gender neutral* ; and that, if more scientists were women who adopted a feminist approach, science would no longer be patriarchal. Fee (1983) voices this cautious approach.

We need not . . . go so far as, to reject the whole human effort to comprehend the world in rational terms nor the idea that forms of knowledge can be subjected to critical evaluation and empirical testing.

This "standpoint feminism" basically maintains the common-sense view of science I described earlier, and is vulnerable to the criticisms I made of it. The radical feminist viewpoint, on the other hand, is that science is inevitably *gender specific* and patriarchal, whoever the scientist is: "scientific thinking itself is constitutionally masculine or patriarchal, and . . . cannot be redeemed for humane, let alone feminist, purposes." (Broom, 1989). Several of the present authors follow this line of thought.

Some feminists also hold that a *feminist science* is emerging gradually, which will develop feminist theories that explain the world as seen from women's positions in society and will enable women to reconceptualize reality so that it reflects their interests and values. Hilary Rose seeks feminist knowledge that takes women's experience as scientifically valid, no longer makes a simple split between intellect and emotion, and emphasizes a holistic approach, including harmony, and complexity (Rose, H. 1986).

Feminist and Male Research Methods?

Few have claimed that there is a distinct feminist method. Rather there may be considered to be general ways of going about research that incorporate certain feminist assumptions. Reinhartz declared that "feminism is a perspective, not a research method" (Reinharz 1992, 240). Her views can be summarized as follows.

> Feminists use many different research methods. Feminist research involves ongoing criticism of non-feminist scholarship. It is guided by feminist theory, transdisciplinary, aims to create social change, tries to represent diversity, may include the researcher as a person, and attempts to develop special relations with people studied and with the reader.

In research methods as used by most men (and some women) it has often been assumed without justification that certain aspects of society were units that could be considered equal to each other, to be added or subtracted, and even measured and compared. Roberts has pointed out how taking a feminist perspective affects theoretical, methodological, practical, and ethical issues in research projects. The public sphere is based mainly on time-oriented rhythms of the workplace, and these can, in general, be measured. But many women's lives also have task-oriented rhythms, for example in domestic work and childcare. Women's experience thus spans both spheres and both types of orientation. But most quantitative research appears unable to take this into account (Roberts 1981). Stanley and Wise showed how gender affects the *process* of research also, including the interaction between researcher and researched, and between researcher and publisher (Stanley and Wise 1983).

Qualitative research has generally been preferred by feminists, for *quantitative* work treats people as objects and can adequately investigate only things that can be measured. Feminists have replaced experimentation and surveys largely with *experiential* analysis, which takes both researcher and researched into account. They have used the methods of ethnomethodology, or in-depth studies of people's lives, because these allow the voices of the persons investigated to be heard, and make it possible to understand the world from their subjective point of view.

One point of view is that feminist research methods must be different from the patriarchal approach. Perhaps Piercy's science fiction helped to show the way.

> Our technology did not develop in a straight line from yours. . . We have limited resources. We plan cooperatively. We can afford to waste. . . nothing. You might say our—you'd say religion?—ideas make us see ourselves as partners with water, air, birds, fish, trees. (Piercy 1976).

It can be argued that in research it is not the *method* that makes it feminist but the raising of women's issues, the alternative hypotheses proposed, the types of evidence given, and the ultimate purpose of female empowerment. Thus there is no feminist method, only methods adapted as required to feminist research projects.

Methods We Have Used

The foregoing feminist critique provided a transition to discovering where, in our "map of the field," we locate ourselves. As a beginning, I will illustrate the approaches taken by the authors of this book to research method.

Methods using experiential analysis are explained in several chapters. Rosemary used the procedure of in-depth focus group discussion as a way of empowering women. In this way, she writes, "they come to *revalue* their lives, even those or perhaps especially those, for which the major achievement has been survival" (chapter 12). Jenny and Pam combine three methods— using the literature extensively; analysis of the content of in-depth, semi-structured interviews with older women; and their own experience (chapter 6). Rosslyn drew on two main sources, a study of older women in the retail industry and a survey of trade union policies on women and mature workers (chapter 4). Again the interviews were open-ended and followed a life-course approach. Her own experience also played a role in framing the research topic and the approach. A guided autobiographical approach was also used by Rosemary (chapter 12), but the outcome is surprisingly different from Rosslyn's. Using my experience working in a group of older women with an innovative approach to housing themselves, I have examined the possibilities of some experiential "routes" to empowerment (chapter 11).

The following account of the methodology of a feminist research project illustrates many of the points made so far about feminist research (Power and Wineke 1994). It refers to the work of Aileen and Chris and others reported in chapter 10:

> *Separate Lives* was envisaged as a collaborative research project involving women from a range of organizations in the health and community sectors, as well as university researchers. While there is no consensus on what constitutes feminist collaborative research, this kind of enquiry emphasizes the participation of those who are the subjects of the study in the research decision-making processes, and aims to bring about increased social justice for participants; underpinning it are notions of equality and openness. Whereas in traditional methods of enquiry, the roles of researcher and subject are mutually exclusive, collaborative research is marked by a spirit of mutuality and exchange. While these principles informed our work, we also acknowledge the

limitations of the project in achieving this kind of inclusiveness. The women interviewed did not participate in the overall decision-making processes of the research. The project could be defined as collaborative, mainly in terms of the interventions of the research team; a very diverse group of academics and service providers working with several older women from the local community. This alone proved to be an extremely complex and challenging undertaking. However, finding ways of moving towards greater degrees of mutuality, needs to be a goal for future projects.

Noeleen's methodology includes exposing some of the cultural images of older women, deconstructing them, and linking them up with the practices of service providers and others (chapter 7) —an effective way of critiquing the discourse on aging.

Most of the papers in this book can be seen as employing research methods that embrace Reinharz' themes outlined previously, and lead into Stanley and Wise's conception of a feminist sociology as follows.

A Feminist Sociology?

Some urge the extreme view that *all theory* is essentially masculine and patriarchal, and that feminist theory cannot and should not be developed. Here we mostly disagree and would rather support Stanley and Wise in their second edition (1993: 8), where they attempt to formulate the basis for a "feminist sociology" which may be summarised as follows (Stanley and Wise 1993: 9).

1. Seeing those we research as being on the same plane as ourselves, and including men among the researched,
2. Regarding both "knowledges" and research as deriving from the position of the person who is making sense of the world,
3. Analysing "structure," "facts," and "inequalities" (and "self"), but recognizing them as socially constructed,
4. Viewing the differences between women as indicating different knowledges and varying ability to exercise power over other women and in society in general,
5. Refusing research that would colonize other groups, whoever they are,
6. Rejecting a positivist view of "reality" as "out there" and available for observation and measurement, but accepting that "there *is* a social reality, one which members of society construct as having objective existence above and beyond competing constructions and interpretations of it."

The last point, which concerns how we understand the nature of reality, seems to be regarded by Stanley and Wise as an essential basis for a feminist epistemology. But I do not find it essential for a feminist epistemology to hold that "there is a social reality" as described. It seems better to state that we cannot know from the evidence whether there is such a social reality. We do not necessarily have to adopt relativism as an alternative, but can simply live with uncertainty until feminist scholarship is ready to proceed further. For the time being feminism can be considered as discovering a "sociology of the lack of knowledge" (Reinharz 1992:248).

We believe that in the feminist work on older women presented in this book, we have moved along with, represented, and further developed the burgeoning feminist sociology outlined above. We believe also that feminist theory and praxis are changing and are improving the representation of older women, their participation in society, their power to claim their rights, and their own view of themselves and their future.

Conclusion

McKinnon has declared that,

As marxist method is dialectical materialism, feminist method is Consciousness raising [which is] the collective critical reconstruction of the meaning of women's social experience, as women live through it (McKinnon, 1985).

This collective critical reconstruction of the meaning of women's social experience, as described above by McKinnon, is the primary method we have employed in this book. Much of the material is indeed involved with what we ourselves have lived through.

But, in addition, this book presents our transformation of male rationality to incorporate some aspects of it in our feminist methodology. We have critiqued gerontology by portraying alternative rationales and methods. We have used and incorporated political economy while developing feminist theory, which interacts with it and highlights new ways of thinking. Deeply *"rational but not detached"* is one way of describing our method. We have rejected the positivist detached observer, for we do not believe detachment is possible—nor even desirable—for us when examining our experience, nor do we believe detachment has ever been possible for men in their attempted value free, objective science.

It has not been easy to write in this different way for a group of trained academics whose daily lives, teaching, and even in some respects, research, are performed under the aegis of a male-dominated academia. There is also the lingering influence of our socialization as women in our earlier years to be compliant, uncomplaining, and unobtrusive. Older women especially are uneasily aware of such well-learned and constraining paradigms lurking underneath our more recent participation in the creation and transmission of feminist thinking. Such hesitations must be overcome, however, for we are committed to using our remaining time to speak out in order to achieve our goal of empowering older women.

Underlying our deconstruction of political economy, Marxism, the dominance of medicine, malestream science, and social science, and underlying the reconstruction we have achieved in this book, there is a common theme. This is the assertion of our deep sensation of an inalienable right to control our own lives.

Gone is the time when we silently adopted the universalism of male theory to describe our lives. Past is the acceptance of research on male subjects as relevant to women's experience. These have been exposed now as ways of imposing limits on us, constraining our independence and participation, and preventing our full potential for development as persons. We ourselves, as older women and women fast becoming older, are the only ones who can validly examine and generalize from our lives to our futures. In doing so we take over the control of our own lives.

Endnote
[1]Portions of this paper are drawn from Sargent, M., Nilan P., and Winter, G. 1997. *The new sociology for Australians*. 4th ed. Melbourne: Longman Cheshire.

SECTION TWO

Deconstructing Age

Introduction

Section two is the center of the book, the solid core. This is the center of our critique, the deconstruction of current perceptions and practices as they affect us. Here we turn our focused attention to specific, functional aspects of our lives. We cannot examine every aspect of our lives, but three areas are central. They are work, health, and housing. Each is problematic to us as women and as aging persons. Because older women are positioned at the intersection of agist and sexist oppressions, we experience each of these three areas as extremely difficult and problematic. We believe that the combined effects of agism and sexism are more than the sum of the parts. Older women, as a homogenized category, as a commodified object of others' attention, experience disadvantages in a way that older men do not and that younger women do not.

We seek , in this section, to unravel the mechanisms by which this double disadvantage occurs. We explore subjectivities and the lived experience of older women. We examine the hegemonic discourses and the contradictions entailed in those: the double messages and contradictory expectations placed on us. We look at the professional and social structures that underpin and perpetuate this disadvantage and seek to identify whose interests are being served.

We turn the microscope first on the world of work and employment. What becomes very clear is that women *work* all their lives, but very little of that work is paid. As Rosslyn, Jenny, and Pam point out, our paid employment, even for professional "high-flyers," tends to be discontinuous, part-time, casualized, and marginalized. Much of our adult lives is spent in the unpaid care of others: children, grandchildren, spouses, aging parents, and disabled or sick adults. This continues until we ourselves are "frail old" and in need of care. Yet even as older women, we give more caring than we receive. To this caring work is added voluntary work in the community, work that is said to underpin social capital and our welfare system, and in which we continue to engage well into our old age. Rosemary explores the positives and negatives of that experience. Yet despite our continued and well documented contribution to society, we are counted as a burden, useless old women unable to support ourselves, a drain on the nation's tax-supported pension. As Jenny and Pam note, few of us are in a position to retire on privately funded superannuation. Few of us had the continuous paid career that makes this sort of self-funded retirement possible. Most of us would like to continue some sort of part-time paid employment at least through our fifties, and, increasingly, through our sixties. Yet, as Rosslyn points out, employers both value the older woman worker in order to exploit her skills, but also to devalue her worth and deny her the recognition she deserves.

Even before we retire we become a commodified object of surveillance and control. Our post-menopausal bodies become pathologized, in need of remedial treatment. And so we are encouraged to make ourselves available, docile bodies in the hands of the medical professions. "For our own good" we are subjected to intrusive forms of medical screening of our distinctively female organs, as argued by Noeleen. As we continue to age we deal with the dreaded threat of Alzheimers or dementia, or other forms of frailty, all of which are pathologized, medicalized, and subject to the regimes of institutional and professional control. As women we are caught up in the apparent inevitability of this process, as nurses, as carers, as patients. Sharyn simultaneously explores the pain of that experience while she attempts to deconstruct the regimes of medical control that produce and are produced by it.

Ultimately, a small percentage of us may "end up" in a nursing home. Here we experience the ultimate end point of medical control; a life entirely controlled by the institutional care deemed necessary to maintain our frail and utterly dependent minds and/or bodies. Townsend (1981), among others, talks about the structured dependency of the elderly, and the creation of massive industries such as nursing homes that are fuelled by the raw material of older women's frail bodies. Friedan (1993) speaks of nursing homes as "death sentences" for those forced to enter them. Rhonda, in this book, talks of "benevolent oppression." Yet as Rhonda and Sharyn argue, it is not that simple. Sometimes, because of the level of personal care required, the nursing home option may actually provide greater independence for older women than is possible with total reliance on relatives.

Nursing homes provide one of two, extreme, structural options for the housing of older women. The other is living alone in the community. Most architecture, planning, and housing options have not attempted to take the needs of women, especially older women, into account. Housing has been designed mainly by men for the earlier patterns of living of small young families and not for single persons. Boarding houses, like many nursing homes, provide little opportunity for control over our own lives. While some people appear to enjoy life in a retirement village, some retirement village managements may exploit people through their conditions of sale and fees. Typically, they offer little say to residents, one of whom said

> when it's all done for you, when you have few decisions to make, when your own physical restrictions prevent contact with the complexities of the wider community, you can feel that you have little power over your life, and little challenge within it (NSW Council on the Aging 1987).

We do know that about two-thirds of older people would prefer to stay in their own homes. Adequate home services, including public transport, would make it possible for many more people to choose to "age in place." Without these services, many older women are deprived of any real opportunity to make a choice. Further, much is said of the loneliness and isolation of older women, living alone in the community. It appears that we have to choose between two extreme structural solutions to housing in our old age: we can either have support or independence, but not both.

Chris and her coworkers explore what it means for women living independently in the community. While women living alone may sometimes feel lonely, or vulnerable in times of need, most of the women they talked to found the experience of living independently in the community to be a very positive one. The key is social connectedness, and a presumption of tolerably good health.

We became increasingly aware, as we prepared this book, that we need a range of options for housing. Nursing homes will remain a sensible option for some. So will retirement villages and independent living facilities in the community. But we need a range of new options, ones that support and empower, that provide the opportunities for connectedness *and* a sense of control over our own lives. This point will be taken up again in section three of this book, in which Margaret explores the possibility of the collective empowerment of older women through community and shared housing.

Chapter Four

The Invisible Woman: Older Women Workers
Rosslyn Reed

The women's movement has always argued that the personal is political. The study on which this chapter is based had its origins in a personal experience. It was the first time that older women in the workforce became visible for me, both as a woman entering mid-life and as a researcher concerned for social equality and justice for women at work.

In the early 1990s, I accompanied my teenage son to purchase a gift of a radio-cassette player. He also required a device for attaching it to his portable compact disc player. In the department store, I observed a game of competitive youthful masculinity as the young male sales assistant and my son of comparable age sparred with each other through the language of modern sound technology—each seeking to score a blow with the level of his specialized knowledge. Having decided which player to purchase and the appropriate connecting device, it was my turn to finalize the commercial transaction. I had not noticed the other sales assistant (or was she the department manager?) talking on the telephone behind the counter until that moment. But the young male sales assistant now turned to her. She told him where the stock was to be found in the storeroom. Then she asked my son what brand and type of compact disc player he had and informed him that the selected device was unsuitable. She told us what type to purchase elsewhere.

I was initially impressed by her knowledge, her confidence, and her control over her domain. Then I noticed her age—very definitely over 55 years and possibly 65 or more. It was hard to tell precisely, but she was not what is popularly called "well preserved." Since that encounter I have been conscious of the number of older women workers in retailing. Why are they there? What are their aspirations as workers and for the future? What opportunities and constraints do they encounter?

Joan's Story

Joan (not her real name) matriculated in Czechoslovakia and began to study for a career in opera. After she came to Australia she was employed simultaneously in two clerical jobs; one while her daughter was at school and another at night. After her son was born, she had a series of casual jobs in delivery, babysitting, and as a shop assistant in a small food store. As a result of this experience, she decided to apply to the large department stores for a better job and has worked there full time for the past fourteen years—twelve with her current employer. Marlene's almost continuous workforce experience has resulted from her need for income. Her late husband was employed as a professional in the public sector but, it appears, at a level below his formal level of qualifications.

Because she has no family in Australia, Joan has had neither family support for childcare during the six years of her husband's illness nor for elder care responsibilities. She did prepare meals for elderly neighbors for a period. While her daughter lives independently, her son continues in tertiary education and is partly dependent on her. His Austudy (tertiary education living allowance) does not cover much beyond his books and car expenses.

Marlene has not had an easy life. She had a fall thirty years ago that left her with chronic back pain and, now, arthritis. While she has needed to take an occasional day of sick leave when in great pain, she did manage to accumulate some sick leave. She had also accumulated eight weeks annual leave that she hoped to use for an overseas visit. She is grateful that her employers allowed her to take all of this leave and some uncertified sick days during the last six months of her late husband's illness. She is also grateful that they allowed her to use the business phone in emergencies although she normally uses the store pay phones for private telephone calls at work. She travels further to work each day than most of the other women in the study because her employer is on Sydney's north shore. She regards her health as "fair," and while not "old" at 58, is feeling a "bit more worn out," perhaps because she is also working through a period of grief at present.

Joan has been a loyal employee. She enjoys selling and assisting younger staff, especially in the fashion area. She thinks mature or older workers can say things to customers that a younger person could not. While she feels older people are undervalued in society, this is not so where she works. Although Joan expresses dissatisfaction with her pay because retail salespersons are "considered as untrained laborers and that's it," she finds the union supportive. She reads their literature and takes up the benefits they offer. Her current income is not adequate for her and her son's immediate needs. Just before her husband's death, they paid out the balance of their house mortgage. There is a small sum in her husband's superannuation rollover fund as well as her own small superannuation payout when she does retire from her current job.

She hopes to retire at 60 because she finds full-time work "a little bit too much." She hopes then to continue in casual work to supplement her retirement income. She is "scared" that she will not have enough money in retirement. She is confused about the relationships between superannuation income, government age pension entitlements and the fringe benefits attached. She is trying not to think about it all while she works through her grief at the loss of her husband. She feels it particularly unfair that she has worked and paid taxes for so long but may not have access to a pension. She says, "just because you're old . . . should you always eat mince and just sleep in rags or just have one good outfit when you go out so people will think you are quite civilised?"

In her retirement, Joan plans to do something to enhance the lives of other older people, like reading to them (but she draws the line at cleaning their homes)! She enjoys singing, especially folk songs, reading, reciting poetry, and loves listening to all types of music. She really would like to have a season ticket to the theatre. This is a great love she has not been able to afford throughout her working life.

Maureen's Story

Maureen (not her real name) is 62 years old. She lives with her retired husband in a leafy middle-class Sydney suburb and works in a prestigious department store in a nearby regional shopping center.

Maureen left school at 17 without matriculating. She had worked in holiday jobs in retailing but because it was not considered respectable then, she entered secretarial work. Varied jobs in Australia, New Zealand, Britain, and Canada followed but retail work like waitressing was confined to the "working holiday" context. After seven years as a mother and with four children under seven years of age, Maureen needed an "outlet" and set out to complete her education. Part-time study for the higher school certificate (HSC—or matriculation) and full time study at University to complete a Bachelor of Arts and Diploma of Education led to a seven year career, achieving the position of head of the history department in a private secondary school. Teaching, like education, had been part of a process of personal achievement. But the accumulated stress of full-time employment and parenting and a feeling that she had not "got out of school really" led her to resign her teaching post.

During this break from paid work in her late forties and early fifties, Maureen researched her family history and took school parties on historical walking tours on a casual basis. She attempted to return to secretarial work on a casual basis but found it difficult after her positions of authority. When she tried to enter management, she was told she was well, even overqualified, obviously efficient, and too old to reenter the workforce. Younger people would not appreciate a manger old enough to be their mother!

After a brief period reorganizing a school office and an encounter with a male school principal who could not accept women in positions of authority, she approached the department store because they were known to prefer a mature, better educated female sales staff. Although seeking part-time work, she was offered a full time job. After eighteen months she was appointed as a department manager—partly because noone else would do the job. After four and a half years in the job she has inquired about promotion opportunities because she is now ready for a new challenge. Her young male supervisory manager has told her she has "no chance."

Maureen has been free of elder and other caring responsibilities undertaken by many other women. Her formerly self-employed husband is partly dependent on her earnings. Her separated daughter has not come home to live, perhaps because independence is so highly valued by her mother. She is entitled to some superannuation in her own right if she did decide to retire, but the time for that decision is unclear. She still hopes her networks may lead her into an opportunity for retail management elsewhere.

Although she had a hysterectomy while still at University, Maureen enjoys good health. Most of her energy is devoted to her work. Work is a form of resistance to aging—she happily taps into her witch side as a source of power and wisdom but rejects the notion of crone as ugly, and she will not allow herself to become ugly. With other women colleagues, she speculates about the potential for post-menopausal women to rule the world and deplores the social devaluation of their experience and contribution. For her leisure she enjoys reading, some occasional tennis, bridge, movies, and the beach. She likes to have time for family and friends. She is planning her retirement: she has joined a political party and hopes to redirect her energy there. This she hopes will be a new challenge.

The Context of this Chapter

Increasingly women are resisting the social pressures that encourage or force them to leave the workforce at around 55 years of age—a decade before the conventional retirement/pensionable age for men and five years before what has been the pensionable age for women in Australia. Their activity and economic contribution are rendered invisible by the expectations of inactivity and passivity resulting from the intersections of sexism and agism and the current moral panic about the burden of a shrinking working population supporting a large frail, mainly female, aged population in the near future (see Noeleen's chapter 1 and Jenny's chapter 2). This view of a large population of dependent aging women ignores the experience of the majority of women globally. Women in so-called Third World countries are likely to be working harder as they age to provide for their families. As a result of the risks of childbearing, poor nutrition due to cultural constraints surrounding food distribution, that the family and other deprivations and disadvantages which are spread across the population, women in these countries have similar or shorter life expectancies than men (Katz and Monk 1993; 5-17).

Within western industrialized countries on the other hand, there is considerable similarity in women's working life patterns. In general, the workplace and its conditions have been set up by men to suit their interests and a typically masculine life course. Women have interrupted careers, earn less than men, are employed in a narrower range of occupations and are more likely to work part-time. As discussed by Jenny in chapter 2, there are both international similarities and differences that reflect particular national policies. For example, research in the United States (but not in Australia) shows the gender wage gap for the 40–50 year age group is greater than for younger age groups irrespective of education, qualifications and broken or unbroken employment (Hollenshead 1982: Nuccio 1989). British research shows that educational qualifications, provide some protection for the level of wages and salaries despite movement in and out of the workforce (Crompton, Hantrais, and Walters, 1990). Australia has higher levels of occupational gender segregation than most other developed countries but a narrower gender wage gap with women's earnings less likely to decline with age than men's (Kalish and Williams 1983).

While it would be unwise to generalize from one single country and single industry study of older women's employment, there are similarities across national boundaries in the structure and organization of the retail industry that make it suitable for some discussion here.

Retailing in Australia has a specific history and structure (Reekie 1993), but its contemporary development, structure, and culture appear similar to other Western countries. For example, there is a gender segmented dual labor market with young male managers and a female sales labor force, as has been shown in United States' research (Jamieson and Webber 1991; Bluestone and Stevenson 1981).

In the past two decades, married women have been recruited to part-time work as in Britain (Cockburn 1991). With improvements in job tenure for part-time workers as a result of union pressure, retailers have shifted their recruitment policies to favor juniors as casual employees (Runciman 1992; Jamieson and Webber 1991), and more recently women in the 35–45 years age group. Some older women are, either by choice or force of circumstances, already continuing in paid work well beyond conventional exit ages of 55 and past retirement ages of 60 and even 65 in department stores in a range of locations in Sydney.

Retailing was, therefore, chosen as the site of an exploratory research project[1] using open-ended interviews of older women as well as department store managers and the relevant union. The results of that study have been reported elsewhere (Reed 1996). The emphasis here is on the possibility of older women remaining in the workforce longer to support themselves economically and to provide for their future retirement plans. At the same time, the interrelationships of agism and sexism are explored in the context of their overall life experiences. The life experiences that are reflected on raise questions about the potential for, and constraints for older women to "reinvent" themselves through the aging process (see chapter 12).

As in other comparable countries such as the United Kingdom, the women's pension age was set five years earlier than men's (Arber and Ginn 1995;71). This is now being phased out to take account of the expectations of the current cohort of women over 55 years of age who did not expect to be financially independent after marriage and may well not have reentered the labor market after bearing children.

Mandatory retirement is now unlawful in NSW (as in other Australian States) because of amendment to the Anti-Discrimination Act, 1977. Penalties are also available for those able to demonstrate age discrimination. As Arber and Ginn

(1995;70) point out in relation to Britain, this provides a theoretical opportunity for women to improve their pension/superannnuation entitlements after child-bearing. Alternatively, it allows the opportunity to accumulate other savings or to maintain financial independence from spouses or the state. In some instances and in contravention of traditional patriarchal relations (Arber and Ginn 1995), women may contribute to their spouse's financial support. In many respects, then, a study of older women in Sydney department stores can be generalized to other comparable countries.

Tracing the Labor Market History of this Cohort
The working lives of Australian born women aged between 55 and 66 in the early 1990s have been affected by two major labor market developments. First, on leaving school they were channelled into a narrow range of occupations that were expected to occupy the time between the end of education and marriage, or at the latest, child-bearing years. Second, they are the first generation to demonstrate the bi-modal pattern of labor force participation, when from the 1960s onwards, married women, including mothers, were drawn back into the workforce to meet the needs of industry for new sources of labor. The first peak in the participation pattern occurs at "twenty-something," while the second is in their late forties, after which women's workforce participation has, in the past, declined rapidly until age 55, as is similar to other comparable countries (Arber and Ginn 1995).

For women over 55 years of age to continue working in department stores, they have had to negotiate a series of changes in employment within this pattern. They are now resisting the construction of them as too old to work.

The women in this study entered the labor market during or immediately after World War II, mainly as teachers, nurses, or, more commonly, as clerical/secretarial workers. The alternatives for the majority of lower middle and working class young women at the time are also represented: female trades like millinery and working in family businesses. Marriage and childbearing constituted direct and indirect "marriage bars," forcing most, but particularly working class women out of the labor force and into marginal employment like babysitting or direct selling. Some women could also juggle childcare and paid work, such as in a family business or atypical arrangements for one child in order for a woman to maintain a tenuous link to the labor market, but interrupted careers were the norm, and a second and subsequent births, the absence of adequate childcare, the dominance of husband's/partner's careers, and expectations of "care" effectively removed most of the women in this study from the labor force for a period.

Incomplete training, occupational, industrial, and techno-logical change, and the unwillingness of male employers to recognize the skills women developed in secondary labor markets or in other unpaid work made reentry to the workforce difficult for this group. But there were economic and social pressures to reenter, just as there had been to find alternatives to formal, full-time employment while children were very young.

Jane, a qualified teacher, had run an employment agency from home while raising four children. Meg found herself with a "little boy to support" following her divorce. No longer employed in her husband's business, she entered retail sales. When she remarried, however, she took up catering as well. "I used to work horrific hours. We'd do weddings and sometimes I'd get home at 4 o'clock in the morning." Meg's career was only interrupted when her second husband developed cancer. After caring for him for three years, and fitting catering around domestic and caring work, she "had to give everything away for a short time." Then for financial reasons and therapy ("a nervous energy thing"), Meg worked at three jobs over seven days a week for a while: "I was selling retirement villages at the week-end and working at (department store) and on my day off, I'd work in a pharmacy."

Women from middle-class backgrounds and typical middle-class nuclear households were more likely to break from all forms of paid work after childbearing. Maureen (see Maureen's Story) pursued tertiary education; others took up technical and interest courses such as interior decorating. In her twenty-five years out of the workforce, Kate became incorporated into her husband's career (Finch 1983). Although her ex-husband is a successful publisher, Kate has made a major contribution. Two of his most popular titles were developed through her efforts in looking for articles of interest to the target audience.

> We went through a lot of years of having no money at all and then having five children . . . (to educate). So it wasn't till later years that things were good. He travelled a lot and I travelled with him . . . I ran the ship as it were and I'm still doing it because he's over there . . . When you live in the shadow of a fairly successful and powerful man who doesn't keep you there—he was very much putting me forward as we traipsed around the world . . . but still, you know, I was (husband's name) wife.

While some women of this age cohort returned to paid work after short breaks, others like Kate returned after more than twenty years absence. Both groups have entered retailing because their choice of career was initially constrained by the limited options available in the 1940s to 1950s. Their choices were then further limited because employers in general preferred masculine norms of unbroken employment records when assessing suitability for higher level positions. Women returning to the workforce with family and caring responsibilities regardless of personal educational attainments or household status had fewer opportunities to fit past careers to "typical" masculine working norms.

Furthermore, some middle-class women managed to use enforced career breaks to upgrade their educational qualifications and subsequently improve their career options. However, if they later desired breaks, because of a range of reasons from the terminal illness of a spouse, as in Meg's experience, to the desire for a break from the stresses of the "double burden" in Maureen's (see Maureen's Story), they found themselves relegated to the ranks of the unqualified when they chose to return to paid work. In this sense, then, women of this generation, regardless of social class and personal achievement, have increasingly come to demonstrate common employment patterns as they age. .

Gender and Age at Work

Women's employment in retailing in the second phase of their careers is a consequence of both economic, social, and personal factors "pushing" them into the labor market. There are also sex and race/ethnicity-biased "pull" factors, as employers draw on particular groups for their labor market strategies (Rubery 1988). As retail sales work became feminized and then casualized (Reekie 1993), mothers seeking to fit paid work around domestic responsibilities were an available pool of labor. Employers found these women to be highly attractive and sought them out as employees: they came to the job equipped to accept greater responsibility, engage in creative sales strategies, and to provide informal supervision of junior sales staff. Personnel departments in the major department stores have been recruiting more mature workers as casuals alongside their full- and part-time female sales workforce at the same time as they are participating in government programs to employ more unemployed youth.

Nonetheless, the value of older women workers is not reflected in higher wage rates. Older workers, including some former full time employees who were denied unpaid extended leave for travel or other personal needs in recent years, have access to employment, but it is insecure employment that is accompanied by increasing marginalization at work. Older women are aware of their competence and value to employers. They can also point to the limitations of their younger, inexperienced male managers. They identify the latter's agist and sexist treatment of them as inequitable and unjust, but also as inefficient and unproductive.

Former teachers, or those who have gained wide experience outside paid work like Kate, have been promoted either to department manager or administration. Kate moved from administration back to a specialized sales role for the same reason Maureen (see Maureen's Story) was promoted to department manager: no one else could succeed in the position. As Maureen's experience shows, succeeding where others have not has not produced career opportunities. At one store, all women over 55 years of age who have years of experience in specialized areas (e.g., bedding) have been moved out of their departments by a young male manager. Helen had the confidence to challenge not only this manager but several higher level managers:

> "Cause I went to the merchandising manager and personnel manager . . . He said you're paranoid about it. He said I think a change would do you all good. You need to have a challenge. Why do we need to have a challenge? . . . All of us have got merit things and we've been . . . top saleslady (sic) for (the month)."

Helen succeeded in returning to her old position after six months. Other have been required to continue in subordinate positions and report to less experienced and successful sales staff. The stresses of these situations are exacerbated because the women placed in situations of tension and conflict with each other have had good personal working relationships in the past. This is, however, more than a simple "divide and rule" management strategy. Young male managers are both reflecting agist and sexist social attitudes and shoring up their own fragile authority by taking formally rational practices to irrational lengths.

Older women are caught up in strategies of unions and management. To some extent these strategies are a management tactic to counter the success of the Shop Distributive and Allied Union in protecting the permanent 38 hour week and the fixed roster status of long standing employees with the shift to greater casualization in recent enterprise (employer-union negotiated) bargaining. This management style partially disrupts an older long-standing paternalistic strategy of "grace and favor" flexibility in rostering to facilitate family and caring responsibilities, which tend to increase with age. Joan's (see Joan's Story) experience is typical of the paternalistic style that generates employer loyalty and commitment to the firm, often at the cost of worker solidarity. Both strategies, however, are consistent with a managerial drive to control even when effective selling requires a degree of "trust" and autonomy for relatively low status "floor" employees (Fuller and Smith 1991).

While coercion and paternalism are managerial styles associated with both men and women subordinates, they are overlaid with both sexism and agism in these instances. As noted above, women returning to the workforce and retail employment bring a range of formal qualifications, experience, and practical and interpersonal skills such as selling through education of customers ("do you know this pattern dates back to 1700") or tactfully persuading customers into fashions that suit them (Joan's Story) (see Beechey 1982; Phillips and Taylor 1980). Employers tacitly recognize these skills and competencies in the way they mix, deploy and occasionally promote (choose cleverly) mature women. But they are not reflected in wage negotiations or career structures because of the paternalism and dominant patriarchal values of both employers and male union leadership.

Agism compounds sexism in, on the one hand, the denial of further challenges to women like Maureen seeking promotion beyond departmental manager and, on the other hand, imposing challenges on other women in positions where they have demonstrated competence, wish to remain, and have industrially protected permanent employment status. This is yet another example of how "trying hurts women but helps men" (Burton 1991). There also elements of the infantalizing process of older women noted by Hockey and James (1993), whereby older men and women are treated more like children but whereby men's status still remains protected. It is questionable that a man who had management experience in another industry like education would receive the same treatment as Maureen because even infantilizing practices tend to protect men's dignity at older ages. In fact, men with experience similar to women like Maureen would be unlikely to accept lower status employment in the first place (Encel and Studencki 1997: 5).

Similarly, the lack of trust of confident, competent, independent older women in management positions carries overtones of medieval images of older women as "wicked" and "evil": the cultural legacy of casting "wise women" as "witches" to devalue their knowledge or perhaps worse, "fragile" and "useless" (Sybylla 1991).

While the influences of the "beauty myth" were rarely evident among the women we interviewed, some women in retailing can be observed trying to avoid the stereotyping of older women (people) by attempting to present a "younger" or "well preserved" image. However, this strategy turns older women into caricatures of the image they hope to project and is unlikely to succeed where obvious ability, educational qualifications, and a high level of performance fail to secure recognition and promotion (see also Noeleen's chapter 1 in relation to images of older women).

These attempts to limit the confidence and aspirations of ambitious older women are not present in other contexts for two main reasons. As has been noted elsewhere (Bernard et al. 1995) some women like Joan (see Joan's Story) have internalized women's subordination. As a migrant she has had fewer social contacts (see also chapter 10 by Aileen, Chris, Lyn and Diane) and was more dependent on her own and her husband's employment for income. Work-related injury and widowhood have left her even more economically vulnerable and hence susceptible to the paternalistic managerial discourse. She has less time, money, or energy to spend on commercial "anti-aging" techniques. She is, however, a well-educated long time Australian citizen of European ethnic background and culturally indistinguishable from Anglo-Australian women working in department stores. In some ways Joan suits employers' interests more than older women who aspire to careers because she has the skills, knowledge, and stability they require without challenging masculine dominance and the existing patriarchal authority relations of the retail industry, which are partially undermined by the reliance on younger management.

Department stores have not been major employers of non-English speaking background migrants, although this is changing as they recruit from Asian communities to attract customers from these populations. They have tended to discriminate against indigenous Australians in recruitment practices (Runciman 1992). Consequently there are few if any of these racial/ethnic groups among older women in retailing. Discrimination on the basis of race, sex, and age, then, constitutes a hierarchical structure that is directly based on race in access to employment, and is systemic/indirect on the basis of sex in the middle and systemic/direct on the basis of both sex and age at the top.

The Impact of Caring Responsibilities

Constraints on career aspirations at work are encountered and resisted at the same time as older women confront increased caring responsibilities as part of their unpaid work. Some still have children living at home while they pursue tertiary education and/or are in lower paid jobs. Two others, like Joan (see Joan's Story) had experienced the death of a husband—in Helen's case also her ex-husband soon after her divorce. Caring for elders may have occurred while they were not in paid work, and others were engaged simultaneously in elder care. Meanwhile, their adult children came and went as they pursued or discontinued career programs or returned home complete with their own children following divorce—even if economically independent of their mothers. Most were "women in the middle" (Brody 1990; Watson and Mears n.d.) with a double (or greater) burden of paid and unpaid work well beyond middle age. Again these caring responsibilities and the prospect of others in the future (e.g., chronically and terminally ill aged spouses) entrenched their dependence on paternalistic managers in the context of increasingly casualized employment structures in the industry as employers seek numerical and time flexibility through collective bargaining (Jamieson and Webber 1991).

Participation in paid work is empowering for women as they age, despite or perhaps because they have had to negotiate these obstacles. Joan (see Joan's Story) is not alone in hoping for continued part-time employment after retirement from full-time work. Two women in this study were already continuing in paid work after their husbands had retired, only partly for economic reasons, as a respite from domesticity. Not all women, however, seek ongoing employment. The desire for limited employment or retirement is more likely for widows. While this can be associated with the effects of the loss of a long-time partner, it is also more likely less an effect of age or aging than of class position.

Joan and Meg had the closest to continuing labor force participation but in lower paid, more working class jobs. They also have had less opportunity to acquire superannuation than more middle-class women such as Maureen. On the other hand, Kate and other divorced women who invested much in their ex-husbands' careers at earlier ages were unlikely to benefit from the sacrifices made to promote his life-time financial security. While some divorced and separated women expected to benefit from former spouses' superannuation/pension entitlements, this seems unlikely when there is evidence that women in continuing marriages do not equally share their partner's retirement benefits (see Jenny's chapter 6).

Those seeking challenges and opportunities for paid work beyond age 60, which has been the age when Australian women became eligible for government age pensions, are those who have been under less pressure to continue in paid work, have had delayed entry or career changes through educational opportunities, and, paradoxically, are eligible for some form of superannuation/pension. For these women, continued employment could be a partial solution to the dependency crisis projected by economists and demographers in Australia and other developed countries in some individual cases[2]. But those with the least opportunity to retire may be the ones most in need of that option at an earlier age. Due to low pay and/or broken careers they have been unable to accumulate savings or investments for retirement incomes during their working lives, and their desire or need for retirement is a consequence of their social contributions as "carers" for children, spouses, and elders. Social justice demands that adequate income be available to support a retirement option at age 60, or perhaps earlier if the burden of care has been or is onerous.

Policies to Support Work or Retirement

Australian public and social policy is silent about older women's continued employment. Policies for older women emphasize services like health, housing, care, carers, consumer rights, and income security. The Mature Age Allowance and Partner Allowance operate as extensions of the age pension to effectively encourage early retirement for unemployed workers and their dependent spouses (Reed 1995). While some policies address employment opportunities for older workers, they do so with the typical life patterns of men in mind, or where they do mention differences in women's working lives, they gloss over the complexities of the patterns outlined above and extrapolate on the basis of the experience and achievements of later age cohorts such as those entering the workforce in the 1960s or later (see Kendig and McCallum 1986: 30). This sort of slippage is also apparent in Australian and British recommendations that the pensionable age of 60 for women be phased out to achieve equality with men who are eligible for age pensions at 65 (Bernard and Meade 1993; Bryson 1994; Arber and Ginn 1995).

Similarly, policies and recommendations related to women's employment treat women in universal terms and ignore the specificity of contemporary older women's experience. When they attempt to address these gender differences, they do so in patronizing ways that are premised on a deficit model of women workers. For example, the former New South Wales government's Mature Workers Advisory Committee Strategic Plan (1995–97) referred specifically to older women. This was, however, as a "special needs" group for whom research was proposed for 1996. While the recognition of women's gendered (and other) "difference" within the population is to be applauded, the construction of special needs categories is disturbing because of the potential for marginalization. This construction of older women within this program is particularly problematic as the evidence is that women have been as successful as men in obtaining employment within the program, partly because they are prepared to accept the lower status work that is offered (Encel and Studencki 1997).

Similarly, the mature workers employment program was not developed with a focus on justice or even the desire of some older women to continue in paid work after age 55. Rather the language of economic rationalism is used to promote the program to employers in terms of the market advantages of employing older people.

Unlike some Scandinavian countries (e.g., Lind 1995: 233), there are no provisions for a range of options such as work/retire/part-time work and part-time retirement/movement in and out of the workforce in later years, as many older women besides those in this study would prefer (see also Wieneke 1993).

The Role of Trade Unions

Older women's interests are also poorly understood and represented by trade unions. The women in the research group were not particularly militant. Nor were they generally hostile to unions. They, and more importantly, their parents, had lived through the years of the Great Depression, which had the potential to radicalize workers. But their working lives had spanned the decades of full employment, economic growth, and affluence, for the Australian born sector of the population especially. Both of these periods had been dominated by union organization around masculine "breadwinner" interests in wage negotiation (Ryan and Prendergast 1982).

While a very small minority of older retailing workers were hostile to unions, reflecting household class position or an intellectual association with totalitarian (communist) politics in their country of origin, this was unusual. A similar small proportion felt that unions had a significant supportive role to play. About half, however, believed unions were not supportive of older women's working aspirations. These and similar observations tend to reflect the marginal position of older women in the labor market.

> They just accept being able to work at all. I think they're grateful for being able to work. These are the conditions for older women.

My more recent research indicated that union policies tend to be silent in relation to older workers (Reed 1997). Emphasis is placed on access to retirement income rather than the right to productive work and to contribute to society. There is little understanding as yet of agism or its relationship to sexism, which many unions have found difficult to address due to past emphasis on masculine "breadwinning." One union policy, however, opposed the recent government decision to increase the pensionable age for women due to women's unequal pay; shorter, interrupted, and part-time employment opportunities, less access to superannuation; and a greater propensity for redundancy than men. This kind of policy, however, is the exception rather than the rule. The union representing women in retailing, however, remains committed to the breadwinner ideology, though the majority of their members are women.

Conclusion

Women are now remaining in the labor force longer and are making a significant social and economic contribution, which is inadequately recognized as a consequence of "gendered agism" (Arber and Ginn 1995:7).

There has been a tendency for women to return to the workforce in the post World War II period. They have been channelled into a narrow range of occupations such as retail sales. Most married women, in particular, have left the workforce at around 55 years of age if not earlier. Women continue to participate in paid work while carrying an additional burden of domestic and caring work. They are further penalized for this in current arrangements for pensions and other forms of retirement income. Governments and unions are equally slow to recognize this and fully recognize the social contribution of older women. While some women are resisting the pressures that relegate them to the ranks of the powerless and poor in later life, others have internalized their subordination and experience injustice as powerlessness. The preconditions for a socially just and personally empowering aging experience for older women workers appear to depend on the development of supportive public, social, and union policies. To date these are lagging behind demographic developments and older women's expectations.

Endnotes

[1]This study was supported by a grant from the Women's Employment, Education and Training Advisory Group (WEETAG) of the Department of Employment, Education and Training (DEET). It was published in 1996 as The Invisibility of Older Women Workers: Women Aged 55 and over in Retailing.

[2] See S. Arber and J. Ginn, 'Choice and Constraint in the Retirement of Older Married Women', pp. 69-86 in S. Arber and J. Ginn (eds) Connecting Gender and Aging: A Sociological Approach , Buckingham, Open University Press, 1995 for a discussion of U.S. literature and British research on this complex and contradictory topic.

Chapter Five

Unpaid Work, Grasshopper Accusations and the Threat to Social Capital

Rosemary Leonard

Increasingly loud and insistent discourses related to individual self-sufficiency and economics demand that a woman should have saved for her old age. The State, she is told, cannot afford to support our aging population. These discourses call for a nation of ants who spend the summer of their lives in preparation for the winter of old age. If a woman cannot support herself financially, the implication is that, like the grasshopper of Aesop's fable, she has wasted her spring and summer in idleness and deserves her winter of hardship. Such discourses place no value on the woman's years of unpaid work, no respect for her caring work in her family or volunteer work in the community. The cumulative effect of years of unpaid contribution is that many women have not been able to make financial provision for their old age. As a gut reaction we can rage at the injustice but beyond rage, how can we respond?

Three responses are explored in this chapter. One is to urge women to refuse to do unpaid work. A second response is to uphold the value of unpaid work in economic terms, such as assessing its contribution to the gross national product or demanding payment for presently unpaid work. A third response is to challenge the economic rationalist discourses by presenting a nonindividualistic, noneconomic understanding of the basis of society. Such a challenge can be mounted through the concept of social capital. These three approaches are not mutually exclusive, and this chapter examines the contribution of each. It argues for a reconsideration of the way in which women engage in unpaid work, the types of unpaid work in which we engage, and a campaign to raise its status.

Urging Women Not To Do Unpaid Work

Second wave feminists, including some of the authors of this book, have treated unpaid work with a great deal of suspicion. We are very conscious of the division of society into public and private spheres. The public sphere, including paid work, government, and civic responsibilities, is dominated by men, highly valued, and financially rewarded. The private sphere within the home includes most unpaid work and is seen to have little value. Women's relegation to the private sphere has profoundly restricted our lives and our ability to prepare financially for later life. Further, volunteering was often depicted as the result of a confidence trick by the State. In her 1983 review of volunteer work, Cora Baldock (1983) identified a range of arguments and studies that address the ways in which the State, as an agent of capital, uses volunteering to obtain conditions favorable to the accumulation of capital while maintaining social harmony. Examples were given of the way in which volunteering can keep wages low and reduce the cost of providing the services without which disharmony and protest would follow. Volunteering was seen as the outcome of guilt generated by politicians' emotional appeals. The above discussion is in gender neutral terms, but feminists who supported this view further argued that it is women who are constructed as altruistic and that the availability of women for volunteering is predicated on the division of labor into breadwinner and homemaker.

In this Marxist-feminist analysis, there was acknowledgement of the potential of volunteering to bring about social change through political action. In the 1974 United States' conference of the National Organization for Women, a resolution was passsed that women should only be change-oriented volunteers. Even those radical feminists working in refuges and other women's services had inadvertently become agents of the State when they were diverted from lobbying into direct service delivery. The potential for change, however, was seen as limited because of a lack of unity amongst organizations, their lack of affiliation with a political party, and the control that governments exert over most voluntary organizations through being their major source of funding (Baldock 1983).

In reference to the other large area of women's unpaid work, family caring, the most relevant research has been on "the double shift." Feminists express concern that the main response to the greater opportunities for women is for us to do both paid work and our traditional caring work, with little sign that men are moving to share the caring work. As Yeandle (1984) says, "employment is not a panacea for women and can be a trap." Many women resolve the problem of their competing demands by giving up much of their unpaid caring work to paid carers. However, with increasing demand for subsidized childcare and aged-care, governments are cutting costs, reducing subsidies, and putting more and more pressure on women to take back this traditional work.

There is empirical evidence that many Australians are ambivalent about caring for their elderly parents. From a random mailout survey, de Vaus (1996) found people did not feel much obligation to keep in contact with their parents and to help them, and even less obligation to live nearby. The gender differences, which might have been expected because the majority of parental caring is done by daughters, did not occur. It is not just a simple case of women wanting to offload their caring work, with the State trying to force them to take it back again, but rather the emergence of a more general social norm of limited obligations to parents.

The Economic Contribution of Unpaid Work

The foremost feminist critic of our global economic system is Marilyn Waring (1988), who argues that the United Nations System of National Accounts (UNSNA) has a lot to answer for in both reflecting and perpetuating patriarchial values about what counts as work and what is to be defined as welfare. The UNSNA guidelines go to extraordinary lengths to make sure that only those activities that are of interest to first world governments, bankers, and multinational corporations can be included in the Gross National Product (GNP). Under this system, munitions and war are of value, and illegal drug dealing is of value but the bearing and rearing of children, growing food for the family, or helping your community are of no value. This approach ignores almost as much significant economic activity as it includes through its devaluing of voluntary social activity.

The contribution from volunteering through formal organizations.

The growth in the voluntary sector over the last few decades has been impressive. Billis and Harris (1992) cite studies from the United States, the United Kingdom, France, Italy, Hungary, and India in which researchers have described the growth as "booming," "remarkable," or "mushrooming." As early as the

1970s, the U.S. and Canada were using surveys to evaluate the contribution from participation in formal voluntary organizations. In Canada, it was assessed as 5 hours per person per week, or about 1-3 percent of the GNP. In the USA similar estimates of 5.4 hrs suggested a total contribution of $22.6 million per year (Baldock 1983). Despite concerns that civic involvement in the U.S. is diminishing, a more recent survey found that about half the population had volunteered in the last 12 months, which show that volunteering definitely makes a significant contribution to the U.S. economy (Hodgkinson and Weiner 1990). Similarly, a more recent British national survey (Lynn and Smith 1991) found 51 percent of people over 18 had volunteered, suggesting an equally large contribution to the British economy.

The pattern of volunteering is similar across western countries, with a higher proportion of mid-life than older people participating. The areas of contribution also vary with age, with older people being the largest group involved in welfare or community work. Mid-life people tend to be involved in sport or recreation or educational groups, probably reflecting their involvement in their children's development (Lynn and Smith 1991; ABS 1995). These age differences are significant because it means that older people are making a major contribution to their own care by not being dependent on the temporarily young. The age differences are even more telling when considered in terms of the hours worked rather than the number of people involved. There is a steady increase in hours worked with age, peaking at ages 65 to 74, but even those over 75 contribute more hours than those under 65. Encel (1997) estimates that older people contribute, in proportion, almost twice as much as their share of the total population. For all ages, women's hours of contribution markedly exceed men's and, in the over 65 age group, women's contribution is 150 percent of men's (ABS 1995). This documenting of older women's significant involvement in welfare and community work is an important step toward debunking the myth of old age being dominated by dependency.

Assessing caring work.

Women's contribution to caring is even more difficult to assess than work in voluntary organizations. However, time-use studies can give some indication. (Note that they do not give the whole story. Talking on the telephone is nothing but passive leisure according to the Australian Bureau of Statistics [1994] but how many of our phone calls fit that description? Certainly many of mine could equally be classified as unpaid work in personal counselling, financial advising, liaison, thesis supervision, or human resource management.) Overall, Ironmonger (1994) estimated that, in OECD countries on average, adults spent 23-24 hours per week on unpaid work in the home compared with 21-23 hours of paid work in market industries (based on figures for Canada, Sweden, Finland, Norway, and Australia).

Women do a greater proportion of the caring work. The Australian time-use study (ABS 1994) found that 37 percent of women (including 5 percent who did not have young children of their own) and 25 percent of men spent some time caring for children, often in conjunction with other tasks. On average they spent 7 hours per day on this activity. It is interesting that childcare was usually not seen as the main activity (for only 2 hours per day was it the main activity), yet children are not like other secondary activities. Most other secondary activities included things like listening to the radio, which you can just switch off. Women's contribution to household chores was over 3 hours per day, which is 150 percent of men's, with men being most occupied with home and car maintenance.

In regard to other forms of caring or helping, we find that although both men and women contribute on average 25 minutes per day, men are more likely to be involved in helping able-bodied adults, usually friends or family, whereas women's energies are directed to caring for those with sickness or disability. Even the most conservative costing of these contributions in terms of the cheapest commercial alternatives would show that their value is enormous.

Clearly we need new models for measuring our GNP and other indicators of people's productive value. These models need to take into account the enormous contribution of unpaid work (and also the cost to the environment of other economic activity). Waring (1988) discusses a number of possibilities. One example is Hazel Henderson's model of a layered cake, with the layers of nature, unpaid work, and public sector activity all propping up the private sector. Another model is Hikka Pietila's concentric circles of free economy (unpaid work), protected sector (public sector and other protected domestic activities) and outer circle of the fettered economy (private sector is fettered by the forces of competition and globalization).

Challenging the Status of Economic Concerns as the Basis of Society

Social capital (Coleman 1990, 1988) is the invisible resource that is created whenever people cooperate. Groups and communities with high levels of social capital have numerous voluntary interconnections between members as well as high levels of trust. High social capital is associated with many desirable outcomes, such as lower crime rates, fewer school dropouts, and higher productivity and economic development (Putnam 1993, 1994). For example, Coleman (1990) found that although the quality of the teachers and curriculum were important, the school's embeddedness in the community was an even more significant influence on student performance, that is, the social capital created by the cooperative activities of teachers, parents, students, and the community was realized in the student performance.

According to the theory of social capital, unpaid work is the basis of society because it is the voluntary exchanges between relative equals that build up the store of social capital, which can then be used for group action. For example, a local football game may appear to be the archetypal masculine aggressive, competitive activity. Anyone unfamiliar with the concept of sport in modern society could be forgiven for believing the two sides were about to slaughter each other. It is, however, the complex web of interrelationships, social meanings, and organizations, most of which are developed by cooperative, voluntary work, which makes this display of aggressive competition tolerable. Social capital is involved in two ways. First, unless each team can trust the other to play more or less by the rules then there will not be a game. Second, for a one hour game, twenty times that amount of time would go into training, organizing, fundraising, transporting, uniform washing, etc. Such responsibilities are usually unpaid and shared by many people other than the competitors. Ongoing involvement in these tasks generates social capital for the community. I would argue that any competitive activity, sporting, commercial, or even romantic, can only take place because of a reservoir of social capital developed behind the scenes.

In terms of social capital, forms of unpaid work would be evaluated as to whether they fit the criteria for adding to the store of social capital. These criteria are that the activity be voluntary, not an obligation, and involve trust among a reasonably large number of people with fairly loose horizontal connections rather than a tightly knit group or a rigid hierarchy. These criteria would mean that there is no distinction between service delivery and political action as practiced by most small community organizations. Both would be highly valued. However, recent government pressure for organizations to become more competitive and professional can lead to reduced social capital. For example, they might reduce community participation because that is time consuming and becomes more hierarchical. In contrast, as argued by Onyx and Bullen (1998), little social capital is generated by large traditional voluntary organizations with rigid hierarchical structures.

Women's caring work within the family would not be highly valued in terms of social capital when it is seen as an obligation, when there is little reciprocity, and when it only involves the small, hierachically structured unit that forms the traditional family.

Women Planning Their Futures

The three approaches discussed above engage with unpaid work at an abstract level. At that level it is relatively easy to make broad statements about the desirability of certain courses of action without considering the complexity of the place of unpaid work in women's lives. The small, in-depth study, entitled Women Planning their Futures gives some valuable insights into the multiple roles of unpaid work in our present lives and future plans. Because the focus was not exclusively on unpaid work, the results also raise questions about division of work into paid and unpaid categories and the implications for social capital.

The study was a collaborative one by a group of nine mid-life women, including myself as the researcher, and a research assistant, who all wanted to exchange ideas about how we could have a positive experience of aging. An important dimension to the study was the diversity of our situations in terms of our income and caring commitments. The study involved, first, brief preliminary interviews to obtain background information and clarify the extent of the contribution being requested; second, a series of three in-depth group discussions aided by exercises and supplementary readings; and third, a meeting to comment on my interpretation of our results. The discussions were recorded and transcriptions distributed before the next session for any corrections and to avoid covering the same ground again. Because our situations are not unique, I think these issues could arise for many women. The first broad issue to arise was that most were preoccupied with issues surrounding family caring. The second issue, which has implications for our understanding of social capital, was that the distinction between unpaid versus paid work was not a very salient one for most of us.

Caring for family members

All of the nine women in the group identified with some form of feminism and all were familiar, at least at a basic level, with the feminist critique of the exploitation of women's unpaid work. Three identify with radical feminists, five could offer a sophisticated feminist analysis of the topic, and Stella had deliberately chosen a life-course consistent with those feminists who suggest that women should avoid unpaid caring and provide for themselves. Nevertheless, family caring was the most dominant topic in the study and occupied over a third of the transcripts and was also being introduced into many other topics of discussion.

The discussions around the issue of adult children caring for elderly parents were the most tense in the project. The interactions were marked by a more emotional tone and more frequent interruptions than the rest of the discussions. Marked divisions occurred between those who did not have children, or had children, but did not want to become dependent on them, and those who felt that there could be give and take and mutual caring in the family.

First, it is important to identify the characteristics of a family caring situation that was not seen as problematic by the group. Robyn talked about her mother.

> She's seventy-nine and she is able to maintain much independence—a lot probably compared to others. One of the family doesn't do anything much but the other four are able to network and work it out between them who can do it at a certain time.

In the discussion that followed, the group responded positively to the fact that the burden of care was not too heavy, the sense of reciprocity as Robyn's mother looks after the children when she visits, and the good sense of mutual commitment amongst the four siblings. Another characteristic of caring that was seen positively by the group was that it was done willingly. Megan had cared extensively for her grandparents and great-aunts. Although she had a lot of expectations placed on her, she responded with love. When Megan was challenged about having done so much work for love, she asserted that she had genuinely wanted to help out of her feelings for these relatives. The questions suggested that the group thought Megan's behavior unusual; however, they appeared to accept her explanation and generally affirmed her generosity

Characteristics of caring that were evaluated negatively by the group were when it interfered with a woman's career or other aspects of life, was seen as unnecessary, involved emotional dependency, or when it was done out of other people's expectations rather than genuine willingness. For example, Megan now recognizes how the time spent caring has meant that her Ph.D. is not complete and, until it is, she cannot look for the better paid, more secure employment she needs to secure her future. The other women in the group agreed that she had done enough and that it was time to focus on her own career. In contrast, Marie is becoming increasingly resentful. For her mother, who lives in a retirement village, Marie and her family are the sole focus of her mother's life. Marie gets frequent urgent calls for immediate attention for trivial matters. She feels she has always played the dutiful daughter and is unable to change her relationship.

It was around the resistance to perceived obligations that the strongest feelings were expressed. As a consequence of her experience as a carer, Marie is determined that, as she ages, she will maintain her interests outside the family so her children would not feel as pressured and resentful about her. Julia, who had married into an ethnic Greek-Australian family, was horrified at the notion of children being obliged to their parents because she had found the system in the Greek community very oppressive: "Grown-ups cannot make their own decisions because they've got to listen to their parents or look after them first."

Stella was concerned about the social expectation that children look after their aging parents, which puts pressure on the children. She drew attention to the material on nursing homes that had been distributed to the group (see Rhonda's chapter 9) and suggested that much of the stigma attached to being in a nursing home came from the expectation that the family should be caring for its older members. In keeping with a particularly western view of the family, she was very critical of the women who thought that children could be expected to help. She argued that you have children in order to give somebody a life, not to have someone to look after you when you're old.

When support from children was advocated, the emphasis was not on dependency but on give and take, responsibility and friendship. Jenny expressed a preference for as much independence as possible in later life but that family should be prepared to give support if your plans failed because you have been supportive of them in the past. There was considerable, in principle, agreement with this model of interdependence. As Robyn pointed out: "it's not total support. I mean some support is just part of the relationship isn't it?" Several practical problems were raised. Julia was skeptical about whether children, especially male children, would cooperate: "I mean it's hard enough getting them to take the garbage out." Erin drew attention to adult children's other responsibilities such as to their own children. Marie strongly agreed that our western culture does not teach responsibility but she was concerned that it could easily become "a total expectation from which they are going to run away."

The issue of whether negotiation could be used to manage family caring opened a heated debate. Erin felt positive about her experience of assertively telling her mother that coming to live with her was not a possibility. The reactions of the other women to Erin's revelation were mixed but in every case it was clear that they thought her behavior extraordinary. Most were impressed with her assertiveness and, in particular, Marie felt that she should have acted similarly but that it was too late now because of her mother's age. Negative aspects to negotiation were that it did not always work and that it may cause unnecessary distress. For example, in response to Marie's recent attempt, her mother initially agreed but then disregarded the agreement within a few days. Stella pointed out that assertion may cause unnecessary distress. Stella knew that she could not bear her father to come and live with her after her mother's death but did not say so. Later he remarried a younger, healthier woman, and Stella now does not expect that she will have to care for him as he ages.

Despite the differences amongst the women, there seemed to be a general agreement that women should not become a burden on their families in later life. Certainly noone expected to live with their adult children. However, there were differences of opinion about what would be too great an expectation. Some argued that they needed to "act responsibly," even if it means making sacrifices so as not to become a burden or put too much pressure on adult children. Others thought that it was possible to develop a relationship of interdependence.

It is not only aging parents but also children, partners, and family members with disabilities who will need ongoing care. Seven of the nine women have such responsibilities. Apart from the twelve children whom we have already raised to, or close to, adulthood, two women are single parents with young children who will need at least another ten years of mothering. Jenny's mother has a mental illness and at times she seeks Jenny's help; at times she keeps her distance. At other times Jenny is treated with hostility. It is the unpredictability of her needs that is a constant low level concern for Jenny. Three other women have children with conditions that mean that they will probably need ongoing care. Helen's child has severe physical and moderate mental disabilities; Julia's boy has epilepsy and his behavior can become a problem, and Marie's daughter had a mental breakdown and has an ongoing anxiety disorder. Erin's husband is twelve years older than her and lately he is under a great deal of pressure at work and his health has been poor. Erin was concerned that, if he continues working to obtain adequate retirement income, then he will not be able to enjoy it. Although the group acknowledged the heavy load of such caring work and the need for more government services, they did not dispute the women's need to take responsibility for caring in these cases.

The other dimension to the issue of family caring was the possibility of future caring for grandchildren. The seven women with children were generally positive about being involved with grandchildren. They differed in the amount of responsibility they wished to have. Julia remembered how much she would have liked to have some help when her children were young and was willing to make herself available. In contrast, Marie was determined to mind her grandchildren only when it suited her. Given that Marie was having difficulties drawing clear boundaries with her mother, the group felt that she needed encouragement: "I'd hold onto that," "write it down," "stick it on the fridge."

Issues arising from these accounts of family caring.

First is that it is unlikely that these nine women are exceptional in their workload of caring responsibilities. Any documentation of a similarly located group of women would identify similar responsibilities that fly in the face of grasshopper accusations.

A second issue is that it was not caring per se that was seen as problematic. A comparison between attitudes to family caring and other caring reveals that many of the issues that emerged as difficulties in the context of family caring were actively sought in other relationships. For example, Robyn's vision for age 66 was to live in a large old rambling house with other women. Erin has a group of friends who wish to stay in close proximity; Helen's goal is to develop a special place where women can come and be psychically renewed. Sharing accommodation, helping neighbors out, and staying close to friends, as well as providing space to foster personal growth, are all approved social activities. Caring was viewed positively when it was done willingly, without hidden pressures and expectations, with possible reciprocity, and preferably spread amongst a number of people so that it is not so great a burden as to interfere with other aspects of the carers' lives. This list is remarkably similar to the criteria for the generation of social capital. It suggests that there would be no problem with family caring if the model for the family was that of an egalitarian, cooperative, voluntary group.

Third, there is the general acceptance of the importance of drawing boundaries around caring for aging parents. These attitudes are consistent with de Vaus' (1996) findings from his broad survey that people have, at best, bounded and, at worst, hostile feelings about family caring, supporting his view that government policies based on the assumption that the families are willing and able to take up the care of older members would be misguided and possibly lead to very low levels of care. Within this group, limits were also set on our willingness to care for grandchildren. Similarly, Coterill (1992), in a study of paternal grandmothers, found that they were willing to do occasional care of grandchildren in exceptional situations such as illness but less than enthusiastic about taking on the long term care of grandchildren while the mother worked. Most let their views be known so they were never asked. Coterill surmises that maternal grandmothers have similar feelings but feel a greater obligation to help their daughters and also that, as state subsidies for childcare are reduced, there will be greater pressure on grandmothers to take on the unwanted role.

Work: Unpaid or Paid?

For most of the women in the group, life is filled with meaningful activities, for some of them we just happen to get paid. Many other issues were more important than economic power. These included personal development, connection with nature, social connectedness, and making a social contribution.

Noone expressed a desire for great wealth. We all saw financial security as being a necessity to avoid the unpleasant alternative.

> It was raining. It was cold and there's this figure in front of me trying to get across the road, swollen ankles, and her head all covered up and I just thought "That could happen to me". It's a fear because, if you've worked in welfare, you can see women who end up homeless on the street and they're not that different to you (Megan).

However, there were differences amongst the women. For Stella, money was not a concern because she had always been the prototypical ant, careful to guard her financial independence, and she had already made substantial provisions for her future retirement. Helen, Erin, and Megan all felt that they were making some progress toward financial security. Megan has been working steadily toward a more secure future of her own design for many years. Having identified as a lesbian in her late adolescence, and clearly not going to be dependent on a man to provide for her, she recognized the need to start saving and investing in property. This was not the norm amongst lesbian feminists, so she felt some disapproval for her "capitalistic tendencies" as a lone ant in a society of grasshoppers. The other five women in the study were open to grasshopper accusations in that a history of little education, alcoholic or violent husbands, and heavy childcare responsibilities had left them with few opportunities for obtaining self-sufficiency before old age. All of us had managed on a very low income at some time and, therefore, were confident that we could do so again, if necessary.

However, seven of us would be open to the grasshopper charge in the sense that it was hard for us to think seriously about money. Very little time was devoted to strategies for making money for ourselves, and we tended to slip off the topic very quickly and move back onto relationships. I raised this as an issue in the third session and found some interesting responses. With money issues, Erin is "uncomfortable and even sort of reasonably sad." She was raised on the edict that "It is not nice to talk about money," and her parents' model consisted of her father's quarterly interrogation of her mother about the accounts. Generally, Jenny has difficulty "seeing herself as a mini-institution," and she wants to leave concerns about marketing and funding submissions, which preoccupy her at work, at work. For Jenny to make money she would need to be less commited to her work. She would need to lobby as hard for staff development for herself as for Aboriginal health programs. Less commitment at work would release energy for her to acquire some formal qualifications. Although we were able, when I pushed the matter, to discuss income strategies in some depth with Stella as our financial expert, our real concerns could be categorized as our social connections, personal development, including and expressing some connection with nature and place, and making a social contribution.

All the women mentioned social connection as being important to them in some form or other. This commitment to social connection could lead to a considerable unpaid workload of caring, as seen in the earlier discussion, but social connection affected our lives and life plans in many other ways as well.

Various ideas for pooling resources were discussed; for example, Erin's daughter and her friends all put in money so that the one who is having a birthday can choose a better present than any one could get on her own. This model, the rotating credit society (Putnam 1993), was discussed with some enthusiasm by the group. It was seen much more positively than as a simple pooling of resources in which the individuals lose control of their assets.

The theme of social contribution is most relevant to volunteering. When we talked about our futures almost all talked about some form of work, but it was not always clear whether we expected it to be paid or unpaid. It was more that there were worthwhile things to be done. Those who have a strong commitment to their work felt that they would want to continue research, writing, and community action even after they retired and were no longer being paid.

> I do a lot of different things trying to put new issues on the agenda . . . so I guess my relationship to work is one of trying to take my life experience and turning it into something (Jenny).

Others envisaged a marked change. Stella would like to move from finance to running a wildlife reserve, which would probably cost her money rather than generating income. Marie would like to change from special education to photography, which would not create much wealth. All of us at some stage had chosen to take less income for more meaningful work. Even during the course of the study, Julia, who was the most frank about her need for more money, had, by our third meeting, resigned from her "good" but meaningless job in the public sector, with its security, super- annuation, study leave, and promotional paths to accept a "bad" but interesting job teaching at a technical college.

The women's plans for the future suggest that it is not that women just weigh their volunteer work against paid work and feel ourselves deprived of money. We weigh paid work against unpaid work and find most paid work lacking in social connection, meaningfulness, and social contribution. The lack of correlation between income and job satisfaction has been explored in the paid workforce with Hakim (1991) concluding that we are not "grateful slaves" cheerfully taking any low paid job we are given but "self-made women" with a different set of criteria for judging our work. This failure to use income as the criterion for judgement has also been noted by Jenny and Pam (chapter 6), whose participants' ambitions often involved a drop in salary or a move to voluntary work. Women's attitudes to work, however, raise questions for the concept of social capital. All the writings to date have made a sharp distinction between paid and unpaid work and excluded all paid work from the accumulation of social capital.

Conclusion

Unpaid work is not a grasshopper activity. It is important to women. We value the opportunity for social connection, within the family and beyond, personal development, and meaningful social contribution that are often lacking in paid work. Unpaid work is also valuable to society. It is not only that older women make a significant contribution through their unpaid work, but it is also that we have been making contributions throughout our lives and thereby have been limited in our access to the activities that would make us self-sufficient in later years. The documenting of our contribution, and the revaluing of unpaid work through the notion of social capital, both have roles to play in refuting the grasshopper accusations against older women.

The argument for social capital as a new way of valuing unpaid work is not advocating that women return to their traditional position of economic disadvantage, obliged to give free services to keep a roof over our heads, nor is it consistent with the argument by some feminists that women should only volunteer for social change work; rather, it argues for the necessity to raise the status of all unpaid work that involves voluntary cooperative involvement and the building of trust.

Although feminist urgings for women to be sufficiently "selfish" to provide for themselves and avoid the traps of unpaid work mean that fewer women will spend their later lives in poverty, the limiting of unpaid work to social action could be disastrous for the accumulation of social capital. The introduction of the concept of social capital, however, is not a substitute for a feminist analysis of unpaid work. The concept does not differentiate between gender, culture, or class, although it could be argued that it supports the breaking down of structural differences because, in a sexist, racist, classist society, people cannot meet as equals across those divisions. We still need our feminist analysis to continue to interrogate the concept of social capital. For example, we can ask whether the distinction between paid and unpaid work needs to be central for social capital when it is not central for women? We need a feminist analysis to show how the men in a voluntary organization take the public glory while the women do the bulk of the menial tasks (Baldock 1983). We need a feminist analysis to see whether men cooperate if women work toward a model of the family as the sort of larger, loosely knit, mutually supportive, collaborative group that would generate social capital. We need an examination of class and culture to see whether social capital should have a wider focus than formal voluntary organizations, which only flourish in middle-class western societies, as the best way to produce social capital. Other cultures and classes may well have models that are equally, or more, effective.

Nor does the argument for social capital replace the need for documenting the economic contribution of unpaid work. It does suggest, however, that we need to document activities that contribute to the accumulation of social capital; for example, the phone calls that are vital for maintaining our networks would no longer be labelled as passive but as significant contributions.

Finally, I would raise the question of whether unpaid work that contributes only to economic capital and not social capital should not be done or should become paid work. Typically such work is caring work for which a woman is persuaded against her wishes to provide extensive care for another. The likely outcome is that she will become resentful and distrusting, leading to a reduction in social capital. In western societies, which value the masculine over the feminine, the public over the private, profit over nonprofit, competition over cooperation, the status of unpaid work is undermined. As evidence for the concept of social capital mounts, it becomes increasingly likely that we do so at our peril. Like our water and air, social capital is the environment we need in which to conduct our society.

Chapter Six

What Does Retirement Mean for Women?
Jenny Onyx and Pam Benton

> I have always been puzzled by the idea of retirement. When I was young, retirement seemed to be something that older men did. There would be a party, and a gold watch, and the person would disappear from my life. What a horrible fate! To lead a busy, fulfilling, engaged life, and then suddenly to stop . . . I could not understand that anyone would do such a thing by choice. I vowed that I would never retire (Jenny 54).

Of course our mothers never retired, but then they never "worked" either. They might have been employed once the children were older, but then they did all sorts of other things, like babysit the grandchildren, or maybe play bridge, or become active in the local bowling club. And then when the fathers retired, the mothers stayed home to look after them.

Our cohort, women who are now in our 50s, have experienced enormous changes in social expectations in our lifetime. Most of us grew up expecting to get married and have children. That was our destiny, our expected storyline. As we got older and the children began to grow up, we were greatly influenced by the women's movement and the growing expectation that we could have, and then that we should have, a professional career as well. Here was a new storyline to follow. But we never thought about retirement. How can you think about retirement when you have really only just started a real job at 40? And during our 40s we were still juggling, still the principal carer and housekeeper, still trying to balance work demands and family demands. If we were still married, then we assumed that he had superannuation and it was his responsibility to provide for our old age. If we had divorced, well there was always the government provided pension. Not that we had time to think about that.

Now that we are in our 50s, the world has changed. We are struggling to make sense of our own historical embeddedness and the contradictory ideologies that impinge on our lives. The traditional ideology of womanhood requires us to care for the sick, the frail, our grandchildren, our spouse. For those of us in senior professional or managerial positions (there are more of us now) there is the pressure to "make it," to break through the glass ceiling, to go for promotion, to work 60 hours a week. At the same time there is a growing sense that if we leave our stressful jobs, we might not get another. It's hard to get a job when you are older. True the new legislation outlaws compulsory retirement, but there is a lot of restructuring and downsizing going on, and that usually means getting rid of the deadwood, the ones who are "past it." Not that we want to work full-time anyway; we're exhausted from years of juggling, doing the impossible, being careerists and mothers and everything else . . . for everyone else.

And then we are told that the demographic time bomb is ticking. By the time we are 70, there will be too many old people to support. We can't expect to get a publicly funded pension; society can't afford it. We should provide for ourselves. But we don not have much superannuation (how could we?), and we can't afford to stop working.

These are the contrary pressures: to work more, to use our skills, to support ourselves, but at the same time to get out of the workforce and make way for the young ones. So what does retirement mean for older women? Are we doomed to a life of poverty and dependency for the last 30 years of our lives, or can we reconstruct more positive storylines for our old age? If so, where does retirement fit?

In the discussion that follows in this chapter, we draw extensively on the literature, and on our own experience. We also draw on two studies of our own: Study One was a small qualitative study that we carried out in Sydney, Australia, of 50 high achieving professional women between the ages of 45 and 65 (Onyx and Benton 1996). Study Two was a later, follow-up quantitative comparative study of 650 employed men and women over 30 years of age (Onyx 1998).

Our story, the story of this chapter, draws on the experience of women like ourselves, professional older women, white Anglo-Australian, well-educated women living in postindustrial countries like Australia, the United States, and the United Kingdom. We don't know how our story relates to professional women in other parts of the world, in third world countries. We suspect that if retirement exists at all there, the issues are different. That must necessarily be another story.

Retirement As Conventionally Conceived

The retirement literature offers some interesting insights. With few exceptions, the scholarly literature operates from an established but unexamined paradigm concerning the nature of work, and consequently about the nature of "retirement." This paradigm had its early explicit formulation in Parson's separation of the public domain of men and the private domain of women (Parsons 1949). He notes, for example

> So far ... as an individual's occupational status centers on a specific "job" he either holds the job or he does not and the tendency is to maintain the full level of functions up to a given point, and then abruptly to retire ... In view of the very great significance of occupational status ... retirement leaves the older man in a peculiarly functionless situation (Parsons 1949: 231).

According to this paradigm, "work" is defined as what men do in a formal, paid capacity, within the public domain. The role of women centers on our function as housewives and mothers, making a home and caring for the family within the private domain of the home. While women are expected to carry out domestic duties, these are not defined as work in the same way that men's activities are. The distinction between the public world that men inhabit and the private world in which women's acts are constrained has been well critiqued by Carol Pateman (1983). That which is consigned to the invisible world of the private domain is placed out of reach of public scrutiny. It is not deemed important; it doesn't count.

Just as "work" is defined as what men do, so is retirement a male phenomenon. The notion of retirement as a male phenomenon rests on the premise that a man's status and identity are obtained through work, while a woman's social position is derived primarily through her family roles (Erdner and Guy 1990; 129). The notion that only men work, and therefore that only men retire is nonsense, particularly if it is premised on the assumption that it is only men whose status and identity derive from their paid work. Throughout history, women have been economically productive. In modern terms, by 1980, 60 percent of women of working age had paid employment in most developed countries (Martin and Roberts 1984) and large numbers of women had held professional positions for 20 years or more. We do retire from these positions, though not necessarily in the same way as men do. Hence, there has been a growing body of scholarly work emerging since the late 1970s that has addressed the issue of women's retirement, and specifically whether there are any differences in the retirement experience for men and women (Fox 1977; Szinovacz 1982; Mathews and Brown 1987; Seccombe and Lee 1986; Hayward, Grady and McLaughlin 1988). However, the bulk of the retirement literature, including that which addresses women's retirement, nonetheless assumes a male model of retirement. That is, the assumption continues to be made that retirement itself is a gender neutral concept, and consequently the characteristics of male retirement are assumed to be normative for women professionals as well. For example, Szinovacz and Washo (1992) note:

> Despite some recent efforts, research on gender differences in the retirement experience remains limited due to its heavy reliance on a "male model" of retirement transition and adjustment process. Studies based on this model typically use predictor variables that earlier research on men identified as important determinants of the retirement experience (Szinovacz and Washo 1992: 191).

The predictor variables that Szinovacz and Washo refer to are not hard to find. Virtually all studies have identified the variables of good health, income security, and social activity of some sort (Seccombe and Lee 1986; Mathews and Brown 1987; Hayes and Parker 1993; Hatch 1990; Riddick 1982). Also considered crucial for many are factors relating to retirement planning (Block 1982; Hayes 1991; Hayes and Parker 1993) and the attitude toward retirement, that is, level of career commitment and whether or not retirement was a matter of personal choice (Mathews and Brown 1987; Feuerbach and Erdwins 1994; Price-Bonham and Johnson 1982) and leisure roles (Riddick 1982).

Although the early literature on retirement presumed retirement to be a largely negative experience that entailed a loss of status and identity (Bell 1978; Blau 1981), more recent studies have suggested that most people, in fact, express considerable satisfaction with their retirement (Jewson, 1982; Mathews and Brown 1987; Seccombe and Lee 1986).

The majority of studies that have looked for differences in retirement satisfaction between men and women have found few consistent differences. Some have argued that men report higher retirement satisfaction, others that women do. The emerging consensus appears to be that retirement satisfaction operates in much the same way for both genders, but that the strength of these factors themselves differs. So, for example, income is equally important for both men and women, but women have a much reduced level of income security, as Rosslyn notes in chapter 4, and so are likely to report greater dissatisfaction with respect to income support (Seccombe and Lee 1986).

The issues that the literature suggests are of special concern to women are income security and the threat of poverty, the lack of retirement planning, the expectations of caring, and the greater stress of life events, including loss of husband through death or divorce (Block 1982; Hatch 1990; Secombe and Lee 1986; Szinovacz and Washo 1992). Several studies have looked for differences between women on the basis of their commitment to their paid work, that is whether they experienced work as a career or simply as a "job" (Connidis 1986; Feurbach and Erdwins 1994; Price-Bonham and Johnson 1982; Erdner and Guy 1990). There is some suggestion that women with strong work commitment derive their identity from their professional employment and, consequently, approximate the male pattern of retirement, while women who see paid work as a supplement to their traditional identity within the home, do not. Until very recently, women's retirement was seen as predicated on the retirement of her spouse, such that she retired when he did.

> Consequently the predominant view of men's employment and retirement was that it is more important and fundamental, and that women's employment and retirement—being chosen and voluntary—should accommodate it because it did not really count as retirement (Mason, 1990; 113).

In all these studies, the view is adopted that either women adopt the male model of work and of retirement, or else that their retirement is subordinate to that of their spouse. There has been almost no recognition of retirement in the context of women's lives as a whole, or of what work and retirement may mean in that context, although there has recently been a call for such an integrated approach (Hatch 1990).

In our own study of 50 high achieving women (Study One), we found little evidence of any difference between those with low and high work commitment. Indeed we found that the distinction itself was not very meaningful. Of the women in our sample, 56 percent reported that paid work was important when they were in their 20s, whereas 86 percent believed paid work to be important now. However, while paid work was usually central to the self image and identity of the women, it was still only seen as one aspect of their lives, and not necessarily the most important. Few of the women's careers appeared to approximate the male model as described by Parsons, and none of them expected to approximate the male model of retirement.

Women Work All Their Lives

The first thing to be said is that women work all their lives. Some of this is the unpaid, and often unrecognized work of caring, or domestic labor. Some of it is unpaid voluntary work in the wider community. Some of it is part-time or casual paid employment. Only some of it is full-time recognized career work. In most women's lives, there is no clear separation from the work that is paid and the work that is not. Often the two are physically juxtaposed so that one flows into the other. We often value paid and unpaid work equally, or even tend to value unpaid work as more intrinsically important. Certainly one can only be understood in the context of the other.

We know that most women have a discontinuous paid work life, with time out for childrearing. Some studies have begun to identify the effects of the time-out on what is called the "bi-modal career" (Silverstone and Ward 1980; Bird and West 1987). Those authors found that few professional women were able to regain the status level achieved before the break. In our own study, we found that two-thirds of the women had spent time out of the workforce; 20 per cent had spent at least 10 years out of paid employment. Even those who appear to have relatively little disruption in their employment, in fact dropped to casual or part-time work during child-rearing. Sixty percent of the women worked part-time for some period of their paid work lives. The complexity of this pattern was such that it was impossible to chart with any accuracy. Nonetheless we found that women were as likely to experience an increase in status on return to the workforce as they were to experience a decrease.

Part-time work was not only undertaken when the children were young. Of the 25 women we interviewed, six were now working part-time in order to have more time for other interests, one had taken a year's leave of absence, two had left full-time employment to work as consultants and give themselves more free time—another four had, or were about to, "retire" for the same reason, but with every intention of continuing some paid work—and three were exploring the possibility of part-time work. Those intending to remain continuously in full-time employment were in the minority.

When asked how they would like to spend their time given an ideal world in the next five years, almost all of the fifty women wished for a reduced emphasis on full-time work. Half the sample (52 percent) would like to "work part-time with more time for personal interests," and a third (32 percent) would like to focus on career but have time for other things. Just 10 percent wished for no paid work, and indeed all of those at or near retirement age were working full- or part-time regardless of whether or not they were officially retired. At the other extreme, only 6 percent wished for a fully committed professional career and indeed several of the younger women had already left full-time work, or were planning to do so, in order to pursue other interests.

Many, perhaps most, women also engage in some form of voluntary work. Rosemary (chapter 5) explored some aspects of voluntary work. Community sector work has often been defined in terms of the voluntary labor of women; labor that is simultaneously honored and devalued (Baldock 1990; Walker 1989). In our study of high achieving women, at least half of the sample also engaged in extensive voluntary work at some period of their lives. Others were more explicitly involved in political or social action when they were young, whether they had children or not. These women tended not to identify these activities as work, or if they did then they made little distinction between their paid and unpaid work. The one tended to flow into the other, and both absorbed much of their life energies. For women like Alice (age 62) it was impossible from her interview to discern which part of her work was paid and which was unpaid, though clearly much of it was unpaid. Others made the distinction clearer, at least in theory.

> I actually didn't divorce work and other activities. They were totally integrated. What I did outside work was informing work and vice versa . . . my entire being was consumed with my social causes (Broni 45).

Nor did unpaid voluntary or social action work end when the women were young. Several women had chosen part-time paid work specifically so that they can have more time to carry out their unpaid work. Others are specifically linking retirement, or partial retirement, plans to expectations of voluntary or unpaid social action work.

> That's my aim . . . to launch out into different kinds of activities either in a voluntary capacity or as a consultant (Anna 58).

Although women typically accept the greater part of the burden of caring for children throughout their young adulthood, it is sometimes assumed that caring is no longer an issue in retirement. In fact, the evidence suggests that over a third of the care of the frail elderly is carried out by the fit elderly (Arber and Ginn 1990). More frequently, a woman may be required to retire with her husband whether she likes it or not, particularly if he has poor health (Mason 1990). The reverse expectation does not seem to hold. Within our study, many women indicated an ongoing responsibility for the care of children (including dependent adult children) and for aged relatives. However, only one woman was required to give up her other plans to care full-time for this dependent. Nonetheless, 40 percent of the sample spent at least 10 hours a week in the care of others.

Although women work all their lives, neither the women or society at large recognizes the enormous weight of unpaid work. Paid work is also likely to continue well past conventional retirement at least for the current cohorts of professional women. However, the particular mix of paid and unpaid work shifts constantly throughout our lifetime, and continues to do so whether we are officially retired or not.

Who Can Afford To Retire?

We explored the issues involved in planning for retirement in our interview study (Study One) and followed up some of these issues with the larger sample in the comparative quantitative study (Study Two). In the interview study, few women had systematically planned for retirement or were even able to discuss it, even those who were near retirement age. In Study Two, we found that only 38 percent of part-time working women and 52 percent of fully employed women (compared with 65 percent of fully employed men) claimed to have actively planned financially for their retirement. Fewer still had planned a retirement lifestyle.

Table 1 on the following page presents the questionnaire results concerning the expected sources of income after age 60. Results are presented separately for women working part-time, full-time and for men. The most likely scenario for our small sample of "high flyers" was to continue paid work after the retirement age of 60, although few wished to continue working full-time. Less than half had superannuation, and of those who did, the existing cover was unlikely to be adequate. Our larger sample of questionnaire respondents were more optimistic about their capacity to cope using their own superannuation (fully employed men and women) or their partner's superannuation (part-time employed women). However, other evidence from the questionnaire suggested that this optimism was not justified for the women; they seriously underestimated the length of time and amount required to save for an adequate post-retirement income.

Table 1.
Retirement Income: Percentage of "very important" responses.

Expected source of income after age 60	Study 1	Study2: females part-time	Study 2: females full-time	Study 2: males full-time
	n=50	n=197	n=203	n=228
Continued paid work	48	14	20	19
Own superannuation	40	25	53	64
Partner's superannuation	24	52	41	25
Own savings/ investment	28	44	50	51
Property	38	51	57	59
Government pension	32	24	22	18
Other	0	4	3	2

This conclusion accords with the urgent calls of the American literature; "it is unfortunate that the popular press continues to ignore the dramatic need to alert and inform women of their need to engage in early planning for the later years" (Hayes and Parker 1993:1). Feuerbach and Erdwins (1994) also found that 91 percent of respondents had not planned for retirement.

The reasons for such apparently poor planning, in Sydney at least, appear to be multiple and complex. In our interview study, most women had difficulty in even responding to the questions. Some of the "younger" group, those between 45 and 50, had simply never thought about retirement, although they belonged to a superannuation scheme. They simply didn't want to talk about it. We found in our larger quantitative study that 50 percent of part-time employed women and 38 percent of fully employed women had received *no* information concerning contribution superannuation schemes. This lack of engagement was especially, but not only, true of women who returned to the workforce after a period of childcare. Their career was just starting to blossom; the last thing they wanted was to even consider retirement. Maggie probably sums up this attitude best.

> I guess as a woman you can get so caught up in raising a family and day to day living and then for me, going back to the workforce, doing some study, going from part-time to full-time work, continuing to have to be the carer and I suppose the main nurturer in the home that you don't tend to take time out to stop and think about your future goals (My partner has superannuation) I've never seen it as a major priority, I tend to get too engrossed in what I'm doing at the time, and put that on the back burner (Maggie 45).

Most women feel very constrained by money. Very few women, even among the high flyers could afford to retire completely. It had not been a requirement in the past that they take financial responsibility for their own future. For many this was difficult to do in any case, having spent years in jobs that were casual or part-time, or under conditions that did not provide the opportunity for superannuation. Many (in both studies) had spent years out of the workforce raising children and so have not had the opportunity to build the kind of financial base that provides retirement income security.

This pattern is even stronger in the U.S. Price-Bonham and Johnson (1982) found that only 56 percent of professional women in their U.S. sample had contributed to a retirement fund. Of those who did not, 50 percent had the opportunity but opted not to do so. Hobbs and Damon (1996) confirm from Bureau of Census data that some of the highest rates of poverty in the U.S. occurred among the "old old" (i.e. over 85) women living alone. Women were about one third more likely to be in poverty than men; in some categories poverty rates for older women were over 50 percent. Of women aged 65–69, 16 percent were employed; those employed part-time rarely faced poverty (Hobbs and Damon 1996). Within Australia, Rosenman and Winocur blame much of the problem on the superannuation rules.

> Much of the problem lies with the character of occupational superannuation schemes. These schemes are designed to "reward" loyal employees, and fit the traditional pattern of male working lives, namely continuous, full-time, paid employment throughout life, with retirement at a fixed age. Workers who do not conform to this pattern have either been explicitly excluded from schemes or exclude themselves by not joining, since they do not expect to adhere to the pattern throughout their working lives (Rosenman and Winocur 1990).

While recent legislation is designed to make superannuation compulsory for all workers in Australia, regardless of status, the effect to date has been to penalize those with short term, casual employment, because the cost of administering the scheme may outweigh the benefits (Wieneke and Arrowsmith 1993; Clare and Tulpule 1994).

In our study of high flyers, this financial constraint often fed into the need to keep working. Even those who are now contributing to a superannuation fund recognize that it won't provide enough to live in the way they want to live, partly due to lack of opportunity for earlier planning and partly because they entered a fund late in their working life:

> My super isn't enough to live on. My super situation is in a mess. Because I've changed jobs at critical times when superannuation schemes changed and got worse, and I've got two bits that don't come together very nicely. Plus I didn't start paying until I was 39. So the combination of circumstances makes my super look very poor indeed I did full time temporary work for years, so there was no super attached. But I wouldn't have done it because I felt as if my youth would go on forever. So even if the opportunity had been there I don't think I would have used it particularly wisely (Freda 52).

Most women see their future as a continuation of the present, but with a shift in the balance of paid and unpaid work. In most cases they are looking for a reduction in the paid work component, perhaps by moving to a part-time position or into consultancy work, in order to have more time for other interests while still earning enough to live. This applies to women of all ages in our sample.

> Yes it (retirement) is definitely planned and implanted. But I never thought I would actually stop paid work. What I thought I would do is to follow some of my loves. I love working with wood, I love doing house renovations. But to actually pay for such luxury you just can't do it. So then you've got to find something that can keep you, and I'm hoping that I might be able to go back to something on a part-time basis (Dinah 60).

For those in conventional marriages, there was a sense that retirement, and the financial arrangements for it, were the husband's responsibility. They expected to be covered by their husband's superannuation, though few have thought much about their husband's entitlements or even know what level of cover is available. Louise found that she could not necessarily rely on her husband's super.

> My various jobs did not have any superannuation provisions but my husband's position provided him with a large lump sum. He did not share my opinion that I should share in this lump sum. My suggestion that a divorce would suit me and give me access to part of the money changed his mind (Louise 62).

In our second, larger study, we found that about 25 percent of those employed part-time (48 percent of those aged over 50), assumed that retirement was their spouse's responsibility. Even among those working full-time, the spouse's superannuation was expected to be a major source of income in retirement.

In another study, Rosenmann and Winocur (1990) conclude that the majority still expected that their husbands would do the planning, and provide the resources to enable them to maintain their living standards into retirement:

> Australian women, especially those aged over 45, saw it as being a man's responsibility to plan for his wife's future. The extent to which husbands do or are able to do so, particularly once they have departed the scene, is questionable. Eighty-eight percent of widowed women and 65 per cent of divorced women, reported being dependent upon an Age Pension or other government benefit for their income (289).

There is no reference here to single women. Where a husband is not available, the state becomes the surrogate husband. Within our samples, up to 31 percent expected to depend on the government pension. Few had made independent arrangements for themselves.

The responses of the women in our studies must be seen in the context of major changes in social attitudes and state provisions in Australia, chief among which are the effect of the women's movement already referred to, equal opportunity and age discrimination legislation (Wieneke and Arrowsmith 1993), and the recent introduction of compulsory superannuation. The general effect of these changes has been to increase the opportunity for women to participate in the labor market while taking more responsibility for their own financial security (Clare and Tulpule 1994). However, it must be remembered that while this cohort of women has been part of making these changes happen, they have not necessarily been in the position to benefit from their effects, particularly in terms of superannuation coverage.

Other Things Are Important Too

As we reflected on our own lives, we became increasingly dissatisfied with the distinction made in the literature, and in general parlance, between "work" and "family life." We conjectured that older women were not particularly seeking either, but rather both, plus something else. Many women in their 30s, we reasoned, were still trying to juggle the demands of paid work and child-rearing, with little or no energy left for other pursuits, caught up in a vortex of competing demands and personal exhaustion, with little room to pursue personal or creative interests. For these women, perhaps later life provides the opportunity to redress the gaps, to reduce the absolute demands of work and family, and to expand the opportunities for new directions, particularly the expression of personal creative interests. If so, then it would make sense that women are neither interested in a career as a total preoccupation, nor in retirement as a cessation of career.

We found little discussion of these issues in the retirement literature, but some attention in the literature addressing life and career issues at midlife. Of particular relevance is an in-depth study of professional men and women in the United States aged, primarily between 35 to 50 (Wolfe and Kolb 1980). This study was at a different time and place, but made similar observations. It noted a very different life course pattern for men and women, in terms of the relative priorities of family, career, self-development, and interpersonal relations. Women in their 20s are almost exclusively preoccupied with family. However:

> The midlife transition for women is much less a turning inward to self. . . but rather, a major reaching outward for career development and achievement. Having denied themselves self-actualisation through career, their priorities in the early forties are not unlike men in their twenties and thirties, though not as extreme. In the post-transition period, family returns as the major investment, with career as a close second. Paradoxically, women idealise the development of self as worthy of more investment of time and energy than they are ever able to devote to it. The demands, first of family and then of career, continually overshadow attention to self and personal friendships, although this may be changing (Wolfe and Kolb 1980:259).

Our own qualitative study suggests that other aspects of life indeed now become important. Women want the freedom to explore new things, to explore the rich complexity of life in its many forms. What the women were saying in our first, qualitative study was that while professional work was important, so, equally, were other things. Most women resented the notion that any one aspect of their lives did, or should, dominate or could only be pursued at the expense of a reduced emphasis on other aspects. While earlier periods of their lives were necessarily preoccupied with family and career at the expense of other aspects, many now sought to reduce the relative time spent on paid work in order to make time for themselves.

The importance of social connectedness for women cannot be overemphasized. In our qualitative study, 96 percent of women regarded friendship as an important priority in their lives. Women place a high value on sociability as a major source of satisfaction within both their paid work and their retirement (Jewson 1982; Depner and Ingersoll 1982; Hatch 1990). The literature suggests that social networks are constructed as resources to be drawn on in later life. They certainly do fill that function. The women in our study, however, portray social networks in a much more fundamental way: as an essential connectedness with other people that provides a rich quality of life, part of what makes life meaningful. As Wolfe and Kolb (1980) identified, women regard interpersonal relationships as important as family and self-development; as they get older, these take on a greater, not a reduced priority. Furthermore, there appears to be little difference attributed between workplace networks and outside friendships; the one generates, or merges with the other. A basic criterion in the choice to stay in employment or to leave it is the relative availability of satisfying social relationships.

Nearly all the women we interviewed also expressed a desire to have more time to develop some sort of creative interest. This took many forms from writing to visual art or some sort of craft, from theatre to music, home renovation to creating a garden. For some this was defined not in terms of their own creativity, but as recreation. Nonetheless, it was always a creative activity that gave immense personal satisfaction that was for the women's own pleasure and only incidentally, if at all, for the use of others.

The desire for creative self-expression often appeared to be linked to the desire to have more time for oneself, often seen as a precious commodity, never fully realized.

> One of the things about my life, I've had virtually no time that was just my own to do things that I did just because they interested me . . . (and later) there are those sort of things, artistic abilities that have never found an outlet. And I would like to explore those. But I'm not one of these people who feel I must paint or I must write (Babs 62).

For many women this was a desire that had never had expression. Most had never had time. It was regarded as somewhat selfish, only to be pursued in private time and never at the expense of being available to meet other people's needs. Perhaps not admitted publicly at all. They felt that it was a sign of their new sense of self, of confidence in who they were, that these desires could now find some expression. Most women were struggling in one way or another to find a way of including all these things in their lives.

> I do put energy into all of them. I spend time with my family, and with friends. I think its important that you do take time to do that. And sometimes you get a bit tired. I'm involved in a few other things. I always want to do more but never have enough time . . . I really have to prioritize things at home so I get time to do things. Having time to do a bit of gardening. Having time to go for a social life. I have to plan more to make sure all those things fit in . . . with demands of the job and also study at the moment (Tora 50).

Key to the struggle to achieve variety was time. Time emerged as a central issue in almost every interview: Too much time required in high-powered jobs. Too much time required to care for family members. Not enough time for key personal relationships, or for a social cause. Above all not enough time for one's self. Finding time to give to a new interest. Prioritizing time. Resisting the demands of others for time. Those who had left their previous high level, full-time position (seven had done so and others were thinking of it) were explicitly seeking to redress the imbalance created by that job. Most women were trying to find a formula that allowed them to maintain all priorities: career, family, creativity, friendships, and social activism. They recognized the importance of having time for others, time to do what seems worthwhile, but also time for oneself.

In this context, the meaning of retirement changes. Retirement no longer means the withdrawal from active engagement in the workforce, to a life of leisure, but a readjustment, a finer balance of time and energy to allow a more creative and satisfying engagement with the many sides of life and self.

A Message for the Workplace

We appear to be moving into a world in which some people overwork in the extreme, but have become resigned to a permanent level of unemployment. Older professional women seem to be no exception. A recent newspaper article quoted a Korn/Ferry International report as finding that among Australia's elite women executives, most spent between 46 and 65 hours in the office. Another 29 percent worked 56 to 60 hours a week and a further 9 percent put in more than 66 hours in the office (*Sydney Morning Herald* 2/12/94). Simultaneously, there is evidence of the greater casualization of labor, including highly skilled labor at all levels.

In the meantime, Australia, like other OECD countries, is facing the prospect of a doubling of the population over 60 within the next few years (Clare and Tulpule 1994). We are told that we cannot as a nation afford to maintain the levels of future dependent older people with the existing levels of health and income support. Yet historically there has been a pressure toward mandatory retirement, and more recently toward early retirement, as a means of organizational restructuring to contain costs and to ensure promotional opportunities for younger generations of workers (Morrison 1986). It appears then that older people are coming under increasing pressure both to continue working in order to be self-sufficient and to stop working in order to make room for younger cohorts. In the case of high profile, highly paid older women, the pressure is to work enormous hours under stressful conditions, and simultaneously, to get out of the work-force altogether.

If the evidence of our study proves reliable, then both kinds of extreme policy are counterproductive. There are many skilled and committed women of energy reaching into responsible positions. These numbers are likely to increase in the next decade. Their skills and experience and energy need to be retained and valued. The loss of these women from the workplace represents the underutilization of a valuable resource.

Furthermore, these women, by and large, are not in a position to be self-supporting without continued employment. To the extent that they leave, they create a double loss to the economy, both by virtue of the loss of their skills, and by virtue of their almost certain dependency on the state. Nor do they wish to be retired in the conventional sense.

However, the vast majority of women in our study are seeking a reduced emphasis on paid work. It is impossible to maintain unpaid caring and other commitments and be any kind of a whole human being with a commitment to paid work that demands sixty hours in the office a week. The greater the organizational pressure to perform better and longer, the more likely that these women will withdraw altogether. The phenomenon of the glass ceiling needs to be reassessed with these findings in mind. It is our belief that very few women are actively excluded from top positions. Rather it is a sane decision in an insane world to withdraw from the race in order to achieve a more fulfilling and enriched life. It is a sad state of affairs if women are forced to choose between objective success and a full life.

Chapter Seven

The "Docile/Useful" Body of the Older Woman
Noeleen O'Beirne

> The Surgeon said, "They're only small breasts anyway. We might as well have it off eh?" No other treatment was prescribed. No inquiries as to how I was handling all of this and no explanations as to why! Just, "Off you go, okay you've only one breast but at least you're alive!" "At least you're alive," is a phrase that I've come to despise (Logue 1995).

Introduction

Recently I received in the mail what I refer to with some chagrin as "my call-up" papers. My name and address had been obtained from the electoral roll, as had many of my friends in the 50 plus age group. It was a personal invitation to attend a free mammography service conveniently located next to a shopping center. Amongst the information provided was "Half an hour of your time could save your life." I experienced a feeling of disquiet (as did several of my friends who received identical notices). I felt that I was suffering an unwanted intrusion because I had chosen not to take part in the mass mammographic program launched two years earlier with the ambitious goal of screening every woman between the ages of 50-69. Although there was no obvious compulsion, there was a definite element of "hard sell" with the reliance on fear as a not so gentle persuader that was combined with a pervasive notion of being under surveillance.

The campaign aroused in me a resistance to the intrusiveness of a process that appears to have an investment in the cooptation of my aging body. As well, tensions arose from emotions of fear and guilt. Fear that lurking within my apparently healthy breasts lies a dreaded, life-threatening disease and guilt that I hadn't submitted myself to this program, with its attendant implications if at a later date, I was to become symptomatic.

Coupled with this was the infantilizing notion that I am not capable of taking responsibility for the healthy functioning of my own body.

As a result of these experiences, questions arose for me as to why well-established regimes in our culture allow a government-sponsored health promotion program to make such assumptions in relation to the bodies of specific groups and to exercise a disciplinary regime through a health promotion practice? And more importantly, why was there such a willingness to comply by the "targeted" groups? For answers to these particular questions I shall look at Foucault's theories of biopower, with emphasis on his notion of the "docile/useful" body - the body that is "docile," coercible in political terms and useful in an economic sense. In her discussion of the body in medicine, Lupton states that "(C)entral to such inquiries is an analysis of the body in medicine" (1994: 20), for in contemporary western societies "our capacity to experience the body directly, or theorize it indirectly, is inextricably medicalized" (Frank 1990, cited in Lupton 1994: 20).

This chapter proceeds from an overview of the cultural perceptions of older women as a normalizing process, whereby social reproduction produces compliant bodies to the use of a particular health promotion strategy, that of mass mammographic screening, as an illustration of how regulatory practices further produce "docile" bodies by which individuals become of economic use to society. Foucault has commented:

> Discipline produces subjected and practised bodies, "docile" bodies. Discipline increases the forces of the body (in economic terms of utility) and diminishes these same forces (in political terms of obedience). (1979: 138)

My particular investment in this topic arises, of course, from my embodiment as an older woman and so focuses on those practices which are directed at the body of the older woman.

A Regular Old Woman

Normative confusion typifies the cultural images that seek to define the older woman, or to produce in Louisa Lawson's words, "a regular old woman." We have the benign, loving and beloved, caring granny; the interfering, demanding, meddlesome, never satisfied mother-in-law—the butt of comedians and the bane of daughter-in-laws; the frail, dependent, forgetful, manipulative older woman; the "old bag," "old boiler," who is past it and over the hill or conversely, "good for her age." What do these contradictory versions signify? When we consider the dichotomy between media releases that accent violence against older women, depict aging as a disease or disability, and the aged as a burden to society, alongside government campaigns featuring slogans like Age adds Value and Growing Older Getting Better (that I discussed in chapter 1), it signals a construction of aging that is responsive to the investments and agendas of particular lobbies and demonstrates that the origins of these portrayals are sited in cultural and/or juridical/political contexts. Missing from these debates are the voices of the older women. Are we consulted as to our experience of age? What contribution do we make to the debate?

Reinventing the Self

In constituting herself an older woman, the individual is confronted with a range of institutional practices, forms of expertise, and "authentic selves" from which to choose. She can reinvent herself for she is not powerless. She can be the adoring granny, the dedicated voluntary carer, the old bag, the interfering mother-in-law, the dependent wife and mother, the pathologized body, the drug consuming "spaced-out grandma," frail and forgetful, or the burden on society. She must choose, for not all of these stereotypes are equally acceptable, and other forms of being, particularly that of sexually desired or desiring, are excluded. It would appear that a feminine continuum does not exist for women who survive into old age. Their gender identity is unintelligible to a society that insists that "you stay young and beautiful, if you want to be loved."

I have set the benchmark for the older woman's "coming of age'," arbitrarily, at the menopause—a time of dramatic biological change and in some cases, role loss; a point where the health sciences intervene, designating the menopause as a time of deficiency disease and decline. In doing so I am aware that the designation of the menopause as a time when women assume the role as older women is open to contest, but it is difficult to define age except arbitrarily because of individual differences in the physiological rate of aging.

The menopause itself is not a unitary experience for women, occurring at different ages and manifesting different physiological and psychological char-acteristics to which each woman adapts through her own interpretation of the cultural meanings attributed to the event. However, the menopause is both a strong social indicator as well as a significant biological change for women, and as such is useful to mark an entrance into a further life stage.

The intersection of biological, cultural, and social factors at the time of menopause serves to deconstruct feminine identity. A natural disruption in the medicalization of the woman's reproductive functions occurs, which may signal an identity crisis for the older woman. Her apparently primary function of childbearing has ceased. Children have often left home and many marriages have ended in divorce, which often leaves the post-menopausal woman seemingly "roleless."

Among the multiple subjectivities experienced by the older woman during her adult life, society has had a heavy investment in one that is influenced by what Matthews terms the ideology of population. This has entailed an "active mothering that was the task and identity that generally coincided with almost all of an adult woman's life" (1992: 186–187), as Johnson observes:

> Woman "choosing" to play her part in this modern citizenry by performing her duties as mother and wife provided a convenient image of a figure who was at one and the same time a loyal subject and modern citizen . . . they [women] had no existence in this context beyond their roles as wife and mother. (1993:146)

Although this is true of the discourses that sought to influence the subjectivity of the present generation of older women, I need not point out that we have witnessed in the present, resistances to, and subversions of, these identities, which were informed by compulsory heterosexuality, reproductive ideology, and a narrow definition of family. Nevertheless, they were the hegemonic discourses that influenced the identity formation of many of today's older women.

So how is an older woman persuaded to take on a new identity that accords with what society judges normal? How does she become an old woman good for her age, sustaining the normative tradition of good girl, good daughter, good wife, good mother? The older woman listens to the experts and in varying degrees complies with or resists their "games of truth." Within role definitions there is room to move, which fosters the concept of individuality, thereby making control appear natural or legitimate. These factors facilitate, in turn, the assumption of a ready made identity at a time of vulnerability when many adjustments both biological and psychological need to be made.

There is a strong possibility that one is just too overwhelmed to again "reinvent the self." As Featherstone notes:

> The individual struggle to maintain a balance between the external stereotypes of age-appropriate behavior and the subjective experience of the self requires considerable energy, tenacity and other resources. (1993:378)

And so the "mask of aging" is assumed. Butler comments that structural interventions influence the production of subjects. To support this she quotes Foucault's observation that "juridical systems of power produce the subjects they subsequently come to represent" (1990: 20) and that, consequently, "the subjects regulated by such structures are, by virtue of being subjected to them, formed, defined, and reproduced in accordance with the requirements of those structures" (1990: 2). Lupton also enters the debate on the cultural production of subjects in her discussion of the relationship between structure and agency. She refers to Frank's (1991) use of a Marxist dictum to argue that

> Bodies pursue ends which are their own, but in so doing, they reproduce structures which require further resistance. Bodies discipline themselves, but they do so within institutions and discourses which are not their own. (cited in Lupton 1994: 22)

The Older Woman's Body as an Economic Unit

So what are the requirements of those structures? Initially, it could be argued that the body of the older woman is neither docile nor useful because she is no longer reproductive, productive, or in societal terms, the sexually desiring/desired object. In addition to which, her viability as an economic unit involved in the consumption of goods has dramatically decreased.

With the diversity of discourses embracing aging, what are the investments that produce a normative definition, the purpose of which is to control behavior that will produce the desired results both politically and economically? There is an economy in this process due to self-regulation and peer regulation. You judge and are judged by the norm. Dissent within boundaries allows the illusion of freedom to be oneself. We have experts informing public opinion as to what constitutes our well-being.

The older woman cooperates in her reinvention by internalizing this information that is accepted and approved. This also creates a space within which she can exercise power. Even in adopting a position of dependency, she is not powerless, for like the character Maggie Beare in *Mother and Son* (that I described in chapter 1) she is able to manipulate others into giving her, her own way.

There are various agencies (government, statutory authorities, welfare agencies, voluntary and private enterprise) who both define and cater to the older person. A friend made a telling remark: "Let's face it. Older women are a growth industry!" Preeminent amongst the institutions, however, is that of the medical establishment.

The Medical Model of the Older Woman

In the twentieth century, the increased medicalization of society has led to high status for the medical profession and a broadening of its influence and jurisdiction by a proclivity within western culture to redesignate social problems as medical ones. Lupton notes the concern of political economic critics "who saw medicine as becoming a major institution of social control, superseding the influence of religion and law as a 'repository of truth'." She refers to Illich's (1976) argument:

> That modern medicine was both physically and socially harmful due to the impact of professional control over medicine, leading to the dependence of medicine as a panacea, obscuring the political conditions which cause ill-health and removing autonomy from individuals to control their own health. (Lupton 1994: 8)

It is in this light that I wish to focus on the health sciences, which coexist with, and often inform, the various discourses surrounding aging. The health sciences have assumed a largely unquestioned authoritative status in relation to the aged, the majority of whom are women. To illustrate my point I shall use a particular example, the mass mammographic screening program, now considered an important adjunct to the maintenance of older women's health.

In Australia, it is jointly funded by the federal and state governments and is an initiative that enjoys broad support and the approval of state cancer councils, women's health experts, women's organizations, and the media. However, there are dissenting opinions that highlight diagnostic, efficacy, and ethical issues and the counterproductive effect of anxiety-raising health campaigns. As well, a parliamentary report found that treatment after diagnosis is a "lottery," depending on geographical and ethnic factors as well as lack of knowledge of some general practitioners about the treatment and management of breast cancer (1995: 4,14,30,39,43). In recruitment practices, these factors are often ignored, with the efficacy of intervention being promoted. Mass mammo-graphic screening, while not preventative, creates that im-pression; it largely ignores epidemiological factors external to the individual (pollution, ionizing radiation, radiation fallout, drug therapies) and is often a cause of anxiety. Studies have shown the negative impact of anxiety on older women.

> In regard to screening in older women, where the substantial benefit in mortality is accepted, many argue that this is not sufficient to outweigh the disadvantages of false positives and false negatives, costs, risks, and anxiety on a personal level, or the societal costs on a population level. (Ellwood, Cox and Richardson 1992: 58)

This does not negate the value of mammography as a diagnostic tool nor mean that proponents of mass mammography are aware of its capability as a disciplinary practice because they too are affected by pervading discourses of community health. Nor do I wish to join the ranks of the proliferating experts who know what is best for the older woman. What I am doing is offering a critique of the discourses surrounding this practice and its objectification of the older woman. I am exercising the freedom inherent in relations of power to use strategies that question where I stand in relation to a particular game of truth. Foucault believed "that in relations of power, there is necessarily the possibility of resistance" (1991: 12). He also believed that the presence of practices of power did not necessarily invalidate the scientific or therapeutic value of an intervention. Power neither guarantees nor cancels it out (1991: 16).

The Gendered Nature of Disease

I have chosen mass mammographic screening for a variety of reasons: because it demonstrates the continuous emphasis in health care on the sexualized fragmentation of the woman's body; the extent and duration of the continued surveillance to which a woman's body is subjected; the continued accessibility of that body as spectacle, even as an older woman, and the embeddedness and privileging of reproductive ideology, which is shown when risk factors in relation to breast cancer are enumerated.

According to Flynn (1993), Foucault saw underlying the concern for the individual's good, both mind and body, "the embarrassing secret of domination and control concealed by our most highminded purposes and stated intentions" (1993: 280). The individual subjects him or herself to a constant self-surveillance that sets in train an accompanying subjectivity that effectively regulates the individual's compliant body. Implicit in these health and hygiene practices is the view that ill-health is primarily a lack in the individual, a lack of vigilance or discipline or submission to preventative or diagnostic measures, a virtual blaming of the victim. Health has become a secular religion with the ideal state being a healthy body. An "epidemic mentality" (Singer 1993) has arisen, which, in its excessive fervor and incitement through fear, views the body as forever ready to produce or succumb within its space to diseases that are ready to destroy the unwary. Similarly, Kroker and Kroker (1988) describe the advent of "panic theories" and "panic bodies" that give rise to "Body McCarthyism," forever on the alert for the invasion of the body by disease (Lupton 1994: 35).

Foucault commented on the origins of clinical practice and the orientation of medicine, subsequently, as a clinical experience which saw

> A new space opening up before it: the tangible space of the body, which at the same time is that opaque mass in which secrets, invisible lesions, and the very mystery of origins lie hidden. (1976: 122)

This fear of what lies hidden in the body ready to erupt has led to the practice of prophylactic mastectomy being offered to, and in some cases undergone by, women who appear to have a strong disposition to breast cancer by virtue of genetic factors. They say they cannot live with the stress.

After a life-time of indoctrination that says that "eternal vigilance" is the price of good health, it is an easy matter to persuade older women, that for their own good they should present themselves for an examination "which combines the techniques of an observing hierarchy with those of a normalizing judgement" (Flynn 1993: 282).

At two yearly intervals between the ages 50 to 69, it is expected that the older woman will present herself repeatedly for surveillance. "Disciplinary power, unlike sovereign power, is exercised through its invisibility while imposing compulsory visibility on its subjects" (Flynn 1993: 282). In mass mammographic screening programs, the mammogram is administered by the radiographer and is then examined by a radiologist who reads the x-ray and decides whether it is normal or not. The role of the radiologist, a specialist who neither sees nor is seen by the older woman in the breast screening program, contributes to a feeling of alienation from her body, which only a disembodied expert can really know. Mass mammographic screening, then, fits within a world of medical technologies that penetrate the space of the body—a world of x-ray scans, ultrasounds, endoscopes, smears, blood tests, and biopsies, where a "whole new system of truth, of knowledge, techniques, and scientific discourses come into being" (Flynn 1993: 280).

Recruitment is through health promotion strategies and willing allies are found in the media, newsprint, women's magazines, and older women's organizations. Fear plays a strong role—the older you get the more chance you have of getting breast cancer! It is this anxiety provoking tendency, which Lupton observes "presents an ethical difference between offering screening to symptomless individuals and providing medical care to someone who is ill" (1992: 120).

Mass mammographic screening is a free service and a condition is that you are asymptomatic at the time of presentation, while 50 is the preferred age for participation, women over 40 will be accepted into the program if they present themselves as will women over 69. Reasons for participating dwell on the frequency and mortality of breast cancer: "One in 14 women in NSW will develop breast cancer each year—875 women in NSW will die" (Boyages 1993). If you invert this statement, you will realize the reliance on the fright factor—13 out of 14 women in NSW will not develop breast cancer. At the present time there appears to be a minimum of risk in the procedures but again it is a calculation rather than a knowledge.

The program has not been in place for a sufficient duration to test this hypothesis. Dr Elizabeth Barrett-Connor of the University of California states that often women have to make decisions in relation to mammograms and prescribed hormone treatment before proper research is done and with the medical profession having only partial answers. For instance, silicone breast implants were also supposed to be risk-free! Also Ellwood, Cox and Richardson (1992) of the Hugh Adam Cancer Epidemiology Unit state in a report to the Department of Health, New Zealand, "that women who are heterozygous to the ataxia telangiectasia gene are at increased risk of breast cancer and may be sensitive to diagnostic ionising radiation" (Sift et al. 1991; Taylor 1992). While the radiation doses are low, they may well have a detrimental accumulative effect over a twenty year period that we are ignorant of at present.

Program Description

The planning of the mass mammographic screenings is regionalized and has the efficiency of a military operation and indeed the language: targets, recruitment, mobilisation. Using the figures from the WBSU (Western Breast Screening Unit) program, the number of women being 'targeted' in this particular region is 111,704 in the 50 to 69 age range with an extended potential of 242,046 between the ages of 40 and 79 (WBSU 1993). The efficacy for women in the 40–49 range is strongly contested in the studies I have cited and is actually seen as potentially dangerous in some. For instance, Ellwood, Cox and Richardson actually recommended to the New Zealand government, who commissioned their report, "that screening should only be offered from perhaps age 55" (1992: 59).

The provision of sites is varied in the region of western Sydney, which covers high migrant and working class populations. As well as a permanent siting of the unit in a public hospital, greater accessibility is provided through the use of mobile vans (often sited near large shopping centers) and shopfronts. Screenings are provided on a supposedly cost effective basis, $85.00 (not borne by the client), as opposed to a cost of $200.00 when done by private operators (WBSU 1993). In this statement, some wizardry with figures appears to be involved when you consider this is mammography, which involves asymptomatic women, whereas a large proportion of women screened privately would be symptomatic.

The emphasis on screening tends to underplay some shortfalls identified by Dr John Boyages, Director of the WBSU.

> Five to ten per cent of breast cancers may be missed on a screening mammogram. Monthly BSE (Breast Self Examination) and an annual clinical examination is important. The risk of a false negative result increases if the patient is symptomatic particularly for younger women (June 1993).

Boyages (1993) has also pointed out that "a patient with a lump does not need a mammogram; she needs a diagnosis—although this may involve mammography, work-up may also include an ultrasound and fine needle biopsy and in some cases open biopsy to exclude breast." Some of these latter procedures also apply to women with false positives. Of nineteen "callbacks" (a term which de-personalizes women), four were found to be positive after further investigation, the other fifteen being needlessly exposed to stress.

Again I draw attention to the fact that breast screening is not a preventative or cure for breast cancer. Despite extensive use of breast screening, the rate is still steadily rising at 1 percent per year (Bricker-Jenkins 1994). However, screening may reduce breast cancer mortality by at least 30 percent, improve the likelihood of treatment by breast conservation (that is avoiding a mastectomy), and reduce the likelihood of more toxic therapy such as chemotherapy (Boyages 1993). Dr David Dalley, an oncologist, stated in a documentary, *Agatha's Curse*, that survival rates, in spite of advances in treatment, remain fairly constant at 65-70 percent.

As opposed to problems associated with the detection of breast cancer through screening, Guillory (1994) states that 90 percent of breast cancers are detected by women themselves. This appears as a far less intrusive method, with perhaps the disadvantage of not being as effective for early detection as mammography, although this could be offset by Dr Boyages' cautions.

So what are the investments implicit in the health sciences' concentration on breast cancer in preference to other diseases that significantly affect women's health? Mass mammography has a high participation rate due to the fear that breast cancer arouses, a fear, not only of the disease, but a dread of the disfigurement of mastectomy. The perceived loss of femininity is heightened in a society that fetishizes women's breasts and is a factor in women's willingness to undergo prosthetic procedures to compensate. My objective here is not to impute these intentions to dedicated health professionals whom I acknowledge work with sensitivity and care in this field, but to highlight how cultural constructions of women's bodies are so "naturalized" that they are masked in everyday practices.

Feminists contend that treatment is influenced by a "cultural emphasis on breasts as objects of male sexual interest and male sexual pleasure" (Wilkinson and Kitzinger 1992: 230), an obvious "deployment of sexuality" in health care. This becomes more obvious when the gender bias in the treatment of heart disease, which is the largest cause of death in older women, is considered. This has been investigated in three studies, two in the United Kingdom and one in Australia. Alan Hildon (1994), who conducted the Australian research, concluded "that women with heart disease are disadvantaged compared with men in that they do not receive the same treatment as men and are more likely to die after a heart attack as a result" (*Sydney Morning*

Herald, 10/9/1994). He attributed this to "agism and sexism." I think it is appropriate to emphasize here that unlike the symptomless women asked to present for breast screening, these women actually had heart disease and had every right to expect appropriate treatment. This research is of further interest in that cancer is claimed to be the second leading cause of death in women after heart disease (Guillory 1993: 151). In 1992, 27,833 Australian women died of cardiovascular disease as compared with 2,438 from breast cancer (Sweet 1994: 13).

The politics of medicine encompasses gender and, in mass mammography, there is a laudable, visible, and popular project that involves women's health and has strong community approval. There is the ease of persuasion of large numbers of a compliant group with less economic viability to submit themselves to mass screening. There is the redefinition of older women's bodies as unreliable and, therefore, to be known, controlled, and a source of profit.

There is the economic advantage associated with the creation of an industry encompassing *well* older women. There are units to be manned by professionals—doctors, radiologists, radiographers, radiotherapists, researchers, women's health nurses, social workers, counsellors, education officers, recruitment officers, administrators, receptionists, and clerical staff. There is housing and equipment: sites, clinics, vans, laboratories, x-ray equipment, ultrasounds, surgical implements, and prosthetic devices. Foucault explains it thus:

> The biological traits of a population become relevant factors for economic management, and it becomes necessary to organize around them an apparatus which will ensure not only their subjection but the constant increase of their utility. (1976: 279)

In addition to gender and economic factors, the "politics of illness" demonstrates that factors external to the individual are largely ignored (e.g. radiation fallout and pollutants). The beauty of mass screening is that matters appear to be addressed. It alleviates the pressures to examine why the incidence of breast cancer is still rising; in fact, the incidence of breast cancer has doubled since 1940 in the U.S.A (Bricker-Jenkins 1994). Another aspect is that an article in the *Lancet*, *Breast Cancer: Have we lost our way?*, maintains that despite claims to the contrary, that the overall mortality rate from carcinoma of the breast remains static. In disagreement with this, Professor Alan Coates, president of the Clinical Oncological Society argues that "while breast cancer may not be curable . . . more than half the women affected will live to a "ripe old age." The latter half of this statement exceeds the most optimistic estimates available at present. He continues that "although *they may still have residual breast cancer*, [emphasis mine] it is not affecting their lives or responsible for their deaths" (Sweet 1994: 14).

Older women's voices are largely ignored. Lupton finds it a significant factor that the women who are deemed at risk are excluded from the debate surrounding mass mammographic screening:

> These women, apart from their breasts have been rendered invisible. The focus upon the positive promotion of mammography has managed to obscure the rights and the needs of the individuals involved. (1992: 122)

The practice of mass mammographic screening heightens and reinforces agism and sexism through emphasis on the fact that a high risk factor is being female and aged; it also continues control over the woman's sexualized body. It disempowers women by removing the idea of a woman in control of her body when it creates a need for that body to be controlled by exogenous forces. It is a continuation of the concept that "women's bodies when unsupervised can create chaos" (Smart 1991: 173). It creates a health industry around well older women.

Resistances can be as simple as asking for more information, making an informed choice providing a critique using "the ability to speak our own truths in our own voice and participate in decisions that affect our lives" (Pharr 1988, cited in Bricker-Jenkins 1994: 33), or challenging the 'truth' of experts, "which disqualifies alternate visions and experiences which arise from the multiple subjectivities of inhabiting [in this case, older] women's bodies" (Smart 1991: 175).

Conclusion

The slippage between the mounting of an aggressive campaign for mass mammographic screening and the lack of access to universal effective treatment for women (particularly poor, Aboriginal, and rural women) who are diagnosed as having breast cancer indicates that medicine, far from being politically neutral, has an investment informed by a class-based, political economy. That it is gendered is also evident in the disparity in the treatment of heart disease in men and women as well as a deployment of sexuality in the fetishization of the women's breasts and the western cultural preoccupation with body surfaces that is shown in the privileging of breast cancer, which affects the exterior of the body, over heart disease (an interior organ), which kills ten times the number of women. A privileging and eroticization of the visible body occurs, curious in light of the fact that in western society, the heart is a signifier of love but a woman's breasts are erogenous zones, and cause sexual arousal. If medicine was an objective science, rather than being affected by cultural, class, gender, economic, and political factors, surely the emphasis would be on the diagnosis and treatment of heart disease in women and the provision of adequate, accessible, and consistent treatment and management of breast cancer once diagnosed?

Another contradiction in the concern for women's health is that breast reconstruction makes the detection of a reoccuring cancer on the chest wall more difficult to detect. Discourses around femininity and sexual attractiveness are compelling reasons for women to submit to this type of surgery.

The quote at the beginning of this chapter demonstrates the lack of sensitivity to a woman undergoing a traumatic experience in which not only her life is at threat, but also aspects of her identity as a woman. As she says so aptly, "I know they are doing their job but the interaction with me—Jill, human being, someone's daughter, sister, wife and mother, someone feeling anxious and vulnerable is non-existent" (Logue 1995: 4).

There is so much more to the detection and treatment of breast cancer than screening programs, mastectomy, chemo-therapy, prostheses, or breast reconstruction. Above all is the welfare of the women involved and a sharing of knowledge and consultation with them. They should fully know the short-comings as well as the benefits of screening programs so that the debate is broadened and an informed choice can be made by older women themselves.

Chapter Eight

Aging: Encounters with the Medical Model
Sharyn Mcgee

my mother's aging

soft lined face
greying skin
unkempt hair
tired eyes
weakening voice
her legs ache
her back hurts
breathless
its so hard to walk
her clothes are dirty
shes forgetting what she just said
the spasms in her legs make her cry

oh god, **my mother's old**
how did it happen?
when *did it happen?*

This chapter will explore critical perspectives on the medical-ization process, its particular relevance to women and aging, and its implications for practice as women, as feminists, and as health practitioners (e.g. nurses). It is both a theoretical and personal exploration of these issues, ideas, and experiences during a specific period of my life: my mother's illness and hospitalization for six weeks. It is based on my journal writings and theoretical reading and writing at the time of her hospitalization.

13/8/95

well, the day has come that i have dreaded and i am relieved too . . . I
received a phone call from mum's neighbour on Friday morning . . .
mum couldn't get out of bed, she was in pain and breathless . . . i
drove over and rang her doctor, he suggested ringing the ambulance
so i did and we spent the day at the hospital, at 8pm they transferred
her to the local gerontological hospital and I came home exhausted,
drained from being there and talking to everyone like my brothers and
mum's neighbors . . . she's there for the weekend and assessment by
the "team" on Monday . . . i went in yesterday and today and just
rang my uncle and aunt . . . i've spoken more to everyone than i have
for ages!!! on Friday i was remembering being at the hospital the day
dad went in for tests and didn't come out . . . i felt sad and scared
that this was it and maybe it is and maybe it isn't . . . i don't know
yet . . . till the "team" looks at her . . . i am feeling like i will have to
stand strong by her and for her and not let anyone bulldoze her even
family! . . . i went for a "quick" visit . . . 4 hours later i got home . . .
her blood pressure was very low in the morning and they were
worrried about her but this kind of up and down may go on for
years!!!! or days!!!!!!!!!!!!

"Aging" is in a sense something we all do from the moment we are born and in another sense something we all will do. "Aging" is a normal part of life that we cannot avoid. At the same time aging is not simply a biological phenomenon, it is a social phenomenon (see for example Estes 1992; Thane 1995; Cole 1992; Phillipson 1982; Russell and Schofield 1986; Russell 1981). In other words, while aging is a biological process that is common to all human groups, as far as we know the experience of aging and the social position of the aged is socially constructed. Aging is the product of social structural forces as much as biological processes.

The social construction of aging occurs through a complex of discursive practices that act to define the notion of age and aging and link it with dependency, poverty, ill health, disability, and rolelessness. Estes (1992) argues that it is vital to explore the interaction between class, gender, ethnicity, and aging as well as the role of the state in the social reproduction of class and gender relations in aging. However, as Margaret points out in chapter 3, the political economy perspective that Estes uses does not adequately identify the gendered nature of aging and its implications for women.

The health and illness system is one aspect of the state that directly influences the "lived experience" and self-esteem of women and the aged (Estes 1992; Russell and Schofield 1986; Russell 1981). It plays a central role in the social construction of aging, particularly through the process known as the medicalization of society. Since the early 1970s, social theorists, practitioners, and consumers have been arguing that we are witnessing a "medicalization of society" which is the process by which the domain of medicine and medical authority is extended over areas of life that were previously considered nonmedical and where lay and commonsense understandings and practices once predominated. The medicalization of society and the construction of professional dominance (specifically the medical profession) are inextricably linked (Margaret, chapter 3; Willis 1983).

i just rang the hospital and spoke to a Dr B.—she said no change in mum's condition and that she's having x-rays of her back done soon, that by the time i come in she will have the results, i told her i was a RN and that i didn't want them to pussyfoot around, She responded in the usual noncommital way doctors who don't know have but i think she took it in and said she will be on the ward till 5.30/quarter to six . . .

The medicalization of aging particularly affects women because women live longer than men, are more likely to be members of the "frail aged" group, and are the bulk of carers, both professionally as nurses and other health care workers and personally as daughters and family members. The majority of volunteer workers are also women (see Rosemary chapter 5; Gibson 1998). Hence women are likely to feel the negative impact of those processes as well as their benefits as patients, professionals, and carers.

15/8/95
i am feeling guilty . . . perhaps i didn't take charge or be assertive enough in my caring for example go to her doctor and suggest meals on wheels, home care, physio and podiatry . . . her feet are a mess, she's got no muscle tone in her arms or legs . . . and the spasms in her legs .. why didn't i notice them??? . . . have i been so caught up in my own stuff for so long???? . . . still i have been there for her . . .

*doing her shopping, taking her to the dentist, the doctor, the bank,
being patient and aware of her desire for independence and her
pride . . . not wanting to usurp her decision making process!*

Feminism and Foucault: Insights on power

The major insights of feminism are particularly relevant in
exploring how the medicalization process works in relation to
women and aging (Margaret chapter 3; Noeleen chapter 7), while
the social theory of Michel Foucault is important in identifying
the process of medicalization (Lupton 1997) and its constitution
of aging (Katz 1997). What these two perspectives have in
common are their emphasis on power and knowledge.

The importance of feminism lies in its analysis of power and
gender relations throughout society: the catchcry of the 1970s,
"the Personal is Political," and the emphasis on consciousness-
raising made very public statements about the relationship
between the public and the private spheres and the role of power
in both. Feminists applied these principles to understanding
medicine and the medical model and so have been influenced by,
and influential in, the debates about medicalization.

15/8/95
*i am waking up confused about where i am . . . at home, at the
psychiatric hospital where i trained . . . with my mother in my mind
immediately . . . her body so frail reminds me of the old ladies in ward
14, incontinent and demented, some were crazy before they grew old,
others just demented slowly over their ordinary lives as their bodies
disintegrated with time . . . and they were the lucky ones . . . we had
one woman who was slowly losing control of her body and mind . . .
sometimes with it and sometimes not . . . she cried when she peed in
her pants . . . i felt so sad for her and her daughter who visited
irregularly . . . probably because it hurt too much to watch the slow
disintegration of a once strong woman/mother . . . and perhaps angry
too . . . i dont know if there was a more specific problem . . . how dare
they grow old on us!!!!!*

In feminist thinking, the analysis of medicine and medical
knowledge is secondary to the focus on women and is an
accidental outcome of it. In contrast to this, Michel Foucault's
interest for most of his working life seems to have been to
understand the relationship between power and knowledge in
their various forms. In doing so he contributed a number of
insights to the "discourse" on power, which are most clearly

articulated in his distinctive (not unique!) analysis of the notion that "knowledge is power."

The focus of Foucault's work was the human sciences and their construction of human beings through the distinctive "knowledges" that they produced and are still producing. By human sciences Foucault means the social sciences, such as sociology, psychology, criminology, law, and anthropology, although his critique of medicine, psychiatry, and psychoanalysis is based on similiar grounds. Foucault argued that these universalizing and totalizing discourses define humanity and truth while supposedly "describing" them. In other words, the human sciences are constructing or constituting human behavior by studying it.

Two of the most important interconnected mechanisms in this process of defining humanity and truth are the categorization of people into "normal" and "abnormal" and the social construction of the body through the "clinical gaze." His work studies the production of different forms of abnormality, such as illness, madness, criminality, and varied forms of sexuality through which forms of normality are constructed. For Foucault, the study of abnormality and its application to the body are the main ways that power relations are established and maintained in society by the processes of knowledge production, dissemination, and therapeutic practice, which can be summarised by the concept of discursive practices (Foucault 1973, 1980; Fox 1993; McHoul and Grace 1993).

> *and then there are memories of the other "gerie" wards . . . walking frail old ladies (mainly) to the toilet and to meals, feeding them and showering them and cleaning them, changing them in bed, lifting them out of bed and into chairs, turning them and washing their bums, changing the sheets and dressing their bedsores, and in the day room, the music lady playing the piano and singing old songs; we did exercises and physio but nobody including me believed they would do anything except use up time, use up time while they died . . . we were young and bored and entertained ourselves by wheelchair races down the corridors, gossip and pool . . . the smell of urine and faeces and disinfectant . . . i don't want mum to live or die like that . . .*

The Medicalization of Aging

According to medicalization analysis there are four main indications of the trend in modern society. These are the growth of the medical institution, the medicalization of life events, the medicalization of deviance and the public acceptance of this medicalization process (Robertson 1989). The process by which this model of understanding human life became dominant remains relevant because medicine maintains and extends its dominance over understanding life processes and more traditional cultural practices (see, for example, Ngaanyatjarra Pitjantjatjara Yankunytjatjara, 1995). The institutionalization of care and control within large sites such as hospitals, asylums, and nursing homes is a central feature of the medicalization process (Katz 1997; Katz 1995; Foucault 1994).

15/8/95

today i sat in the sun with a cup of tea and a sandwich, reading and listening to the sounds of this land, a white cockatoo screeched over head as well as the normal chattering of the regular birds, the sun was hot and i stripped down to my t-shirt . . . life in all its glory . . . and . . . sadness, grief, letting go, challenges, movement and growth . . . i can't find the right word to describe it today . . . all things come to pass .. i feel i want to grab a hold of life, my life and live it fully, strongly . . .

The consequences of the medicaliztion of society are summarized by Russell and Schofield (1986) as being twofold: the development of problems arising from medical interventions and the application of the medical model to nonmedical areas of life, especially social problems. The concept of social control, practices developed by social groups of all kinds to enforce or encourage conformity and deal with behavior that violates social norms, is a fundamental one in sociology. Medicine is considered by sociologists to be one of the key institutions in the organization of social control in industrialized societies.

later, 15/8/95

i am feeling relieved—i spoke to the doctor today and the tests show no reason for the pain, no underlying pathology so far and no expectation of any! So their focus is on getting mum up and about and able to go home . . . with homecare and meals on wheels etc . . . mum seems a lot better . . . color in her face and life in her eyes . . . she's eating well, breathing a lot better and she said the pain in her legs isn't as bad. She only had one cramp while i was there which was pretty mild compared to the other days . . . the physio took her walking around the ward today supporting one side and with a walking stick, she walked to the toilet and the sink to clean her teeth . . . i'm feeling less frightened . . .

The core of the medicalization process lies in the application of the medical model to more and more aspects of life (Russell and Schofield,1986). In a general sense the public acceptance of medicalization has confirmed the tendency to see all undesirable behavior as illness that requires medical intervention and to see medical intervention as justified in every and any situation.

Our society, like many others, defines desirable and undesireable behaviors in ways that hide the process by which these definitions are socially constructed. When experiences like aging, which in the past were valued positively (Cole 1992), are seen as undesireable they too become subject to the medicalization process. The outcome of this process is that images of the aged and aging are dominated by those of sickness, disability and dementia, poverty and dependency. Dependency is in itself defined negatively in a society where being independent is highly valued (Hockey and James 1993; Gibson 1998).

15/8/95

i didn't like the way mum's doctor responded on the phone on Friday saying he would "get more sense from you quite frankly" when i asked if he wanted to speak to mum . . . this seems typical of doctors' negative attitude to elderly people, women especially . . . the hospital i found as impenetrable and cold emotionally as usual while it seemed efficient, generating that busy knowing air . . . they were busy, every bed was full! No one initiated communication with me until i stood around the nurses' station . . . then they noticed me!

The modern medical view of health and illness is a mechanistic one and has three main characteristics: a focus on cure, individuals, and intervention. This mechanistic and individualistic view of health and illness that emerged during the scientific revolution differs from the traditional view of health and illness because the body is treated like a machine that malfunctions "occasionally" rather than as a part of a "whole person" in relationship with his/her social environment (Russell and Schofield 1983).

23/8/95

The last few days have been challenging . . . . the news is her arterial circulation is so bad the doctor has asked a surgeon to assess the possibility of a bypass probably femoral but as my friend who is a doctor said they would do it wherever the blockage is! Her doctor at

*the hospital seems to be talking with her and me fairly openly and
honestly. Yesterday i asked her what are the implications of not
having surgery and she said mum would need to not smoke again and
that she would need more care, more painkillers etc, although no
amputation would be necessary at this point. This is a scary future
especially if the pain gets so bad and she becomes more disabled!*

The medical approach to illness involved in its initial stages a
sharp division between the body and the mind. However, this
sharp division has not been sustained as the medical model has
been applied to more and more human experience. As Peele
(1989) points out, three groups of life experiences have been
described as diseases within the last two hundred years. These
"generations of diseases" as he calls them, are physical ailments,
mental disorders, and addictions.

30/8/95
*Doctor R. thinks mum may have had a heart attack: her heart was
beating very fast this morning and the ECG suggested she has had
one ..... afterwards i read an article that suggested women's heart
attacks are often misdiagnosed because their symptoms are not the
"classic" ones (ie male) and tend to be breathlessness and stomach
upsets .... which have been getting worse in mum!*

The first, physical ailments, are defined by their "meas-
ureable" physical effects and are clearly connected to the
functioning of the body, and the damage disease does to the
body whereas the second generation of diseases are the so-called
"mental illnesses" or emotional disorders. These disorders cannot
be defined by their physical effects and become visible to us
through what people say and do, no matter what evidence or
lack of evidence exists (e.g. EEGs, blood tests, cat scans).The
third generation of diseases, the addictive disorders, are
indicated by "the goal directed behaviors they describe" (Peele
1989: 6) and are concerned with physical/emotional desires
and/or appetites such as drinking, eating, and sex.
    Although aging was taken up as a biological problem to be
studied in the early stages of the medicalization process (Cole
1992; Katz 1995; Katz 1997), it has also been constructed as a
mental illness through the diagnosis of the group of conditions
known as senile dementias one of which has now been named
"Alzheimer's" which is often referred to colloquially as Old-
timers' disease.

30/8/95
Today (at the larger hospital she's been moved to) her new doctor said
that "dementia?" was down on her notes but he had spoken to her
and thought she gave a good account of herself although not in detail!
i said she was forgetting things a bit more especially short-term
memories but not in a way that was abnormal . . .

Historical Perspectives

Although a dominant trend of this century has been the way in which aging and old age have been constructed through their medicalization, medical thinking dominated the study of aging even before the field of geriatrics became established as a special branch of medicine at the beginning of the century (Russell and Schofield 1986). Hence the study of old age (or gerontology) is dominated by biomedical perspectives that focus on the problems of aging, in particular the biological decline model of aging (see Margaret, chapter 3) and the social problem perspective (Gibson 1998).

The birth of the modern system of clinical medicine can be seen as "simply one more construction or perception of the nature of illness" (Armstrong 1993, p. 56). The "fabrication of the body by means of the 'anatomical atlas'" (p. 56) is central to this new perception, which demanded the construction of "normal" and "pathological" bodies. This construction of a particular way of interpreting the body as the truth was based on "mechanisms of power" particularly techniques of surveillance that analyzed, monitored and fabricated the body, such as clinical examinations, post-mortems, and photographs of the mentally ill. These techniques are often referred to as "the clinical gaze" (Armstrong 1993; Fox 1993; Foucault 1973).

The "clinical gaze" has created the search for "normal" and "pathological" aging. This search began in the nineteenth century through the fledgling disciplines of gerontology and geriatrics, which were deeply embedded in Victorian values and social realities (Cole 1992). The scientists and physicians involved in research were looking for "the mechanisms of senescence and the pathology of old age" (p. 18). They assumed that the biology of aging (like all science) could be cut off from cultural perceptions and values. Hence, Jean Charcot, a major influence on the emerging disciplines whose work is another example of the "clinical gaze" (Katz, 1997; 1995), rarely referred to or recognized the class or gender of the population upon which clinical research was conducted. The implications of this rejection have been hotly debated by feminists and other social theorists in the twentieth century.

2/9/95

. . . i just realized that the geriatric hospital's behavior was secretive and insulting—they never suggested to me that they thought she was dementing except when i questioned their informed consent process and then doctor B. said in a defensive tone they had told her but she was very forgetful . . . i don't think they took into account the strange surroundings or her educational background!!!!! and lack of knowledge of the system!!!! which they should in a geriatric specialist unit . . . is it an example of tunnel vision? . . . they see what they want to see and dementia is what they want to see!!!!

Throughout the nineteenth and early twentieth centuries, research was primarily conducted on the poor and working class, who were housed within the growing public welfare institutions, such as alms-houses and public hospitals. Charcot's treatise on the diseases of old age was primarily based on large numbers of women living in the Salpêtrière (a large public hospital in Paris) who belonged to "the least favored portion of society" (Charcot 1861, cited in Cole, 201). Their health was already diminished by their social location and the social conditions of their lives.

The search for normal and pathological aging reflected a middle-class dualism and "a decidedly masculine flavour" (Cole 1992). Pathology was primarily documented among the poor, while normality seemed to exist primarily amongst the middle and upper classes. Male scientists, themselves aging, expressed concern about declining influence, sexual potency and productivity in their writings (Cole 1992, 197–201).

At the beginning of the twentieth century the belief that biomedical science could someday develop "a solution to the problem of old age" (Minot 1908, cited in Cole, 197) began to grow and the division of the disciplines into those scientists who studied the normal processes of aging and the clinical physicians who studied the pathology or diseases of old age was established. Geriatric medicine was born (Katz 1995, 1997).

8/9/95

i am my mother's next of kin—this feels weird and strangely adult! the hospital registrar rang to get my permission for a test this morning . . . he wanted to get my permission as well given that the information on her file suggested dementia. i told him that i thought

that the other hospital had got it wrong: that she was forgetful but
not dementing and that she had been quite confused by being in
hospital, that she didn't have an understanding of the medical stuff
and her background didn't prepare her for understanding it . . . he
kind of ignored me and just clarified that i was her next of kin—i
hesitated as i thought i should say my eldest brother and then i
realized i was her next of kin and the best person to be nominated as
that!

The Diagram of Power: The human sciences

The "diagram of power" was rearranged in the twentieth century and the human sciences of sociology and psychology have played a more important part than in the previous century (Armstrong 1993; Katz 1995, 1997). The "clinical gaze" began to move from the microscopic detail of the individualized body to the "undifferentiated space between bodies" and into the "social body" itself. The space between bodies became a social-psychological space and not just a physical space (Armstrong 1993: 57). Hence the techniques of examination that have developed in the twentieth century, such as questions to elicit the patient's history and mental functioning, exemplify and contribute to the construction of this social-psychological space.

The disciplines of sociology and psychology contributed to the construction of the division of life processes into "normal" and "pathological" as they emerged as distinct and autonomous disciplines. Sociology, for example, contributed to post-war medicine through its survey techniques, which extended the "clinical gaze" to new areas such as the health experiences and illness behaviors of ordinary people (Armstrong 1993).

Psychological and sociological interest in old age was aroused more strongly in the twentieth century when increasing numbers of older people again began to be seen as a social problem (Russell and Schofield 1986). The public health and welfare institutions provided a basis for research as they had for medicine in the nineteenth century. Cole (1992) argues that old age had become "a condition to be explained and regulated by scientific management" (p. 211) by the middle of the twentieth century. This focus on the "problem of old age" has become in the latter half of the twentieth century the "problem of old women" (Gibson 1998).

as i was about to leave she asked me about the money . . . she needed
$5 change and she put 5 ten cent pieces on the table and asked is this

$5? . . . i responded in a patient and loving way explaining "no it
was 50 cents here was $5" putting 5 one dollar coins on the table . . .
then i said next time we go to the bank we'll get 20s,10s and 5s in
notes... in other words i was problem solving as a nurse but my heart
sank . . . and i felt scared and sad . . . it's a little incident but means so
much about her cognitive functioning—only another person with a
similiar sort of experience could understand its loaded meaning . . .
she is fading . . . her body is here and relatively healthy (compared to
others) yet she is fading . . . the person i know as mother, the woman
i know, the person i have shared so much of my life with in so many
ways (not only as a child/mother) is fading and i am missing her: her
energy and gentleness and the ongoing support she gives
us . . . she is fading and i must let her go with as much love and
support as i can give . . . i think i need to find some way of being with
her as friend and daughter and maybe even as nurse . . . as i would
with a friend.

The diseases of old age were being mapped, especially the
deterioration of social competence in old people. These
conditions, known collectively as the senile dementias, are
commonly believed to be physiological in origin, yet Kitwood
(1995) argues that even the dementias are socially constructed
and that Alzheimer's is "a deeply paradoxical category" (1995:
93). He points out that there is a huge variability and
arbitrariness in the diagnosis of dementia and that social and
psychological factors are systematically ignored. While
accounting for only a small percentage of problems in these over
65 an "Alzheimer's culture" has been produced in the wake of the
concern of the aging of the population (Kitwood 1995). Chetley
(1995) argues that health problems of the elderly including
dementia, may be compounded by the overprescription of drugs.

A reluctance among health personnel, patients, and carers to
identify dementia and develop management strategies suggests a
stigma akin to mental illness. The voice of the person with
dementia is rarely heard in research, and their presence as people
entitled to information and with rights is ignored by professionals
and family alike (Knapman and Waite 1995).

15/9/95
. . . i spoke to mum's doctor (G.P.) today and we talked about her
condition. He said she has mild to moderate dementia . . . It was a
relief to talk about it straight forwardly although i don't trust his
knowledge of management . . . there is no cure, no treatment so there

is no hope in his opinion . . . while i arranged to be there when he starts home visits he didn't seem to grasp why and made no comment on developing a management plan! We are doing what we can in organizing social supports etc in his opinion . . . he reckons she has had it for a longish while so why didn't he speak to me about it? !!!!!

Recent Trends

Two related trends that have occurred in the rearrangement of the "diagram of power" in the late twentieth century (Armstrong 1993) are particularly important for health practitioners. Firstly, the perception of the body has changed from a passive object of study to an active participant in "the health continuum." Secondly, the development of the "new public health" has meant that a vast network ranging from the post-war integrated and comprehensive health care system to community and "informal' care" (Armstrong 1993: 65) has emerged in which the patient is an active member as well as a consumer.

30/8/95
According to the hospital doctor mum has begun talking about the possibility of going into care rather than home—like a hostel! This is a shock that i'm still processing, Last night i dreamt about going to the house and opening the door with a key for the last time, i felt sad and scared . . . the possibility of mum's moving raises issues for me! i need to be conscious of that so that i can be open to what is best for her and help her decide what is best for her, to look at all the options open to her!
later
when the doctor said mum wanted to go into care . . . i was shocked but willing to support her in any decision she made but when i asked mum she said no she wanted to go home . . . i feel manipulated as if the doctor had planted the idea because they thought supported accommodation was the right thing to do!

These broader trends can be seen in the management of the aged and the aging through, first, the increasing dominance of discourses in the health and welfare systems that emphasize healthy aging amongst the aged and aging ; second, the movement of the care of the "frail aged" from large, segregated public institutions to small, privately owned institutions such as nursing homes and hostels situated within the community, and to within the home itself (Dalley 1993; Fox 1993; Power and Bevington 1995; Gibson 1998).

The high percentage of nurses and nonmedical personnel amongst health practitioners is well known, but the focus of most of the medicalization literature (including feminist and critical theory) is on the role of medical practitioners. Yet the role of nurses and other nonmedical paid personnel in health and welfare is crucial in enacting the many levels of social control in relation to the aging process.

At the same time it is obvious that the vast network of surveillance techniques known as community care, to which the patient belongs as both carer and consumer, has also engaged the family and local community as members of the "health team." Women as daughters and wives play a key part in this expanding network, as they do in the health field. Social research supports the emphasis of family and community care in that these networks are seen to play an important role in the health and independence of people as they age (Kendig 1984; Gibson 1998) and so produce an "independent but parallel gaze" (Armstrong 1993).

> . . . *the caring and support mum has received from her friends and neighbors is incredible—as one said mum is like family. This says a lot about mum and the nature of our neighbourhood! i wouldn't like her to lose that by moving too far away so whatever happens we need to be looking nearby. . .*

An Independent and Parallel Gaze: Nursing and feminism

The medicalization of society has had an impact on the discursive practices of nursing and other health and welfare occupations in Australia and other countries (Davis and George 1988; Palmer and Short 1989; Willis 1983). It has also constructed the caring practices of women in the family (Dalley 1993; Ehrenreich and English 1979).

The care of the elderly and infirm, or gerontological nursing (one of the many historically and socially distinct forms of nursing), is historically linked in Australia to a variety of other nursing specialities (including community nursing and psychiatric nursing) as well as geriatric medicine. The role of the nurse includes far more than the care of the "oldies" or "geries" in nursing homes and hospital wards.

Nurses are affected as much by the dominant images of aging and women as the rest of the population. Rhonda's chapter 9 shows how nursing the "geries" is considered to be the pits of nursing and that gerontic nursing lies at the bottom of the nursing status ladder. In addition, research seems to suggest that nurses prefer nursing men (Knowles and Sarver 1985; Evers 1988, both cited in Nay 1995). The dominant ungendered construction of aging people in health policy (Power and Bevington 1995) permits nurses and others to ignore the need for a gendered approach to their practice.

6/10/95
mum is home and both of us are feeling relieved and scared . . .
The intrusion of medicine and the hospital continues of course with my blessing in some ways . . . a nurse visits daily . . . she/he organizes her medication and checks that mum is going okay . . . mum thinks this will end soon and she will be both relieved and scared when this happens . . . she has begun to recognize her vulnerability and frailty and the fact that medicine can do nothing about the problem has disappointed her and left her feeling hopeless . . . they have also left her, of course, without any suggestions for management other than medication and social supports such as meals on wheels and home care . . . no referral to any pain management clinic or complementary therapies (not even physio!). This attitude of "we have found out what's wrong and there's nothing we can do so here's some tablets you take care of it . . . "!

Two limitations of the critical literature on the medical profession is that it seems to suggest that nurses and others, including the family, are totally embedded in the medical model and powerless to resist its demands personally or politically (see Lupton 1997 for discussion of this in relation to Foucault) and that there is only one discourse on aging, which is the negative one of decline (see, for example, Thane 1995, for discussion of this).

Nurses and family are not completely powerless to resist the totalizing aspects of the medical model within their daily life (Brown 1995; Fuller 1995; Gray and Pratt 1995; Hewison 1995; Knapman and White, 1995; Wicks, 1995; Gibson, 1998) and can use the diversity of discourses to struggle against and construct their own experiences of aging (Thane 1995). Short, Sharman, and Speedy (1994) argue that nurses can affect change in substantive ways through the use of critical social theory such as feminism, while women have shown through the Women's Movement that social change can happen by linking the personal and the political (see, for example, Broom 1991 and Short and Sharman 1990 for discussions in relation to health).

Two of the insights of Foucault's analysis are, first, that no one profession or institution is wholly responsible for the medicalization of society and, second, that no one discourse is completely dominant in any society. His focus on the human sciences in general and their construction of human life and behavior demands an ongoing exploration of the relationship between the discursive practices of science, health and welfare agencies, and our own actions.

Feminist theory also challenges us to analyze our practice. Both Foucauldian and feminist theory create personal as well as political dilemmas for clients, practitioners, and carers because they emphasize the constructive and interpersonal nature of power within discursive practices that cannot be ignored yet cannot be easily resolved.

11/1/96

since i asked her G.P. to stop the new drug . . . she is more present and herself—even smiles and cracks jokes occasionally! For the first time for ages she rang me about the groceries and to tell me the man was coming with the commode . . . she was even chatty! When i went over there yesterday i talked to her about her forgetfulness and suggested we all talk about it with each other and her doctor. . . Mum was not enthusiastic and said we'll talk about it when she's feeling better . . . !

She said she just tries to forget about it!
Then Mum's nurse rang me to take a stool sample to Mum's doctor. . . well i immediately began to think the worst, bowel cancer etc and i also felt like i hadn't being doing my job properly! Mum hadn't mentioned any pain to me . . . i recognized the roller coaster ride i was about to get on and so didn't to the same extent . . . a relief! When i rang her later to check whether she had produced anything she hadn't and she spent the rest of the conversation talking about whether she can do it or not and how she does both together! Do i want to know this!?

While the persistent media image of lonely, isolated, disabled old women living (and dying) at home alone without anyone noticing for weeks or months is not well founded in the majority of women's lives these dominant discourses construct old women as problems and ignore their strengths and contributions (Gibson 1998). This middle-agist perspective means that women as daughters and women as health practitioners need to create alliances with each other and the older women in their lives so that the emphasis on community care is not simply another extension of the clinical gaze.

After three days of talking about bodywastes she produced something and i went over and for a little while played competent nurse . . . i put my best nurse face on . . . but i'm not sure i could play nurse again in that way!
i took the sample to her doctor's . . .

Conclusion

The dominance of the medical model and the medicalization of aging has shaped to a great extent our understanding and experience of aging as women. As Estes (1992) argues, older women are treated as permanent members of the sick role, no matter how healthy they may be, in two ways: as women and as old. The challenge for feminists and practitioners is in exploring how medicalization works—both historically and in our personal lives—so that this informs our practice!

The construction of aging within a medical framework is usually construed as a repressive force that needs to be resisted. Yet as Armstrong (1993) points out, Foucault stresses the contradictory nature of power and that the tendency to describe the effects of power in negative terms ignores the way it produces reality. Surveillance is a productive force, has no inherent moral charge, and may, in fact, benefit individuals and the community (Dingwall and Robinson 1993; Thane 1995). We need to look at ways of exploring these issues without a dualistic mindset so that we can appreciate the pitfalls and the benefits of the clinical gaze and the medical model and so construct new understandings of aging that can enhance individual and social life.

The most powerful encounter with aging in my life so far is what I am encountering now in the process of sharing my mother's aging and, when the time comes, her death. I often feel the sadness and powerlessness that we encounter as we age and come to accept that there are some things in life we cannot control or change. Rather than wasting energy and time raging against the world I am enjoying my mothers company, her life, in snatches, and the growing I see in us, neither being obsessed with her aging nor denying it. I am picking up her life and doing what she can't or doesn't want to do anymore. At the same time it is not all one way, she still helps me and my brother financially. She listens to me rave on about work and frustrations in my life. She is even now supportive and kind. Sometimes I want more from her in terms of emotions and advice but I am learning to accept who she is and what she has to give. She is a gentle loving soul my mother even as she fades!

I remember a friend saying how beautiful old women were: their soft and lined skin, I was shocked at the time especially because she is younger than me in her 30s and I thought it weird . Yet now I am beginning to see what she meant. I visit my mother and her body wrinkling and shrinking is beautiful to me, her wispy grey hair is dear and elicits a sweet tenderness in me, a sadness and an appreciation of the frailty and shortness of life and the demands it places on us all. I'm glad I made the decision to share her aging with her, our aging together as women.

Chapter Nine

Benevolent Oppression: Experiences of Older Women
Aging "Out of Place"
Rhonda Nay

Introduction

Most of us dread the possibility of entering a nursing home. It is our least preferred option for accommodation, and is seen as the last resort (e.g. Kendig 1989; Rowland 1991; Day 1991; Nay 1993). In fact the proportion of the aged population residing in nursing homes at any one time is approximately 5 percent in most OECD countries. However, the proportion estimated to spend some time during their lives in a nursing home is between 25 percent (Rowland, 1991) and 43 percent (cited in Friedan 1994: 479). Of this group, the vast majority are women.

Nursing homes have poor reputations. They are associated with suffering, dementia, and death. In a society where dementia attracts stigma, death is denied, and people constantly receive the message that all suffering can be "cured", it is hardly surprising that residents entering nursing homes do so with less than enthusiastic anticipation. Nursing homes have always suffered very poor reputations and research has demonstrated that relatives generally provide care "at home" for as long as is humanely possible and often beyond the point where their own health and that of the person receiving care suffers (Nay 1996, 1997; Pearson, Nay et al. 1996). Such care by relatives assumes the presence of (usually) a spouse or daughter who is not otherwise employed but who is in good health (de Vaus 1996).

There is increasing policy emphasis on encouraging older people to "age in place"; those older people who are admitted to nursing homes can be seen within this context as "aging out of place". It could be argued that the greater the emphasis placed upon growing old in the community, the more immense will be the sense of failure, guilt, resentment, and loss associated with nursing home admission.

Nursing homes are largely populated by women: women as residents, women as informal carers and women as nurses. It is important, therefore, that a book that explores the experiences of aging/aged women includes some discussion of the experiences of nursing home life. Although I have not had the experience of residing in a nursing home, I have had approximately twenty years experience as a nurse and researcher working with residents, relatives, and staff. In addition to my own experiences, the research study upon which I am drawing involved, in part, in-depth interviews with nineteen nursing home residents (fourteen women and five men) and seventeen nurses (sixteen women and one man) who worked with them, from five nursing homes. The study explored nursing home life as it is experienced by residents and nurses. For the purposes of this chapter I will emphasize the residents' stories and only use the nurses' stories where they illuminate the lives of residents (the study is fully detailed in Nay 1993). It is not appropriate to generalize from this study alone, however; the themes that arose were remarkably consistent with other Australian, U.S. and UK studies (cf Schmidt 1990; Friedan 1994; Bartlett 1993). What is most important to emphasize is that although the analysis situates this study more broadly and draws upon other works, where I refer to my study I am reporting the experiences of the residents and nurses *as they described them* to me.

Although the interviews did not always follow a chronological sequence, for the sake of clarity I will present the discussion commencing from the relocation to the nursing home and then moving on to life after admission.

Relocation

Relocation to a nursing home has been the focus of quite a number of research studies. However, the findings remain inconclusive (Coffman 1981: 483–495). There is evidence to suggest that moving to a nursing home has devastating consequences for the elderly, even death. Coffman reviewed thirty-one investigations and found that, of fourteen statistically significant results, "eight showed lower mortalities for the relocated groups and only six show higher mortalities" (Coffman 1981: 491). Coffman's conclusion was that "serious deterioration in the support system—either actual or perceived was" responsible for the negative results of relocation and that relocation per se need not be hazardous, and in fact relocation could be revitalizing and beneficial provided the person enjoys an adequate support system. Hooyman and Kiyak (1993: 306) also pointed out that physical and cognitive functioning have been shown to improve where people move to environments that foster independence, rather than dependence. They also noted that positive outcomes are related to individuals "wanting to move." There is other evidence to suggest that if the older person freely chooses to move into a nursing home the impact of relocation is more likely to be positive (Minichiello 1986).

The positive aspects of nursing home care are unlikely to be publicized in societies where the public purse relies so heavily upon relatives caring for the vast majority of those elderly people who need care and thus are carrying the financial burden. The aging in place policies have a vested interest in nursing homes having a less than inviting reputation, older people resisting placement, and relatives feeling guilty if placement becomes necessary. Equally, however, women are not going to want to move into a nursing home that fosters dependence.

None of the older participants in my study wanted to move or *freely* chose to relocate to a nursing home. It was more like choosing to have a leg amputated rather than die from gangrene. I asked the participants to talk about when the decision was made to enter a nursing home, who made the decision, why, and what the experience of relocating was like for them. Some decided that they would move because it would take the burden off families, and others had the decision made for them by family and/or health professionals. In both cases older people felt there was no choice. For those who made the decision themselves, it was a case of there being no other viable option available. Their perceptions of relocating were of overwhelming loss; that "everything went": home, possessions, friends, family, affection, pets, freedom, favored locations, and the environments, roles, and lifestyles that were known and predictable. Residents spoke of these losses in terms such as

Leaving home [was the hardest part].

The hardest part was being away from family . . . it was all a bit of a wrench. I shed a few tears, but I come [sic] to accept things, which is the only way.

Forty-four years we had lived in that house and we had to sell every single thing. You know, the place, the farms, the cattle, the house and the furniture. Everything had to be sold. . . . That was the hardest part

having to part with the home and the furniture and everything we had
lived for.

I miss them all, my lovely neighbors. . . . It was hard to say good-bye to my
friends; leaving the coast; Ohh I love the seaside, I used to go out with my
beach umbrella and go over to the beach after [my husband] died and
read and I used to feel so lonely. Oh I loved the beach.

Giving away all the things that I possessed and was very very fond of
and then to leave the home which I had lived in for fifty-five years, and
that was a terrible decision to make.

All residents perceived themselves to be potential burdens
and either refused to place that burden on relatives or understood why their relatives could not accept it. The language used
by the residents also implied a sense of a devalued self. One
resident even spoke as if she had already ceased to exist. "I *was* a
Libra" she said. Entering a nursing home was perceived to be the
"end of the line." The residents could not see any real future and
simply lived one-day-at-a-time.

The nurses with whom I spoke described relocation in terms
that reflected a good appreciation of this transition. The
residents also felt welcomed by the nurses when they arrived at
the nursing homes, and in describing the staff they said: "the
nurses couldn't do enough for you'. So, relocation was a
desperately difficult experience of overwhelming loss, but it was
cushioned to some degree by feeling the nurses were welcoming
and understanding.

Aging Out of Place: Living in a nursing home

Numerous studies have been conducted into nursing home life.
Many of them draw upon the work of Goffman (1968) on "total
institutions". Goffman (1968: 11,18,19) defines a "total
institution" as:

a place of residence and work where large numbers of like-situated
individuals, cut off from the wider society for an appreciable period of
time, together lead an enclosed, formally administered round of life . . .
Staff tend to feel superior and righteous; inmates tend, in some ways at
least, to feel inferior, weak, blameworthy, and guilty. . . .
Characteristically, the inmate is excluded from the decisions taken
regarding his [sic] fate.

In addition, inmates are stripped of identity and the
institution is identified with, and organized for, the benefit of
staff. Staff control mealtimes, bedtimes, and all activities of daily
living. According to Goffman (1968: 28–33) identity stripping can

take many forms, including not calling people by their given, preferred name; not permitting the person to retain personal possessions; removing the "identity kit" that people use to maintain their public selves, for example, mirror and make-up; expecting humiliating verbal responses, for example, humbly asking for cigarettes and permission to do things; and removing personal space and privacy. Many studies, such as Schmidt (1990) and Bartlett (1993) have found nursing homes often do reflect some, or many, of the aspects of total institutions.

Another area of work that has some bearing on how nursing home life is experienced relates to theories of labelling. It has been found that individuals tend to accept and often mirror labels applied to them by health care institutions (Waxler 1981). The most notable definition or label applied to nursing home residents is that of "dependent." Again, research abounds on the notions of dependency and learned helplessness. Seligman (1975) undertook the definitive work on learned helplessness. His theory was that the expectation that an outcome is independent of responding (1) reduces the motivation to control the outcome; (2) interferes with learning that responding controls the outcome; and if the outcome is traumatic, (3) produces fear for as long as the subject is uncertain of the uncontrollability of the outcome, and then produces depression.

Admission to a nursing home can precipitate learned helplessness because of the lack of control asociated with nursing home care (Foy and Mitchell 1991: 21). There are numerous studies that provide convincing evidence to demonstrate an association between lack of perceived control and physical, psychological, and emotional disturbances (e.g., Langer and Rodin 1976; Rodin and Langer 1980; Sarason and Sarason 1984; Petrou and Obenchain 1987; Learman, Avorn, Everitt and Rosenthal 1990). Faucett, Ellis, Underwood, Naqvi, and Wilson (1990) found, in their research, that although the maintenance of control was recognized as beneficial and the nurses stated that they encouraged resident control, observation demonstrated that, in fact, the nurses reinforced dependent behavior and were reluctant to allow residents to make their own decisions. Learman et al. (1990: 802) also noted how nurses give residents nonverbal "let-me-take-care-of-you" messages and reward dependent behavior.

It is important to recognize that the literature often polarizes the debate on nursing home versus community care of older people. Both the community and the nursing home have been perceived according to stereotypes. The community has been idealized as a place in which older people live happy, integrated lives over which they maintain control, while nursing homes have been portrayed as miserable institutions in which neglected older people are dumped to end their days (Clough 1981; Fine 1984). However, older people who are at home can also suffer neglect, abuse, and loss of control (Hailstones and Sadler 1993, Friedan 1994; Penhale and Kingston 1995). On the other hand, some nursing homes have demonstrated that it is possible to provide excellent care that maximizes choice, control, and independence. Keeping this balance in mind, however, there are still very real problems in long term care that must not be ignored or glossed over. Most nursing homes struggle with the situation of trying to provide good care in the face of insufficient funding, a largely unqualified workforce, and continuing rampant agism.

For the residents in my study, life in the nursing homes did involve loss of freedom and control over their lives. There were rules and regulations governing everyday life. For some residents, it was described as a prison; all acknowledged that "you must do like the rest". The rules and regulations were less offensive when residents felt that they were being "asked" to comply, rather than being "told." Being instructed by the nurses resulted in the residents feeling like children. Requests permitted at least a sense of control and, importantly also, the feeling that they were "making themselves useful" to the nurses by complying with the requests. Privacy, or lack of it, was significant to some residents. They spoke of the need to entertain visitors, display their own possessions, and retreat from public areas. A minority were prepared to tolerate the lack of privacy to meet a greater need for company.

The nurses recognized that they exercised control over every aspect of the residents' lives. All acknowledged that this was a problem; some perceived a need for, and possibility of, change, while others saw the situation as unavoidable. Both the nurses and residents expressed vulnerability and fear of retaliation if they were to "buck the system." The residents reasoned that if they did not comply with the nurses' wishes "they will get a set on you" (or in other words, take a dislike to them and their care could suffer). The nurses were constrained by concerns of loss of employment; peer pressure, and/or disciplinary action from superiors.

The residents' sense of self, which was devalued prior to, and as a consequence of, relocation, was further "spoiled" (Goffman

1968) after admission. In describing their loss of individuality, they asserted "you are just a number." Aging in a nursing home involved loss of control, fostered dependency, infantilization, fear of retaliation, and lack of "presencing" (being with them as real, valued, whole people) on the part of the nurses. These experiences all contributed to further self-distortions. While these residents endeavored privately to maintain the identity they associated with their former selves, publically they presented a "self" that complied with the stereotypically "good" resident. They did this because of their vulnerability and to negotiate the care they needed from the nurses. The "cheerful face" presented in exchange for care masked the emotional pain that accompanied each resident's loss.

Lack of time was the most common explanation given by the nurses for "batching" (Goffman 1968) the residents and not supporting the maintenance of individuality and identity. The nurses realized that they did not really know the residents and that loss and grief were generally ignored. However, they felt that they did not have the time or the skills to rectify this situation.

Despite the negative experiences described by the residents, they continued to maintain that the "nurses can't do enough for you." The interviews with the residents were constantly punctuated by glowing references to the nurses and comments that indicated that "it could be worse."

Survival Strategies

Often the impression is given that older residents are passive victims of their situation. Given the predominance of women in nursing homes, Gilligan's work (1982: 68, 69, 143) is instructive. She argued that

> For centuries women's sexuality anchored them in passivity, in a receptive rather than active stance, where the events of conception and childbirth could be controlled only by withholding in which sexual needs were denied or suppressed. The strategies of withholding and denial that women have employed in their sexual relationships appear similar to their evasion or withholding of judgments in the moral realm. The reluctance to claim one's sexuality bespeaks a self uncertain of its strength, unwilling to deal with choice, and avoiding confrontation. . . . The image of drifting along or riding it out is common.

Further, Gilligan (1982:143) asserted that because women have given a lifetime of service to others and have been rewarded for self-sacrifice and the desire not to hurt others, they cannot see any way of exercising control without risking an assertion that seems selfish and hence morally dangerous. Assuming Gilligan's assertions to be accurate, it could be expected that most nursing home residents who are still mentally competent would select nonconfrontative coping strategies, that they would seek affiliative relationships, and would look for ways in which they could help, and not hurt, other people. Certainly the literature suggests that aggressive behavior is more common in male residents and those who are cognitively impaired (Mentes and Ferrario 1989: 23; Meddaugh 1990: 28). McLellan (1992: 81) also contended that women learn to repress their own needs and focus on the needs of others. She maintained that when women experience anger it causes them discomfort, and so they "immediately (often unconsciously) turn those feelings into something else" more acceptable; usually guilt and self-recrimination (e.g., I am unkind, ungrateful, I could be worse off, etc.). Kjervik (1986:4) contended that women are well practiced in the art of compromise and Porter (1991: 31) proposed that while she is "not suggesting women voluntarily accommodate themselves to positions of inferiority and subjugation . . . through dependency, or submission to convention and ignorance, women often have not envisaged the possibility of refusal, resistance or opting for change." This view is supported by Friedan (1994: 490) when she tells of a conversation she had with Elias Cohen:

> He suggested that older people themselves "have bought into an elderly mystique which holds that the potentials for growth, development and continuing engagement virtually disappear when disabled." Seeing themselves already solely as passive objects of "care", "without high aspirations or even a sense that empowerment was a real possibility," once they enter or are "put" into nursing homes, they collude in that living death.

Whereas once I would have agreed without hesitation and believed that nursing home residents were total "victims," my experience and research speak to me of another interpretation. Older residents do, it seems, typically avoid confrontation and try to play out the "good patient" role. However, I was able to identify numerous strategies that were employed by the residents to help maximize the positive aspects of living in a nursing home and cope with the negative experiences. The strategies included

1. Having something to do, such as watching television, reading, or being involved in an enjoyable activity;

2. "Distancing," which means getting away from others and creating either physical or psychological space;

3. "Escaping," which is a specific strategy knowingly used to reduce the intrusion of unwanted thoughts or feelings, such as reminiscing about the past to avoid thoughts of the present, "hiding in a book" and so on;

4. "Comparing" and "thinking yourself lucky" are similar but not identical strategies—in the former the residents compare themselves with someone or some situation that is worse, whereas the latter involve concentrating on positive characteristics of their situation—instead of looking at a negative situation and saying "I am better off'," the residents looked at a positive situation and say "Aren't I lucky?";

5. "Steeling your will," which without exception involves the residents in having the will to survive;

6. "Living for today" avoids the need to confront the often unpalatable/frightening nonspecific future; however, residents do think of the future to the extent that it provides specific events to anticipate, and thus, another strategy is looking forward to family visits, Christmas, and so on;

7. "Laughing it off'," the use of humor is a frequently used strategy, and

8. Drawing upon lifelong coping skills. Here residents make comments such as

"I think in every case the person gets lonely but I have been a loner all my life."

"I have seen a lot of people die and I am not frightened."

"I have lived on my own all my life and have always been able to cope."

"I came from a family of six girls and two boys, eight children. There were always lots of people around. I think that helped me a lot. You must be able to deal with other people."

"I have always had a Christian upbringing and I thought about it and prayed about it and so I just I resigned myself to it as it were."

"I am not a person to feel sorry for myself because I think that is the wrong attitude to life."

All of these strategies were nonconfrontative and involved either altering the way in which they perceived their situations or avoidance. These were self-sufficient strategies. Other strategies that relied on the cooperation of others included

1. "Making yourself useful": Making yourself *useful* was doing things for *others*, it was helping, and thus increased the sense of worth and self-esteem:

    "I used to cut another lady's food up; I feel it is lovely to do something for someone else. Sometimes the jug of water is not near her and I get it and she said the other day: "Oh I am glad I have a good neighbour." Well, isn't it good you can do those things."

2. Having "someone to listen" required another person to be willing to participate. Although this strategy emerged as being one of the most significant facilitators of a "good" experience, it was also the most difficult strategy to adopt because so often there was no other person to listen:

    "Everyone likes to talk about the old days or days gone by and just as long as they have someone to listen to them they seem happy."

    "Having the nurses talk to you more would help but they don't get paid for that, do they."

    "It does help to talk because I feel that I am a nuisance to everyone; an old person is far better off dead and gone. The nurses don't get time to sit and talk. That is not their work really to sit around and talk to you."

3. Feeling independent.
    The majority of residents valued independence. Acting independently increased their self-esteem and quality of life. Being dependent had the opposite effect.

    "I try to maintain my independence by pulling myself around in this chair. I can get from A to B but when I get there I need someone to help me at B point. Going to the toilet, getting into bed, it is terrible having to rely on people to do that for me, it is terrible."

and,

4. Deciding that the nursing home feels like home:
    Despite the problems associated with living in a nursing home, many of the residents claimed that the nursing home felt more like home than the hospital. Most clarified this claim with a reminder that there is no place like your own home:

    "It must be a pleasure for visitors to come in and they'll make you a cup of tea, no charge. I'd call it a home away from home. What did we ever do without these homes? It's wonderful."

"I look on this, well to put it bluntly, like a large boarding house, or
something. You know it feels like home, like a big family home."

The most difficult strategy to implement was having
"someone to listen." The residents differed in their opinions as
to who could facilitate the implementation of this. Some would
have appreciated it if the nurses could have fulfilled the role of
confidant, but "recognized" that it was not within the nurses' job
description. Others would not have talked to the nurses about
personal feelings, even if the nurses were available, because they
believed that a confidant was an intimate friend and nurses were
inappropriate for this role. The residents tended not to develop
close relationships with each other, and thus, if they did not
have close family they were deprived of any avenue for
expressing intimate thoughts and feelings. The "brave front"
replaced empathic communication.

In summary, residents were actively trying to maintain/
control their sense of self and self-worth using the nonconfrontational strategies that they would have learned and
internalized as appropriate behavior for women. They were also
generally very grateful and gave the impression that they felt,
given their "worthless" status, they were lucky to have care.
Nevertheless, the picture is not one of totally passive, powerless
old women. In fact, these women were actively resisting
definitions that they feared may reduce further their status,
and/or more importantly, the level of care that they received.
The women were using numerous strategies to boost their self
esteem and to present themselves as they wanted to be
perceived.

Older Women as Invisible and Asexual

Women in nursing homes are simultaneously defined as
female, passive, and asexual. In a youth oriented, male
dominated society, older people, especially women, have been
devalued (Sontag 1978; Hooyman and Kiyak 1993). Agism
affects older people generally; older women are faced with agism
and sexism. It has been argued elsewhere (Nay 1993) that
masculinity has been constructed as "active, resisting,
authoritarian, superordinate, well-armoured and aggressive,
rational, unemotional, reliable, strong, objective and intellectual";
further, "men are defined as 'acting' rather than 'acted upon' and
'independent' rather than 'dependent'". Femininity is associated
with passivity, submissiveness, subordination, defenselessness,

powerlessness, compliance and nonconfrontative coping strategies. The picture of these residents' lives in nursing homes is colored by the same characteristics.

Women, especially of this cohort, have learned from an early age that their identity is tied to being wife, mother, and sex object. Such identity definers are relational and require sacrifices, distortions and denials of the self. Women are socialized to perceive these sacrifices, distortions and denials as expressions of femininity, caring, and goodness. Any assertions of self, as other than that ascribed, are defined as selfish, uncaring, immoral, and unfeminine. Despite the oppressive nature of these social constructions and definitions, men and women actively work to maintain the status quo. Those women strong enough to defy their socialization and accept the inevitable sanctions associated with deviating from the taken-for-granted norms and values may resist being labelled wife and mother by refusing to marry and have children. The centrality of sexuality to their identity and the defining of them as sex objects is essentially outside their control. Given that sexual attractiveness is defined in terms of specific characteristics, for example, youthfulness, slimness, and heterosexuality, women may choose to be obese, lesbian, and to accept age changes without attempting to disguise or delay them. Nevertheless, others may still choose to treat them as sex objects, regardless of their efforts to define themselves in other ways.

It has been demonstrated that the majority of women do not/cannot resist the pervasive and overwhelming pressure. Their acknowledgment of the centrality of youthful, sexual attractiveness to their identity is shown in the painful, often embarrassing and generally expensive, treatments that they seek out and tolerate in their efforts to comply with social expectations (Wolf 1991). The paradox is that despite their greatest efforts, eventually, assuming death does not intervene, they will lose their youthful appearance and consequently their ascribed sexual attractiveness. Although women frequently complain that sex is disappointing and that they want to be appreciated as people and not just objects of physical sexual pleasure, it would seem that being a sex object is preferable to being socially invisible (see Rosslyn's chapter 4). For some older women the cessation of sexual intercourse is probably greeted with relief. For many, however, age brings with it an increasing need for sexual satisfaction and, with greater experience and fewer pressures, achievement of their desire. Although publicly they are perceived to be asexual, privately older women are often more sexual than they were in their youth. They engage in more intimate sexual activity with others and alone and they also define sexuality more broadly to include intimate physical activity, affection, cuddling, warmth, and so on. In their youth, women are more likely to accept the traditional male definition of sexuality as being penetration (Rubin 1982; Nay et al. 1997). The traditions of sexual silence and negative sanctions that are applied to those who deviate from socially prescribed norms have ensured that the agist stereotype obscures reality. Young people still believe that they have a monopoly on sex, and old people feel obliged to maintain the myth.

Upon admission to nursing homes the myth usually becomes reality. Older people may not lose their feelings; however, they are forced to deny and repress them. Thus, sexuality as the central definer of female identity is prescribed in youth and prohibited in old age. In the nursing home there is no place for the private lives that allowed resistance to the asexual definition prior to admission, so most residents are forced to play out the asexual script that has been written for them. That this is accepted as readily as it appears to be can be explained in terms of the broader female situation. Being female required a capacity to cope with objectification, self-sacrifice, lack of control, low status, and being other-defined (Gilligan 1982; McLellan 1992). Women develop over their lifetimes numerous nonconfrontative coping strategies. They are manipulated into compliance by the moral imperative to care for others and the concomitant sense of martyrdom, self-righteousness, and self-worth that accompanies feeling needed. The guilt associated with breaching the moral imperative also constitutes a strong controlling influence. Older women, having internalized the socially devalued status that attends being old, asexual, and female, experience the invisibility that is consequent upon being ascribed this status themselves. In other words, women grow up in a context that defines being a woman and being sexual as synonymous so when they are no longer defined as sexual it follows that they are no longer fully human. They were objects of sexual desire; now they are merely objects!

In a context in which the majority of nurses have only their personal experiences of caring to inform their practice, and appropriately qualified nurses are few and far between, it is hardly surprising that objectification, depersonalization and dis-empowerment result.

Gerontic Nursing

The majority of gerontic nurses are female and, hence, share the "being-female" experiences. This is compounded by their "being-a-nurse" experiences: nursing, as a predominantly female profession, has been constructed as inferior to the male profession of medicine. Nurses have had a history of being handmaidens to doctors. Doctors appropriated the "rights" to cure and permitted nurses to care (Ehrenreich and English 1973). In the process, curing has been valued and caring devalued. Many nurses accepted the male definition of value and moved away from the caring role as they attempted to increase their status and value (Colliere 1986). Aged care has traditionally not been seen to attract the best and brightest nurses (or other health care professionals). Society, the health professions, and older people themselves have tolerated care that would not be considered even mildly acceptable in acute care situations. The majority of staff in aged care who provide nursing care have no nursing qualifications, and most nurses say they work in aged care because it suits their family circumstances and they need the money, rather than because they have chosen it as a career option. As a result there is little support for anything that requires additional effort outside work hours, such as education. Those nurses who are career minded and committed to improving nursing home care often become disillusioned with the lack of support, the constant resistance, and the fears associated with taking responsibility for the practice of unqualified workers.

Consequent upon sexism and agism, gerontic nursing has been considered to be *the pits*: bringing together devalued older people, predominantly women, and devalued nurses, predominantly women, all of whom have experienced the objectification and oppression that is typically associated with growing up female in a society that privileges maleness and masculinity. Objectification permits depersonalization and abuse (Porter 1991).

Nurses and residents often have had as their only, or major, experience of caring, that of mothering. Thus, caring is equated with doing for, knowing what is best for you, being cruel to be kind—or in other words, fostering dependency. Such caring is disempowering, infantilizing and oppressing, all within a framework of benevolence and kindness. The "caring for" is equivalent to "power over" (Tong 1989) and, therefore, consistent with oppressive behavior; it is also associated with typical mothering behavior and thus perceived to be benevolent.

How often has a mother punished a child and justified her actions as "for its own good"? Elderly people in nursing homes are dependent upon the nurses for having their most intimate needs met; thus, it would seem predictable that these elderly people would need to think well of their carers, almost in the same way as a child prefers to think well of parents, even those parents who are kind but controlling.

Conclusion

Older women who age "out of place" in nursing homes experience tremendous loss. Most, for example, have suffered the loss of home, pets, friends, spouse, control over their lives, and central to this experience, loss of identity. The nursing home culture is dominated by "femininity." Feminine identity has at its core sexuality. The older women in nursing homes are defined out of sexuality and concomitantly out of identity. With loss of identity comes objectification and loss of rights. Women's lives have typically been grounded in objectification, self-sacrifice, and caring for others. This "caring for" is perceived to be benevolent. The "power over" aspects of "caring for," in practice, are not recognized as disempowering for the recipient. Just as mothers typically do what is best for their children, the nurses in nursing homes tended to do what is best for the residents. The majority of women who work as nurses in aged care have little or no formal gerontic education. This lack of knowledge and skills results in the care that is given as being modelled on the mothering experiences that the nurses have experienced. Consequently, the lived experience of nursing home life for older women is one of benevolent oppression. The older women were grateful for the kindness but suffered unnecessarily because of the oppression. Although most residents presented a grateful, cheerful public face to mask their suffering, they had also developed many strategies for resisting identity loss. The resistance was typically nonconfrontational, and its purpose seemed to be about managing the tension between holding on to past identity while presenting a new identity that they felt was expected from nursing home residents.

There were residents who covertly resisted the loss of identity and objectification. There were residents who seemed to have given up. There were nurses who recognized the oppressive nature of nursing home life. There were nurses who wanted change and were committed to improving the quality and status of gerontic nursing care. This chapter does not purport to reflect the experiences of nursing home life in *all* nursing homes, nor even of *all* residents and nurses in the nursing homes involved in this research. Nor does it deny that there are many ways of interpreting nursing home life and that this is but one. What it does do is provide a picture of how *some* residents experience life in nursing homes, and if it reflects accurately these experiences, then it adds to understanding, increases awareness, and hopefully alerts nurses to the "power over" nature of "caring for" and provides understanding that will assist older women and their families in resisting oppression, rejecting benevolence, and demanding care that recognizes the personhood, individual identity, and adult status of older women wherever they age.

Chapter Ten

Separate Lives: Older Women, Connectedness, and Well-Being

Chris Wieneke, Aileen Power, Lyn Bevington,
and Diane Rankins-Smith

Editors' note: Chris Wieneke was one of the key members of the original Women and Aging Research Network (WARN). She was a respected and prolific academic, a committed feminist and activist, and one who had initiated several research projects concerning the predicament of older women. As original coeditor, she made a valuable contribution to the work of developing this book. Her death late in 1994 was unexpected and devastating for the network. However, her work, and indeed her death, continued to influence the direction of the book, and we resolved to dedicate the book to her memory. We also resolved to include something of her work. What follows are excerpts from a report of a collaborative research project initiated by Chris as leader of the research team. The research was a collaborative effort between the University, the local Area Health Service, the Older Women's Network, and the women who participated in the study. Other members of the research team, apart from the authors, included Mavis Bickerton, Chris Kemmerer, Nance Cooper, Alison Sneddon, and Michelle Noort. The excerpts are included here because they relate to our exploration of alternative options for housing for older women. The previous chapter explored the nursing home as one favored social option for disposing of older women who are frail. At the other extreme we here look at the benefits and costs for older women who chose to continue to live in the community. We locate the research findings within current discourses on housing for older people.

The literature on women and housing is characterized by two contradictory lines of argument. On the one hand, it is assumed that the ideal situation is one in which women may "age in place" (Sax 1993), that is, in which they remain at home for as long as is practically feasible so that they may remain independent and a part of the community. On the other hand, women who remain in the family home after children have left home and the husband has died are often assumed to be isolated (Chappell and Badger 1989). Accommodation itself may be unsuitable for a single, older woman, and home maintenance may become an increasing burden (Johnson and Falkington 1992; Sax 1993).

The very concepts of "home" and "community" carry powerful positive images in our society. As Peace (1993) argues, home and community is widely assumed to be the appropriate "place" for women's activities, the embodiment of family and domestic life within the private space of the home and extending to the semi-public but enclosed sphere of the local community. Although the home may thus serve to isolate some older women from the wider world of work and public affairs, and thus reinforce their disadvantage, it also provides a sense of safety and self identity. As women age, the home may represent important memories and possessions and provide a sense of defensible space over which women can maintain personal control.

Of central importance is the issue of companionship. A common assumption is that the home provides security through the relationships of those who live in it, normally that of husband and wife. Indeed there seems to be a direct relationship between marital status and well-being for men. Those who are married experience less stress and emotional pathology than those who are single (Coombs 1991). However, for women the issue appears to be the presence of peer confidants and companions, rather than the presence of a husband (Chappell and Badger 1989). The presence of a husband who is not a confidant may well increase the woman's sense of isolation.

It is likely that for the present older generation, it is the maintenance of family and neighborhood networks that is important, especially the maintenance of extended family networks. Kinship networks may well continue to be important for the next cohort as well, especially among immigrant communities. At the same time we can catch a glimpse of newer types of social networks not based on kinship at all. There is at least some evidence that older women can create their own social networks, which more than compensate for the loss of a spouse (Francis 1991; Friedan 1993; Jewson 1982). Nor should we assume that these social networks are simply a compensation, second best to "normal" family relations.

There is also a growing emphasis on individualism which is exemplified in the high rates of single mothers and older women preferring to live alone and refusing to join the households of relatives. It is not that they have become isolated by deaths and departures of family members, but that some women themselves have a positive preference for the freedom of the single person living alone. At issue here is the apparent contradiction between "community" and "independence." As Margaret explores further in chapter 14, more and more of us older women are seeking ways of maintaining our human rights and independence *through* sharing and mutual support among social networks of our peers.

Despite the apparent centrality of housing and home to the experience of aging, there has been little research on the meaning of home for older women, and almost none that reflects the voices of older women themselves (Davidson, Kendig, Merrill, and Stephens 1994; Gurney and Means 1993). Surely Chris's perception of ongoing changes, and the importance of hearing the voices of older women themselves, helped inspire the research project, "Separate Lives" which follows.

Separate Lives

As a contribution toward countering the dominance of the biomedical approach to aging, we undertook a research project specifically exploring the experiences of aging among a group of older women who identified themselves as living independently within our local community. We recognize that notions of "independence," "connectedness" and "isolation" are conceptually complex when applied to individuals in their social environment (isolation, for example, may be geographic, social, cultural, or some combination of these in different contexts), so we agreed to explore the meaning of these concepts as part of our unfolding research.

There is little research relating to older people who might be characterized as "independent" and "well," and almost no acknowledgment that the experiences of older women may differ from older men's because of their different and unequal social and material circumstances. In debates about identifying needs and creating equitable conditions for an aging population we should be making a concerted effort to access perspectives of older women living in varied circumstances, and particularly those who may not normally be involved. Experience with community consultations demonstrates that it is very difficult to encourage the "silent" members to express their views. In this project, we sought to develop ways of accessing older women who had not participated in community consultations and who, if judged by their lack of membership of community organizations, could have been characterized as "isolated."

The range of strategies we adopted (print, electronic media, brochures, and networks) had varying degrees of success. It is probable that those women who came forward to participate in the research project were fairly confident and articulate. On the whole we did not reach women who are often characterized in the media as "truly isolated" and in desperate need of "support services." Nineteen of the thirty six women who participated lived with another person, usually their husband, and twenty one were in paid or voluntary work (for detailed discussion of methodology, see Wieneke et al. 1994). Nevertheless, having accessed a range of older women within our local community, we explored with them issues around independence, connectedness, and isolation. We asked them about the importance of the connections they had to their well-being.

Older Women Speak about their Lives

As we have argued throughout this book, diversity, above all else, characterizes the experience of aging (Russell and Oxley 1990; Minichiello et al. 1992). This view was confirmed by the responses of the women to the question "What is it like for you, to be an older woman?" For many, the experience was positive.

> "I'm free of all the old shoulds and shouldn'ts that I grew up with. I don't have to say "yes mum" and "no mum" to anyone . . . my life is my own . . . it's the best time of my life" (Narelle, aged 55–59).

> "I am delighted. I can become more eccentric. I can say what I want and I can wear what I want. I always feel that I can be what I want to be" (Lucy, aged 55–59).

Others spoke about older age in less enthusiastic terms of the losses they have experienced.

> "I'm starting to feel a bit resentful that time's running out. It seems such a waste" (Caroline, aged 55–59).

> "It is frustrating. You don't have the time . . . the energy and you don't have the health to do the things . . . I miss the money that I was earning when I had a professional career. It's taken me a long time to come to grips with being alone" (Louise, aged 60–64).

Some women who lived by themselves found that being alone was a very positive experience. Others missed the companionship of a partner and/or work colleagues.

"It's very stressful because I don't have someone to talk to . . . and I find it very exhausting to look after the house and garden by myself" (Pauline, aged 55–59).

"Lonely, because I worked until a year ago and now I'm very lonely" (Robyn, aged 60–64).

But for many, older age meant greater freedom from the responsibilities of family and paid work. Women commonly talked about their pleasure in being able to take up or renew hobbies, travel, spend time with friends and family, do voluntary work, study, and so on.

"I like being retired; it's wonderful to have the house to myself and do what I want, when I want" (Hilary, aged 65–69).

Meanings of Social Connections for Older Women

Even with the small number of women we spoke to, there were enormous differences in the amount of contact they had with others, and in what this meant for them. The concept of connectedness needs to be explored and understood as something highly complex rather than being seen as having some unified meaning, such as "support." Women overall tended to have very complex interconnecting relationships of varying intensities and frequency of contact. Those who had few family members or close friends were largely maintaining patterns that had been established much earlier in life. Most of these women said they were quite content as they "enjoyed their own company" and "liked their space." Reading, gardening, and having pets were often especially important in the lives of such women, though these were also commonly mentioned by other women as well.

For women with many close connections, family members were generally more significant than friends, although some women described friendships that were intensely important to them. A reminder needs to be given though, that the term "friend" is likely to be applied to a family relationship as well as to one that might conventionally be understood as a friendship. Adams' (1989) observations about the problems of categorization were confirmed by the responses of women in the study. They did not necessarily see (or experience) "family" and "friend" as mutually exclusive terms. Some family relationships were described in very positive terms of "friendship." Neighbors were acknowledged by most women, but were usually described as "just there" and "neighborly," though for a few, neighbors were the focus of their social connection; important in terms of both emotional and practical support. Although women clearly appreciated opportunities to meet with their age peers, a number talked about the pleasure they experienced from being with younger people as well—either family members such as grandchildren, nieces, and so on, or young people in the neighborhood.

The impact of change, and the ways it affected their lives and connections, was a common theme discussed by many women. For some, change was very positive—a freeing time with more opportunities to do the things and be the kinds of people they really wanted to be, without the constraints of full-time employment or childraising responsibilities. Many spoke of a sense of adventuring into a new and exciting part of their lives. For others there was a strong sense of loss accompanying the death of a spouse, relatives, close friends, and so on.

> "Honestly, I was counting up . . . all the crowd we had were all gone, moved away, the others have died . . . I've always had people around, and then . . . they left (Sarah, aged 80 plus).

Women spoke of the ways they had adjusted to these changes: the importance of the support and encouragement of friends and family; volunteer work; developing talents neglected during years of heavy commitments; and taking up new interests. Connections into the community through recreational and cultural activities were also the means by which many women enriched their lives. While some women's well-being is enhanced through their use of available support services (including medical ones) these were not used by the majority of women. Being connected to others and feeling valued by others through the giving and receiving of support and assistance were reported as being important in developing and maintaining a sense of identity and self-esteem.

> "I suppose it all comes back to one's own identity . . . people, I presume, who have no connections never feel they really belong somewhere" (Lorraine, aged 55–59).

> "Connections are a mixture of responsibilities and dependency going one way or the other. [They] also create a sense of who I am or how I see

myself in what I see in the response from other people" (Narelle, aged 55–59).

Many women spoke of enjoying the independence of living alone and combining this with rich family and community connections. They described needing "their own space" and enjoying having time to themselves—though this was qualified by the acknowledgment that this contentment was based on knowing that they could have contact with others when they chose to do so.

"I like my own space around me; I'm quite happy to be alone sometimes" (Tessa, aged 55–59)

For the few women who spoke of preferring to live alone with very little social contact, this seems to have been a lifelong pattern, not the result of growing older (it was not part of our study to examine what the reasons for this may be).

I suppose in a way I'm an independent sort of person. This sounds a terrible thing to say, but I don't really like having visitors because it upsets my routine and I like reading and I'd rather be reading than being with people (Susan, aged 70-74).

I've not got a lot of friends because I had too much to do and I didn't go out (Leonie, aged 80+).

But it would be a mistake to accept that all women who have little contact do so because they actually prefer this as an option, even where it has been a lifelong pattern. Jennifer (aged 65–69), for example, explained that she had been brought up in a way that discouraged her from forming friendships. She felt that she didn't have the skills to do this now. Nevertheless, she expresses some regret about this, and seems lonely.

"I've always been a lonely child; mother didn't like people coming to the house. She kept away from people. So I was brought up like that and I got used to it, . . . lived in make believe. But I would like to have more friends I think . . . but I'm not a good social mixer . . . I can't chat" (Jennifer, aged 65–69).

For some who had made a transition to living alone, the process was a difficult one and had heightened the importance of social contact and involvement in various work and community activities.

"I think it means a lot because when you live by yourself it's very lonely. When we were first separated I was extremely lonely and to have this daily contact with people both at work and at home . . . is good for your morale. It's a self-esteem thing. I hardly ever get depressed and I enjoy my life. It's very, very busy but I enjoy it to the maximum" (Kay, aged 55–59).

Other women expressed mixed feelings about the benefits of living alone, weighing these up against factors such as the company (especially at night) and security of having another person in the house. For instance Janice, (aged 70–74) talks about her surprise at the way she was able to adjust to living alone - and that this has been very positive for her, realizing her own capacity to live independently.

"I had no idea how I'd react [to being alone] because I'd never ever been alone until my husband died; I'd always been at home with my parents and family or with my husband and I was absolutely astounded how I, you know. . . it didn't worry me at all" (Janice, aged 70–74).

She then goes on to question in her own mind, "whether I like this living alone." She speaks of her feelings of apprehension as she recounted the story of an older woman living in the area who was attacked in her own home.

Most women valued living in their own home and while they were able to identify things that would improve their quality of life, only a few spoke about considering supported accommodation. Even those who expressed considerable reservation about the loss of control and decision making power that they saw as an inevitable outcome of such a move.

"I'm quite happy . . . if I could have somebody who comes daily or twice daily or something or somebody at night and if I'm as well as I am now, well I don't want to be in a nursing home. But because I'm booked for it and because the doctor and everybody said if it's available I should go, not wait until I'm too bad. But at the moment I'm quite happy at home. [and if I went to a nursing home] I'm a bit scared . . . whether I might pine for my little home . . . I like to have a little bit of responsibility . . . for paying my own bills ..and what I'm going to eat and all that, I'm still in control of myself; when I go there I wouldn't but at the moment I'm very happy" (Amy, aged 80 plus).

But feeling isolated wasn't simply a matter of living alone. Some women living with a demanding spouse or dependent relative experienced a strong sense of isolation. Other women spoke of the impact that their former marriage relationship had made on their current level of social contact.

"That's [community services and phone calls to family] the only connection I've got; well I didn't have the time when I was younger . . . I think I had a very strict husband too . . . he thought that (indicates kitchen) was my place" (Leonie, aged 80 plus).

"I was married to a very bossy, overbearing person . . . and getting divorced was a good decision for me [but] I do find things stressful because for one thing I don't have someone to talk to, to bounce things off. That's what I notice mostly, I don't want someone to help me or tell me what to do . . . I would just like to confide in someone . . . even get their ideas . . . if maybe helping them in the same way . . . it makes your life more, full" (Pauline, aged 55–59).

Thus "isolation" cannot be understood in any simplistic way, and is not necessarily a direct outcome of living alone, or related to the number of contacts women have. Narelle, who is very active and seemingly well connected, when asked about friends and connections in the community, answered that she had very few.

"It's an area of my life I've been looking at lately, and thinking, Hey, I'd better get out there and do something . . . subconsciously expecting that kind of reception from anyone else if you go to them with something, and not getting it and feeling angry and disappointed. So, that interdependency which I'd like to have in close relationships is very, very rare. So that, in a sense I'm isolated" (Narelle, aged 55–59).

For some, feeling isolated had to do with where they were actually located, and was associated with difficulty in getting to places easily. This in turn was linked to the availability of public transport and whether women had a car and were still able to drive.

"I'm a little bit far from the station and shops . . . a bit over three kilometres . . . I think [there are] about two [buses] a day, so I really sort of think I should think of trying to move nearer so I can walk to the shops" (Juliet, aged 60–64).

Feeling lonely was for some, particularly those in their late 70s and 80s, connected to the fact that they were not able to get out and about in the community as they had done in the past.

"We used to see hundreds of people. We used to see them here and there and they used to come and visit, but when you get old and you're not in it, people tend to forget" (Amy, aged 80 plus).

Women often had difficulty articulating any single reason for feeling lonely or isolated and spoke of varied and multiple factors that might account for their feelings. This was the case with Pauline (aged 55–59) who spoke of not liking the town she lived in, but going on to include her concerns about trying to cope with the practicalities of running a house on her own and how this increased her feelings of being alone.

> "I think basically I feel very isolated because this is an isolated area and I don't really like living here; I'm actually a town person . . . and I find living by myself is lonely—but it's not so much the loneliness—but I find that I get exhausted from doing . . . from having to do everything myself" (Pauline, aged 55–59).

But Drusilla (aged 55–59) described another aspect of feeling invisible in the community. She experienced this after her husband died, and she was no longer somebody's wife, part of a couple. This raises an important issue about the impact of changing roles and relationships on older women.

> "You know I heard and read that when her husband dies, a woman just disappears, yeah, and I thought, oh that won't happen to me—and it did—but luckily I don't mind my own company so it hasn't bothered me that much"(Drusilla, aged 55–59).

Although some women did talk about feeling lonely or isolated it was usually at certain times or in particular situations. It is also very important to acknowledge that feelings of loneliness and isolation are not restricted to older people and can be experienced throughout life in various circumstances and for numerous reasons.

For most women, whether they lived by themselves or with a spouse or other family member, various forms of social contact were highly significant to them. Contact with family was especially important to most women, even though there were often tensions within these relationships

> "They're like a rock. They're always there" (Bronwyn, aged 60–64).

> "You don't feel alone. They are most important to me. We have always been a close family" (Janice, aged 70–74).

> "I wouldn't like to live without them. But at the same time it makes you sick if one of the relationships is out of whack" (Ruth, aged 55–59).

Relations with neighbors were described by some women as being important sources of connection, though most women valued just knowing neighbors "were there." Practical assistance, such as reciprocal arrangements for looking after gardens, pets, and so on when necessary, were commonly appreciated aspects of relations with neighbors.

"We have very good neighbors on both sides. They are supportive. This one on this side takes me shopping once a fortnight. The other side neighbor helps keep an eye on the place. The one on the other side comes shopping with me" (Sharon, aged 80 plus).

"I don't see them a lot but it is nice to know that they are always there. If I'm stuck I can ring them" (Amy, aged 80 plus).

"Neighbors have always been important" (Larissa, aged 55–59).

With friends, companionship and shared interests were central to the relationship.

"The sheer fun of sharing things that are interesting or funny . . . I learn from people. They enlarge my perceptions and enlarge my focus. I'm getting stuff, in that sort of sense. They're fun and support" (Narelle, aged 55–59).

However, close friendship was sometimes specifically avoided with neighbors.

"Well I don't make friends with neighbors, my mother warned me about that, but they're good . . . they're wonderful if I go away. It's real neighbourly support" (Susan, aged 70–74).

The emphasis on wider community connections was also on practical support.

"Well I've got to eat. I've got to get taken out by taxi to buy food" (Karen, aged 75–79)

But, as with family, this support was often given by the women as voluntary community work, rather than received by them. The meaning of "support" needs to be constantly questioned in relation to older women. Often there is an assumption that the support is given to, or needed by, the women themselves. The responses of the women in the study indicated that this is far from true. Support (both emotional and practical) is often given by older women to others (family, friends, neighbors and the community at large) or is given reciprocally by them, depending on changing needs and circumstances.

"I've always been helped and that is . . . giving something back to other people ... that's all part of it . . . to make my contribution" (Juliet, aged 60–64).

"My brother, he lives in Sydney, well I'd say he's very supportive. If I ask him to do anything for me he'd do it, but he wouldn't volunteer

—we're all [brothers and sisters] like that; if any of them asked me to do anything for them I would, but I don't volunteer" (Susan, aged 70–74).

"We (daughter) used to do a lot of talking; there was a lot of two way support, but that has changed quite a bit now . . . I guess at the moment I'm the one offering the listening ear when she rattles on and on, and you know, if she desperately needs something picked up in the car . . . " (Narelle, aged 55–59).

Some women spoke of making conscious attempts (though not without considerable struggle) to break with a lifetime pattern of supporting others, to focus on their own needs, and using this time of their lives to be freed from the requirement to always "be there" for other people.

"It sounds terrible but I've got to the stage in my life where I've spent so much of my time giving it out and running and doing things for other people and you know. . . I'm desperately trying to get out of that mold . . . sometimes I think I really should . . . [then I think] No. I must not. This is my retirement. There are plenty of other community people and friends who can do it now (Lorraine, aged 55–59).

If You Really Need to Talk to Someone, What Would You Do?

One indication of whether people feel isolated relates to their opportunity to talk with someone about important issues or concerns. We, therefore, asked the older women participating in our research project what they would do if they really needed someone to talk with. The women either nominated a person or suggested that they could deal with matters on their own or had never needed to find someone to talk with. Of the twenty women who identified a particular person or category of person, thirteen specified close family members, particularly daughters, or, in one instance, a daughter-in-law.

"I'd ring my daughter. She's got a very balanced point of view. She comes up with such sensible solutions. She's quite well balanced, I think. I don't know what I'd do without her" (Drusilla, aged 55–59).

"Well, I've never been in that predicament. I suppose I'd ring up the children and sort of talk to them. Well, I do. Especially my eldest daughter. She's a very kind-hearted, understanding, lovely person" (Danielle, aged 60–64).

"[My daughter] we're very sharing companions. She rings me up and asks me for advice. I ring her and ask for advice" (Bridget, aged 60–64).

Only one woman unequivocally nominated her husband. Many women indicated that they had options on who they would talk with, depending upon the nature of the issue or concern.

> "I'd phone my daughter. I phone my husband and poor thing, he can't really talk very much because he's only got partitions round his office and so everybody can hear what's going on. I'd rather ring my daughter or even maybe my psychiatrist" (Robyn, aged 60–64).

> "I'd probably ring one of my friends at work or my daughter. It would depend on what it was" (Ruth, aged 55–59).

> "Ring one of my friends or ring someone depending on what you wanted to talk about. Depending on if it is "classified information." Just depends who it is, what it's about. The kids are very good and my friends are very good with advice or if you want someone to listen" (Louise, aged 65–69).

Some women nominated friends or other people outside the family network, including counsellors or other professionals.

> "I'd go to the Samaritans down here. I mean I've never been, but I'm sure that's where I'd go. Otherwise, one of my friends or M or somebody, I don't know" (Lorraine, aged 55–59).

> "That has to be friends; you'd have to unburden yourself to friends; the friend of mine in [suburb] has been the biggest support to me through my marriage crisis. She's been marvellous—couldn't have done without her" (Kay, aged 55–59).

A small group of women said they didn't have problems requiring discussion or would work them out by themselves.

> "Never needed to do that. I am part of the cosmos. So therefore your voice goes out to the cosmos to the universal thought waves. I try to put myself outside myself and look in as another person rather than being overwhelmed by your problem. They're not problems. They're projects that you've come into life to overcome. That's my philosophy" (Rosemary, aged 55–59).

> "Not necessarily family, I wouldn't. I'd try to cope with it. Work it out myself, logically, I hope. No I wouldn't involve the family" (Bronwyn, aged 60–64)

Some of the older women among the participants either would not talk with others or had outlived those they may have talked with in the past.

> "I've never felt the need, love. I've never felt the need because most of them are not on the same plane as me; I just sit down and forget it. I sit down and work it out for myself" (Karen, aged 75–79).

"Well, I'd just have to talk to myself (laughs); [talk to home care person] She's one that doesn't repeat anything; [No other family] They're all done in. I'm the only little petunia living; most of my friends have all died" (Sarah, aged 80 plus).

Conclusions

Part of being connected was clearly having people to relate to—though not all connections were positive ones. And support (emotional, practical, financial) was given as well as received by the women. But connection was more than just people. It had to do with being able to take part in the everyday life of the community; shopping, visiting, doing voluntary and paid work, and so on. It was also about feeling pleasure with one's surroundings—enjoying the bush, being able to walk along the streets, taking the bus, visiting the library. As with studies conducted by Anne Moyal (1989) and Kirsty Williamson (in Smith 1994), the phone was an extremely important means of contact with family (and also close friends). Whether family members lived locally or not, phone was indicated more often as the means of contact than personal visits. Letters and cards were used mainly to keep in touch with interstate or overseas family members. For those unable to move about easily, visits of service providers, family, and friends were generally valued. But, the importance of pets in women's lives was often mentioned in the interviews. For many women pets were the source of joy and companionship. The concern they had for the adequate care of their animals, often despite very limited budgets, was a recurring theme.

But not all women talked about having lots of connections. Some enjoyed their own company and some private space where they could "suit themselves," after years of "doing for others.' Some had always led fairly solitary lives and continued this lifelong pattern in relative contentment. Though most women lived in their own home, they described all kinds of different arrangements; living alone, with a spouse and/or offspring, mother or other family member. On the whole, family members and close friends were described as very important connections, while, in the main, neighbors were appreciated, but not vital relationships.

So, even within the small and demographically homogenous group of women we spoke with, there was amazing diversity! Because of this it was very difficult to prioritize things they identified as contributing to well-being. For most women, well-being was constituted by numerous interacting processes that came together in very particular ways in the lives of each person. It is true that some themes were common, but to segregate them out of the interconnections that gave them meaning and treat them as isolated issues needing attention would be a mistake.

How then do we move from examining the complexities and interrelationships of the daily occurrences and interactions in women's lives, to using this knowledge to improve services and enhance the lives of older women in specific ways? Perhaps one of the most valuable contributions of the project is a reminder about the danger of constructing categories like "isolated," "dependent," "alone," "support" and imbue them with meaning that is not informed by, or checked out against the reality of people's lives. Women are not simply "isolated" OR "connected"; "dependent" OR "independent"; "supported" OR "unsupported." If anything, they are all—and yet none of these. For each of these words have come to be associated with distinctive meanings when used in relation to older women. All these terms, including "older", need to be constantly challenged and those practices informed by them and in response to them, need to be rethought and reworked.

There is a great danger in continuing the negative stereotypes associated with older people in general, and older women in particular. The "separate lives" project sought to examine some of the assumptions about the terms isolation, connectedness, and dependence when used to refer to older women. Although we believe that this kind of work is vitally important to the enhanced well-being of women as they age, we warn against any polarizing of meaning. To be overly optimistic and deny the possibility of very real cultural, social, and geographical isolation that may be experienced as a result of poverty, homelessness, language barriers, distance and so on, would be foolish and unjust. But these understandings too need to be explored by talking with people living in diverse locations. We need to avoid slipping into polarized, "either/or" thinking that denies or obscures the diversity of situations and experiences that are part of women's lives. We also need to reject the tendency to assume that we "know" what the lives of others are like, without taking the time and devising ways to really find out.

An acknowledgment of this diversity, and a commitment of resources, including time, needs to be part of the process of developing policies and programs for older people. If policymakers believe that it is important to incorporate the diverse perspectives of the full range of older women, then greater effort and resources need to be devoted to seeking out and heeding their views. It is only through such participative processes that the perspectives of people affected by policies can be incorporated into their development.

SECTION THREE

Revisioning Aging

Introduction

We have expressed in this book considerable anger at the narrow and unjust way in which aging is constructed in our society, and at the oppression of older women in particular. But we do not want this to be an angry book. We express a determination to end with celebration.

So we must act. This book is a part of that action, using our anger in a constructive way to change what needs to be changed. This is not a book on social policy that advises government on steps they need to take, though there are many potential policy implications in what we say. Nor is it a book directed at the medical and caring professions, advising them on more effective modes of care, though there are many potential treatment implications in what we say. Primarily this book is directed toward ourselves, and toward the millions of older women, like ourselves, who are beginning to see the possibility of a better future for older women. Revisioning aging *is* empowerment. As Margaret correctly identified in chapter 3, this book is about the empowerment of older women by older women. It is about the action that we can take for ourselves to create a more exciting and fulfilling and deeply satisfying storyline for our old age. That means revisioning what aging means for women. It means taking more control of our own individual lives and making real choices. It means acting together in the public social domain to change the parameters of our social context.

There are many paths to empowerment. Some of these are individual acts, though they are difficult to take alone. Many are social acts, taken in concert with others. All are political acts because they are about change. The personal is political as much for us as older women as for anyone else. Some paths to empowerment are also explictly political because they entail lobbying and advocacy at the formal level. The chapters that follow explore some of these paths. Margaret explores empowerment through housing. She explores the multiple aspects of empowerment: the getting of results, of real services, and obtaining the kind of lifestyle and housing structures we want; but also the more intangible empowerment of coming together and articulating our wishes and learning to speak out in government forums, to take a stance in changing public attitudes and policy. Rosemary, too, explores the potential for change at both the individual and the collective levels. Life review can have a powerful effect for women who wish to review what life has meant, to construct a new storyline for ourselves, to plan new futures, and identify strategies for achieving these. Organizations of older women, for older women, can have a catalytic effect, not only in increasing the skills, mutual support, and confidence of its members, but also in challenging government, the media, and the wider society.

The chapters that follow explore but a few of the options of change. Personal development is a lifelong process and can itself take many forms for older women. As older women we can explore our sexuality. We *are* sexual creatures. As Rhonda noted in chapter 9, sexuality is not just about orgasm. sexual preferences, or producing babies. It's about exploring our capacity for sensuality, the pleasure of the senses, the pleasure of touching and being touched. It's about exploring identities, about self expression, about being freed of conventional and narrow constraints that define who and what we are. It's about experiencing pleasure in our bodies. Gaining confidence and pleasure in our physical bodies can have profound social and political consequences, as the story Rosemary relates shows. A group of older women in a working class suburb of Sydney joined a program of physical fitness. They entered the local health club gym, that forbidden arena of youthful vitality and beauty. They claimed a right to be there, to improve their own health and fitness, a right to their own kind of beauty. In a way that noone envisaged, they tapped into a deeper reservoir of collective strength and determination, and turned to act in the political arena. What started as a physical exercise program became a process of powerful personal and social change. This is what it means to focus on health and not illness. This is also the nature of education, which we see as a lifelong process. We hope and expect that the day we die, we are still learning something new, about ourselves, about life, about our planet.

Empowerment can and must occur at more formal levels, within the public domain. We demand that older women be consulted about issues that affect us. Real consultation, not token consultation. But we believe that consultation is not enough, and will always be vulnerable to manipulation and tokenism, important though it is. We need political representation. We need representatives elected at all levels of government. We need older women in active public life. We need older women employed in positions of power within government offices. We need older women employed in positions of decision making about older women, and in positions of resource allocation for older women. Why, for instance, do so few older women come to be employed as policy officers in various "Offices of the Aging"?

Empowerment will also occur through our active engagement with the structures of power, from outside those structures. We must address the media by monitoring and challenging the prevailing negative media images. We need to institute our own counterpropaganda, alternative media messages about how we wish to be represented. We need to address the unions, to seek alliances within the union movement, to encourage unions to seek improved employment conditions for older women, to fight age discrimination in the workplace. We need to make greater use of anti-discrimination legislation within all spheres of public life. We need to encourage more active research into all aspects of older women's lives, but research that uses methodology that includes and consults us as older women, not research that reduces us to objects.

The many paths to empowerment all begin with a renewed sense of our individual and collective worth. This is different from demanding our right to be treated with respect and dignity. We do indeed demand that, and demand the removal of the negative images of the decrepit, the ridiculous, the helpless, the hapless old hag. At the very least let us be seen in neutral terms, cleared of the unjust stigma that oppresses. But we are not satisfied with mere neutrality. No, we revalue ourselves in much more positive terms. We are, individually and collectively, rather wonderful!

We suspect that we need to reclaim the title of *crone*. Like all the other terms that describe older women, like "witch" and "hag," the word "crone" is now used as a term of offence. It was not always like that. In fact, in ancient times, all those words were terms of respect and awe. The crone, in particular was "a woman of age, power and wisdom" (Walker 1988). It is time we reclaimed the right to such status. Not that age guarantees wisdom or power, but we can aspire to that greatest of all roles for women, the status of crone. As crones, we take an honored place in society. We are valued for our experience and insight into some of the deeper dilemmas of life. It does not mean that we have current technical expertise, but it does mean that we have a better grasp of the fundamental principles, something of the bigger picture. It does not mean that we lust for temporal power, but that we are the storytellers, the advisors, for those who seek a greater meaning. As crones, we are freed from the grind of everyday survival, though this is not so for all older women. We are freed of the pettiness of conventional social expectations. We are free to be who we are and to speak out as we must. We are also free to taste life at its best, knowing that we are now in the last phase of our lives.

Chapter Eleven

Which House?
Margaret Sargent

Ways in which certain social groups have been disempowered through housing have been explored (for example, in Watson 1986 and 1988). The people who have been marginalized in this way include women, people with disabilities, people from a non-English speaking background, older people, homeless people, indigenous people, and other social groups. Two main cultural assumptions prevalent in Australian discourse appear to have contributed to this disempowerment: the preference for owning one's own home in an economy that treats accommodation as a commodity and an index of class and status, and the priority given to the housing needs of the nuclear family. People are, therefore, disempowered if they cannot afford to purchase a dwelling, and if they are not members of nuclear families. Virtually the same groups tend to be excluded from higher education and training, well paid and high status jobs, adequate health care, and other benefits of our society. Their actual experiences with housing vary with their sex, class, race, age, education, income, and so on. Older women can be considered to be marginalized through their sex, advanced age, low income, and variable state of health.

Over a surprisingly short period the predominant patterns of living have changed from extended family to nuclear family to new forms of "family" (such as single parent and "blended" households) and patterns that include shared living for unrelated people (including numbers of single people). This trend is not only a western phenomenon, but seems to be similar in many societies all over the world.

A contributing factor is the growing phenomenon of fragmentation of ethnic groups and nations. One notable response to this has been the Jewish Kibbutzim, which were communities founded in Israel during World War II to ensure the survival of Jews as an ethnic group. At a macro level, unrelated people are increasingly living together for their survival after war and displacement. A major factor in family change is the increasingly high level of women's education and their desire for empowerment. In particular, older women are claiming the right to independence, continuing through old age.

Occasionally, marginalized groups reverse their disempowerment and achieve housing that is appropriate for their needs. The ways they achieve this can be described as routes to empowerment through housing. These routes and the kind of housing preferred will vary with the particular group and its sex, class, ethnicity, and so on.

In basic ways, older women all want the same: a living environment conducive to retaining control over our lives for as long as possible. But not all want to organize together as a group that consciously seeks empowerment through housing. Older women are mostly still in the process of discovering and working toward our rights. The social discourse that devalues older women, representing them as dependent and a burden to society, is still a strong influence on us. But we are changing the discourse in order to value the contribution of older women to voluntary caring and community activity, to recognize that a few older people (mostly male) own a high proportion of the country's wealth, and to acknowledge the feisty efforts toward empowerment of some groups of older women.

This chapter continues with a preliminary discussion of concepts of empowerment, independence, and community. This is followed by an examination of empowering aspects of housing, five routes to "empowerment," and the nature of empowerment. Next I shall look at some options in housing to discover which could be considered empowering and why. Shared or community housing is advocated as an empowering option. An account of a housing venture by one particular older women's organization called Women in Community Housing (WICH) follows. Before going any further, let us ask what we mean by empowerment, independence, and community.

Empowerment, Independence and Community

Relatively little is understood about either empowerment or power. Here we are primarily concerned with analyzing these concepts in connection with social organization rather than with person to person relationships. Nevertheless, the feelings and subjective experience of empowerment of older women are an important aspect of empowerment.

Neither power nor empowerment can be seen as a thing or commodity possessed by certain people and exercised at certain times. They are rather the capacity to affect social activities through a dynamic process, even against the resistance of others. Power and empowerment cannot be observed by looking at overt decision making because they are exercised in a more hidden way by influence behind the scenes (Bachrach and Baratz 1962). Foucault (1980) pointed out that it is mostly through hidden power that discourse itself, including "reality" and "truth," is established and changed in our society. "Power," he said, "is a name we give to a complex strategic situation in our particular society."

In the 1970s, poverty was analyzed as due to lack of power. The poor were seen as needing power over relationships, information, decision making, resources, and so on. Self help was seen as the way for the poor to achieve empowerment (Liffman 1978).

Members of a marginalized group who come to see how that group is devalued and oppressed in society may regard themselves as powerless victims. This response is endorsed by the welfare attitudes of governments who follow the deficit model, viewing them as disadvantaged groups or "groups with special needs." The literature on powerlessness has also fed this response and failed to take into account that all groups have varying degrees of power and a relative amount of autonomy. As Weedon (1987) said, thorough understanding of power relations is vital for feminists, who need to know that through strategic resistance and struggle it is possible to increase their social power.

Wearing (1990) has applied these ideas to the ability of individual mothers to overcome the repressive aspects of motherhood and transform their control over labor and gender power relations. But, as Staples (1990:36) said, "individual empowerment is not now, and never will be, the salvation of powerless groups . . . Empowerment must be conceptualized, operationalized, and measured in collective as well as individual terms." Neither power nor empowerment can be simply bestowed on one party by another. Yet in current bureaucratic jargon, government bureaucracy is now employing a new strategy of giving "personal packages" which are said to empower individuals. However, according to the sociological approach taken here, power must be taken or seized. Empowerment is not passively received but actively achieved. Collective social action rather than individual effort is likely to be effective in changing the power relations in society. By these means women, including older women, can become the kind of people we want to be. We can change our positioning in power relationships and our image in discourse. By thus increasing their social power we can be said to be transforming ourselves and achieving empowerment. Thus, by embracing marginal status and our positioning as older women, the group becomes enhanced.

In order to avoid vagueness, Gore (1992) suggested that the exploration of meanings of empowerment should be "context specific and related to practices." I have partially followed this advice, for it is important to ensure that empowerment is not defined solely in terms of perception and experience. In my analysis I was influenced by Staples' assertion that "empowerment is a product as well as a process" (1990: 39). As an ongoing process it strengthens control over conditions of life and the ability to plan and act in order to achieve goals. Empowerment can be observed also by practical outcomes that may have wide empowering effects but, in the example explored below (WICH community housing project), I found it an oversimplification to call these a product.

According to Ward and Mullender (1991), empowerment is associated both with right-wing welfare consumerism and with the user/consumer/community movement, which "demands a voice in controlling standards and services." (Needless to say, the project described in this chapter is concerned only with the second category.) The social work literature continues its attempts to find a role for the professional worker in empowering projects developed by client and community groups.

Mullender and Ward (1991) consider it possible to integrate professionals in group discussion and action by "self-directed group work." But Power et al. (1994) carried out a research project in which women academics encouraged older women to participate in group work intended to empower them. As a result of this experience they warn researchers that academics "will inevitably experience tension between being at one and the same time oppressor and oppressed," having embarrassingly greater access to resources, struggling with authoritarian leadership styles, and with participants' expectations about the nature of research and education.

The word "independence" has at least three meanings, including having control and capacity to make choices, having the capacity to do practical things for oneself without assistance, and lastly the capacity to live—perhaps at home or in a retirement village—without the assistance of relatives, friends and so on. In general I intend the first of these meanings, but occasionally the second. The third meaning may alert us to the fact that independence is a socially constructed notion, not necessarily observable nor agreed upon, and varying according to the eye of the beholder.

One form of shared living for a group is community housing. "Community," as a term for describing forms of accommodation, has too many connotations to be very satisfactory. *Webster's Dictionary* reminds us that it derives from the Latin *communitas* and *communis*, which mean "fellowship" and "common," respectively. It defines a community as "a group of people residing in the same locality and under the same government . . . a group or class having common interests . . . common ownership or participation." This is the sense of "community" intended here when reference is made to community housing or living. (In "community group" or 'community of women" the word is used in a different, more popular sense and does not refer necessarily to a group existing in a particular locality.)

Housing and Empowerment for Older Women

There are several different aspects of housing that may be empowering (Sargent 1996). Through women's experience and social research (Wieneke et al. 1994; Older Women's Network 1994) we know that many older women accept the importance of social connectedness, social networking, and continued activity to our health and well being. To a large extent these have been absorbed into our ideal lifestyle and our concept of community housing. Both survival and degrees of empowerment can be achieved through shared living, so forms of community housing may be expected to proliferate in the future. Porcino declared confidently that "community living/shared housing will be the fastest growing housing design in the decades ahead" (1991:xxvii). Forms of housing can certainly be regarded as empowering when they promote continuing independence and control over their lives for older people.

Research into architecture and design has shown that women tend to use domestic space differently from men. Linda Baker has emphasized how space can be adapted to the concerns of women in, for example, allowing supervision of young children at play. This was illustrated in the Sitka Housing Cooperative in Canada (Porcino 1991). An earlier connection between community living and the emancipation of women was made in 1859 by Fourier (Porcino 1991), who advocated creating a cooperative society based on "phalanges." These were common buildings with collective housekeeping. The design of community housing for older women offers many innovative possibilities for empowerment, including considerations of access and ecological sustainability (Fromm 1991).

For accommodation to be empowering—because of the relative poverty of the majority of single older women—it must also cater for our economic needs. Among older women, it was found that 75 percent of all Australian single women over 65 years experience "housing stress" (i.e., must spend over 30 percent of their income on rent.) (Howe, 1992). This is where the need for government assistance is important.

The kinds of housing we select as empowering should take into account the wider aspects of urban design (Urban Design in Australia 1994:8), including the goal of social equity.

> Through good urban design, urban change can be made to respond to the needs of less advantaged groups, by distributing benefits through places and neighbourhoods that are more accessible, satisfying and empowering to its users, are well connected to the rest of the city, and provide safe and educative environment for all children and adolescents.

The use of government resources to house only persons seen as disadvantaged is frequently required by law, as in the Australian Commonwealth State Housing Agreement. The housing of older people is usually seen as a welfare matter, and sometimes there are patronizing attitudes toward those who are considered as the objects of welfare. But housing is a social institution that affects every member of society (Sargent 1994). It is important to see the whole picture and to consider the accommodation needs of older people and of whole populations, whether they are economically disadvantaged or not. Older people, whatever their income, have difficulties of access, transport, isolation, house and garden maintenance, and so on.

Housing is one of the ways in which the population is organized into social classes (Watson 1988). Housing in general helps to create and maintain class divisions, the dependence of women, and discrimination against immigrants. Renters are divided from owners. Public housing and accommodation for the frail aged have generally been built only in certain localities, very rarely on waterfronts or in leafy suburbs.

Future official housing policy, especially if there is increased flexibility in its rules, can potentially encourage social mix. Mixed tenure can be encouraged by selling to occupiers, possibly at lower than market prices. Shared equity will allow residents to part-buy while their community organization pays the rest. In this way property can be redistributed more equally and greater urban consolidation can be achieved.

Five Routes to Empowerment Through Housing

In the planning, completion, and future habitation of the project of Women in Community Housing (WICH), there seemed to be five routes or more for older women to achieve empowerment.

1. The development of the concept and ideology of the pilot model,
2. The individual and group experience of the process of working collectively toward the common goal of empowerment through housing,
3. Finding means to successful outcomes through the bureaucratic structures,
4. Finding means to successful outcomes outside the official structures, and
5. Reaching successful outcomes related closely to the goal.

Nature of Empowerment

The nature of empowerment differs in the five routes mentioned. In the first route empowerment consists in developing creatively the concepts and ideology central to the plan. These form part of the process of empowerment that will strengthen the organization, inspire the social movement, and enable strategies to emerge.

In the second route, empowerment lies in the subjective experience of participating in the process and activities planned for the advancement of the social movement. The experience includes that of both individuals and the group as a whole. The sense of empowerment, which may emerge as part of the experience, may derive from collaborating with other members of the group, thus increasing its cohesiveness and force, creating a sense of belonging and purpose, joining in with consultations and negotiations, having input into decision making and political processes, and extending knowledge, skills, and political awareness.

The third and fourth routes are concerned with discovering the means that lead to success. In the case of the housing project, the means involve working either with or outside the state bureaucracy and political apparatus. Both routes require the community group to defy the patriarchal split between the private sphere of the domestic and the public sphere of politics and finance, and, therefore, to operate in areas with which some older women may be unfamiliar.

Working with the bureaucracy (the third route) may ease the way for successful outcomes for marginalized groups in the future by redirecting government policy and priorities, by setting a precedent, by changing the inflexible ways the rules and guidelines have been applied, by improving the consultation processes, or by drawing attention to the needs of groups of people hitherto ignored by government.

The fourth route involves finding means to achieve outcomes by working outside official government structures. It may involve negotiating with corporate fiscal institutions or collaborating with a commercial developer or using other resources that are difficult for community groups to access on account of their marginal status. As noted by Jones (1985), access for marginalized people to any form of housing ownership is extremely difficult.

This route will not necessarily alter future government policy, but can show a pathway through the public sector for other community groups to use in the future.

In the fifth route the group realizes certain outcomes that are closely related to achieving the goal of empowerment.

The five routes could be interpreted, as by Rosemary (chapter 13), as empowering in personal, organizational, and social-political ways. They mostly contribute, however, to more than one of these three types of empowerment.

The five routes cannot easily be interpreted as process and outcome. It would be misleading to speak of a single product or of clearly defined stages of development. Success and empowerment may not always be observable or self-evident. Even when the project is built and functioning, the goal of empowerment is not complete but is still in the process of developing—or it may diminish or fluctuate with the state of health of the group of residents or with the financial status of the project. The various incidental events or stages reached in the process can then be viewed as a succession of outcomes achieved, even though they may not necessarily seem empowering.

Who is Empowered by the Five routes?

The process as a whole produces empowerment for the particular group and the individuals within it. It may also change the conditions and reduce the obstacles for other marginalized people who may strive for empowerment in the future. Successful outcomes may have widespread empowering effects, including the following.

1. The experience of empowerment by the individuals and the group of people involved, not only through participating in the process, but through the continuing process and pleasure of living in the housing complex.
2. The experience of others more indirectly involved, such as allied women's groups and older people's organizations, individuals and organizations who gave donations and other support, various housing organizations and bureaucracies and their individual employees, and so on.
3. The enhancement and strengthening of the organization.
4. The wider community of women, improving the opportunities for those with housing needs. For older women there may be effects of greater visibility and influence in society and adding value to the image of the group in discourse.
5. The wider community of older people in general;
6. Other community groups and marginalized groups who may be working toward improved housing or other conditions of their lives.

As further projects of various kinds are undertaken by community groups, a continuing analysis of routes to empowerment may be possible. In this way it is my hope that the ways of achieving empowerment by marginalized groups can be promoted and extended.

Human Rights for Older People

Following on the United Nations Habitat II Conference in 1996, a basic level of housing became accepted as a human right. The provision of appropriate housing in the future then should be seen not as a welfare response to need but as enabling all citizens to attain their rights. Two of the United Nations' Principles for Older Persons refer to minimum standards for accommodation.

1. Older persons should be able to live in environments that are safe and adaptable to personal preferences and changing capacities.
2. Older persons should be able to reside at home for as long as possible.

I would like to see a third principle added:

3. Older persons, regardless of their state of health, should be able to maintain continuing independence and control over their lives.

If this principle was followed, it would ensure that older people's housing is empowering for them.

Housing "Options"

Many governments and future planners claim that in a liberal democracy older people's right to choice is fulfilled by the availability of "options" in housing. The implication is that this choice enables marginal groups to achieve their will to independence and liberation.

The options include living (often) alone in houses, flats, or mobile units and living with relatives on dual occupancy sites or in movable, prefabricated units (whose Australian nickname, "granny flats," in itself suggests dependent status in the occupant), retirement villages, hostels, nursing homes, boarding houses, and cooperatives (Lazarowich 1990). Through a variety of housing programs governments claim to increase the availability of options, especially for low income groups.

Yet, such are the constraints on choice in housing from the point of view of many older women that agency seems to play little part. As Rosemary (chapter 12) found in women's autobiographies, "choice is not a construct that is used by women who become wives and mothers." Most of the options listed above deprive older women of their independence in one way or another.

Most architecture, planning, and housing programs have not attempted to take the needs of women, especially older women, into account. Housing has been designed mainly by men based on their preferences for the earlier patterns of living for small young families, and not for single persons. The limits of adaptability of such accommodation are in themselves disempowering. In the assumed split between public and private spheres of life, women may still be confined to the private domestic sphere, implying the traditional female role. This situation is not inevitable. For example, Wajcman (1992: 102) refers to a "self cleaning house" designed by a woman architect. Amazingly enough, this desirable model has not been adopted although it would cost no more than conventional housing.

Some of the more obviously disempowering options for older women include boarding houses, nursing homes, and others where the circumstances reduce control over our lives. Cheap, unsanitary, and exploitative boarding houses are all that are available to many deinstitutionalized clients of psychiatric centers.

Nursing homes are also for sick people, most of whom have nowhere else to go or no opportunity to state a preference. Hostels, originally created for well older people, are now filled with the sick and frail for lack of available nursing home beds (as in Australia in 1998). Some retirement village managements may exploit people through their conditions of sale and fees, and offer little say to residents, one of whom said (NSW Council on the Aging 1987):

> When it's all done for you, when you have few decisions to make, when your own physical restrictions prevent contact with the complexities of the wider community, you can feel that you have little power over your life, and little challenge within it.

Some residents, however, accept and enjoy retirement villages.

From several sources we know that about two-thirds of older people would prefer to stay put in their own homes. Adequate home services (such as those of Australia's Home And Community Care) and public transport would make it possible for many more people to choose to "age in place." Without these services, they are deprived of any real opportunity to make a choice.

Some accommodation options offer a transition back to the mainstream—for example, Housing Options for Women, Victoria (Forsyth 1992), intended mainly for homeless women. At worst, such housing may alleviate conditions for women with no abode. At best it may not be disempowering and may provide an opportunity to increase control of their lives.

Shared Living and Community Housing

Shared living for unrelated people takes many forms, large and small, the simplest being sharing a house or combining houses, as in the case of the two traditional houses that have been joined by a group of women in Prinsengracht in Amsterdam.

Reasons for preferring community living include the following:

- companionship, sociability,
- mutual support,
- reduced need for long residence in hospital and nursing home,
- health and well being through activity and social connectedness,
- alleviation of isolation and loneliness,
- continued independence,
- control over your own life through group self government,
- shared values (social, religious, political),
- economy of resources for low income individuals,
- economy of resources for environmental or group reasons,
- group provision of stimulus to activity, training, recreation, and so on,
- survival of minority group, and
- empowerment of minority group.

Community Living Options

Community living experiments are frequent in Denmark and Sweden. One form, cohousing, which began in Denmark in 1972, now has projects in Sweden, the Netherlands, France, Norway, Germany, the U.S.A, Australia, and Canada. Cohousing provides grassroots, affordable, economical housing, in a community house and other shared facilities, and offers the kind of support and freedom needed by young families.

Perhaps more suitable for some older women are the Abbeyfield Houses, which originated in the United Kingdom (UK) in 1959. These are set up largely by community leaders who see a need for low-cost rental accommodation for the needy. With the assistance of a housekeeper, the residents largely look after their own physical needs. But residents seldom have any part in setting up or managing the residence, nor in organizing the activities provided.

The UK also began "gifted housing," a scheme known as Help the Aged. Older people can donate a large house, which is turned into apartments where the older person may live with companions for the rest of his/her life. Variations to cater for the same problems of large, unmanageable houses, isolation and financing have been adopted in the U.S.A by the National Institute of Senior Housing, and in Australia and elsewhere

(Friedan 1993; Office of Local Government 1991). Many other projects for low income older people exist in various countries (Regner et al. 1991).

Examples of community living for the propagation of particular values or lifestyles abound. Gilo Sheltered Housing is maintained by the Israel government for the integration of older people and youth in a farm setting. Findhorn in Scotland combines ecological and spiritual values.

Development of a Concept of Shared Housing—The beginnings of WICH

A concept of shared housing was fostered in the late 1980s by an Australian association called Housing Options for Older Women (HOOW), women who found that the existing options in housing were not appropriate for them. This organization carried out research, collected and distributed information, consulted with other organizations, and organized seminars to develop and broadcast the concept and ideology further. The members of HOOW came from diverse socioeconomic backgrounds. But they had two things in common: their present accommodation was inappropriate for them, and the existing options in housing were not appropriate for their needs.

They found that many older women felt isolated by their housing and unable to find the companionship they valued. Their various mobility problems, disabilities, and health conditions led them to believe that in a few years they would be forced to give up their own homes and the independence they enjoyed in order to receive basic support for daily living in frail old age. Inevitably, it seemed, they would lose control over their accommodation, have no opportunity to make decisions about how they would live the last third of their lives, and become the proverbial burden on either relatives or the state.

The concept of shared housing was developed in conjunction with an ideology that proposed that shared housing for older women can provide mutual companionship, support and security, sharing of skills and learning new skills, control over our own lives, collective involvement in and responsibility for administrative decision making, and continuing independence. The ideology also maintained that women of all socioeconomic backgrounds must be able to find a place in shared housing projects.

It was decided that HOOW's initial housing venture would be a mixed equity housing cooperative situated in an inner Sydney suburb. Unfortunately, the late 1980s in New South Wales were a time of political stagnation in the area of housing, and the group's proposal to government met with little response. After a period of inactivity, HOOW was formally disbanded, and its remaining funds were passed to the Older Women's Network (OWN).

Development of a Housing Project

The Older Women's Network housing group was set up in mid-1993 in response to the offer of the government's Hostel and Care Program to consult on the development of a housing project. The group consisted of four former members of Housing Options for Older Women.

The project developed gradually over a period through meetings and consultations about the concept and ideology, the needs and preferences in management, ownership, title and design, and the methods of funding the project (Sargent 1994). The project plan followed a pilot model that could be used again in the future with modifications as needed to suit other community groups. It was planned to purpose-build or refurbish existing accommodations to produce the complex, which would consist of twelve self-contained units and community areas in an attractive setting in the inner city, for women of all income levels. The community areas would be locations for collective activity in order to foster both companionship and informal support for the residents. It was expected that the usual support services of Home and Community Care would be available to eligible residents. It was hoped that the government might assist with funding the units for low-income women and with bridging finance (loans to span the period between being required to make payment for new accommodations and receiving payment for the old house). Some of the other units would be sold at full market value rather than the actual cost of construction so that the profit could be used to cross-subsidize women unable to afford the full cost of purchase.

The OWN management committee decided it did not have the capacity to proceed with such a large project. But the housing group was able to survive and continue by setting up a separate, but very small, organization. There were also advantages of being independent of the management committee, such as the power to make immediate decisions. Nevertheless, the housing group experienced serious feelings of disempowerment at that time. However, we also found to our delight that the new body could appropriately be called WICH (Women In Community Housing)!

Government Housing Policy Response

In the Australian government housing provision, it has always been assumed that the needs that the government should consider are essentially and solely economic. The idea that government should be concerned with noneconomic housing needs in the population (such as maintaining independence in older women) is quite novel. So, for example, in public housing frail older people have been accommodated side by side with disturbed ex-psychiatric clients, apparently without consideration for the security needs of one group or the behavior of the other. So the government response has been almost entirely confined to the provision of low rental public housing (Donnison and Ungerson 1982).

In the early 1990s, under the National Housing Strategy, the response of federal and state governments to older people's complaints about the inappropriateness of existing options and unavailability of alternatives was to declare a new flexibility in housing programs and funding, the encouragement of joint ventures and innovative schemes, and arms length administration of projects.

WICH's submission for funding of the three rental units, intended for women eligible for public housing, was made to the state government. The proposal certainly qualified as innovative for it did not fit with the guidelines in government housing programs at all, and would clearly need all the flexibility promised by the government.

What happened? The government turned down WICH's submission for funding, giving several reasons for this—the government's investment would not be secure and the group should move out to middle ring suburbs where medium density housing was more feasible. Furthermore, the government would want to choose the residents from the top of their public housing waiting list.

Unlike most applicants for funding, we are not a large, established organization with money in hand and already owning a plot of land—so we could not offer the government security. The group members who were eligible for public housing, after contributing to the project for a period of years, insisted they should be among the residents. Nor did any of us wish to move out of our familiar surroundings and social networks in the inner city.

Unanimously we decided to attempt the project without official funding. But that proved difficult. A mixed tenure project that would include women with neither assets nor income (other than the government age pension) is especially hard. One by one women decided to leave the group. But a few WICH remained.

Were we empowered after all? Yes, I think so, in personal and social-political ways. WICH as an organization was weakened, however, by losing our identity as part of the Older Women's Network and by the government's disinterest. As for the five routes to empowerment, we experienced the first two—the pleasure of developing the concept and ideology of the model and the process of working collectively toward a common goal. We also learned a good deal about housing, whether provided by the state or privately, and its bureaucratic structures.

The political climate was not receptive to older women developing their own housing model, aiming to free themselves from the controlling system of public housing, and owning their own project and their own support system in order to remain independent into old age. In the future WICH's work needs to be directed toward changing the male culture pervading bureaucratic housing structures and strategies so that women's projects and preferences may be supported by the state.

The housing group were angered and politicized by our experiences. As a result, when we discovered how little interest was being taken in the coming United Nations (UN) Conference on Habitat, we decided to alert and inform women's housing organizations and to act as a channel for their submissions to the Australian government. For a year we devoted our energies, although still without funding, to conference preparations that might change the political climate for women's housing. Indeed, WICH's lobbying of the Australian government at the conference in Istanbul may well have influenced it to leave the U.S.A isolated in its opposition to the proposal to make housing a human right. As the American position became untenable, the proposal was finally accepted. An empowering feeling for WICH.

Conclusion
At this stage I believe we have found that the collective action of a community group can empower the group in a variety of ways, which have been here analyzed as five routes to empowerment. Housing can be empowering for older women and for others, both through the process of achievement and through the experience of living together there.

As for the WICH housing model, it has been developed with much thought, incorporating concepts of maintaining independence and developing community. Various aspects of housing that may be empowering were built into the model, including social connectedness, continued activity, health and well being, housing design with older women's needs in mind, innovative financial arrangements to purchase/rent accommodations, and broader aspects of urban design, such as social mix among urban residents. The possibilities of shared living and the values that may be incorporated in community living were canvassed and were considered more likely to be empowering for marginalized groups.

I described the plans of Women in Community Housing (WICH) in some detail. But as yet the model has not been built. It remains hypothetical, an abstract concept. If and when it is built, we will need further experience and more analysis to prove the model is empowering in practice.

Postscript

This is an interim report. WICH expects to have both further subjective experience of empowerment through housing and, perhaps, to achieve successful outcomes that will have empowering effects in much wider circles. Our concept and pilot project have been taken up by a commercial developer who considers such schemes as the only possible way for the provision of housing for people on low incomes in the future. He also has ingenious proposals for financing our plans and the government is taking an interest in these.

For the next installment on WICH's progress, watch this space!

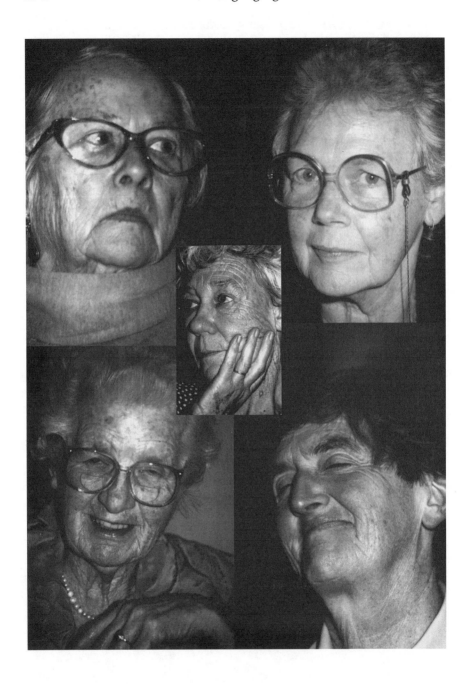

FACES (1) by Helen Leonard

Chapter Twelve

The Potential for Empowerment from a Life-Course Approach
Rosemary Leonard

Apart from the five years at home with young children, I have felt, with increasing age, increases in my abilities, self-respect and respect from others. This is a trend I would like to continue but, somewhere up ahead, I know that the respect from others will decline and, unless I am superbly resistant, my self-respect and abilities will decline in response. In my current optimistic frame of mind, I cannot engage emotionally with that downhill process. I just hope that the world, or at least my microcosm of it, changes before I get there. So I write books to change the world and plan a personal life of mutual respect to decrease my vulnerability to the onslaught of negative messages about my worth: and I find that I am not the only woman thinking so seriously about her future.

Imagine seven women in their forties and fifties from very diverse backgrounds and life experiences. They could each be identified crudely by words such as housewife, recovering alcoholic, lesbian or former nun, and this shorthand might superficially suggest their lack of commonality, and that working together as a group might be problematic. However, they will meet together with a facilitator for the next nine weeks to explore their life-course through guided autobiography, a process developed by James Birren (Birren and Deutchman 1991). The strength of this process is that working through themes together emphasizes what their lives have in common, as well as encourages a reflection of diversity. None of the women are in distress or wanting therapy, but they are all at turning points and thinking about future directions.

In the course of their exploration they will come across many of the issues that are the concern of life-course researchers. By engaging with these key issues in our life-course, whether to plot our own futures or to contribute to the more abstract world of research, we have the opportunity to write a more powerful future for ourselves and for possibly other women as well. This chapter identifies some key issues experienced by the women in the guided autobiography group, and as studied by academics.

Research from a life-course perspective emphasizes the path through life of people within their social and historical context (Elder 1995). That is, it considers both the intrapersonal factors such as people's interests and anxieties and also the external factors such as social expectations or access to resources that shape a life path that maintains some coherence and yet is open to change. Explanations using a life-course approach, therefore, need to allow for two sets of contradictions. One is the tension between individual agency and social determination. The other is between the need for coherence through the life-course versus the possibility of change.

Life Storylines

It is not a coincidence that I and the women in the guided autobiography group are thinking about our future directions in middle-age. Up until our forties we have been aware of socially prescribed "life storylines." The storyline is a concept borrowed from narrative theory for understanding coherence through the lifecourse (Gergen 1990). We choose, create and at times revise our life stories, and it is these stories that both direct our future choices and goals and make sense of past experiences. Out of the stream of everyday life, certain events are labelled as important because they contribute to the plot: others are seen as trivial. However, life story writing is not a purely individual activity. In each society there will be a dominant plot, which most women will approximate, and a few alternative plots. As a young woman, I felt, like many others, that the range of alternatives was rather limited and we were given the impression that those other alternatives held little promise of happiness.

Traditionally the dominant storyline defined women's identities in terms of biology as daughter, wife, and mother (Gergen 1990). The principal role of her education was to prepare her for roles as wife and mother. Paid work filled in the gap between education and marriage or motherhood but was not part of one's identity. However, voluntary work was possible as an extension of the nurturing function. Twenty-five years ago, the women's movement started to challenge that storyline. The more radical feminists such as Germaine Greer (1970) were encouraging women to throw out the old story, while the more conservative, such as Betty Friedan (1963), were telling women they could have much more than the old story allowed. While Epstein (1970) argued that women wishing to pursue a career faced a normless task, Conran's (1975) bestseller *Superwoman* told women how to manage their extra workload. The strongest response has been the shift to a new dominant storyline in which women return to paid work in addition to, not instead of, their mother and wife roles (Helson and Picano 1990). This additive response has occurred despite feminist warnings that "employment is not a panacea for women and can be a trap" (Yeandle 1984). The trap keeps women overworked or exhausted so they cannot protest against their oppression (Balbo 1992). The women in the guided autobiography group have not all followed one of these dominant storylines. The lesbian actively resisted them. The ex-nun started to follow the recognisable, but increasingly less common, alternative storyline of the single woman in a religious order. Nevertheless, the dominant stories have stood as reference points against which decisions were made.

After midlife, however, the clarity of the storylines for women in western society fade with the implication that the only theme is one of loss (Gergen 1990). If, in her forties, a woman was mothering, working, married, and doing community and housework, she will first lose her children, then her job, probably when her husband retires, then her husband; but she may be able to hold on to the community and housework until she loses her health. It is not a very attractive story, certainly not one I would like to follow, but hopefully through our plans with or without the aid of guided autobiography we will write new stories for ourselves.

Even to have come to that first session, the women have made a significant but relatively unusual move. They have decided that their lives are sufficiently important to be worth spending the time to write about, analyze, review, and plan. The relatively small amount of life-course research that has been done with women in mid-life suggests that we generally do not seriously review our lives and only have a vague notion of our futures.

For example, in my study of the lives of the women from my school year who were then aged just under 40, I collected information about our involvement in education, paid and unpaid work, relationships and children over the past twenty years and our thoughts on the future. Overall our plans did not extend too far into the future. Most did not foresee any radical changes in the next ten years. A small proportion planned to continue with a traditional storyline. These women stressed the importance of the children's and partners' needs. There was an absence of references to one's own needs and goals except perhaps in terms of a goal for the family.

The majority planned to continue in the new dominant storyline. Here the demands of family, education/personal development, and work are all taken into account. Those who were happy with this approach comment on its interest and diversity and that "there is a time for everything." Those of us who were not happy reflect frustration at being pulled in too many directions. Chronic tiredness was also common. The last group emphasized career identity. These women, who either did not have children or saw their children as becoming independent, had a clear sense of gaining satisfaction from their work and were often gaining extra qualifications to get further into their areas of interest. By and large we do not fit the stereotype of "tailored, briefcased career woman." It was more a case of believing in the value and interest of our work.

A second example of women's vagueness about their futures comes from Onyx and Benton's study of women's concept of retirement. Although they were ten to twenty years older than those in my study, those women were also vague about their futures. The study is discussed in detail in chapter 6, but it is useful to note here that the women did not intend to follow the male storyline of retirement at 60 or 65, and the only story they seemed to have to replace it with, if they had thought about it at all, was a feeling that they wanted to continue in paid work but decrease their hours so that they could pursue other interests.

Critiques of the Psychological Bases of Guided Autobiography

In the following weeks the women's guided autobiographies will cover nine topics each with its set of trigger questions. The topics are major branching points in the life-course: family; career, one's major life work; money; health and body image; sexuality; death; loves and hates; the meaning of your life. The facilitator, a feminist, points out some of the sexist and classist assumptions in the topics and trigger questions: for example, asking why a woman became a wife is not the same as asking why a man became an accountant.

The reason for the sexist and classist assumptions in Birren's guide appears to be its origins in traditional psychological theories of personality development through the lifespan (Erikson 1980; Levinson, Darrow, Levinson, and McKee 1978). Such theories often describe the development of the self in terms of apparently biologically predetermined stages.

While there is empirical evidence that the stages described by these researchers fit the experiences of certain groups of North American males, many women, myself included, feel a lack of identification with those stages, and there has been strong feminist critique of both the concept of stages and the content of them. First the concept of a stage is that at a particular age one needs to complete a particular developmental task or one cannot move on to the next stage. The order is immutable. Further, if a person does not complete a task at the appropriate age then there is the implication of retarded development.

Critics of stages emphasize the role of the social environment, as set by the cultural-historical context, in defining what constitutes a normal progression. Those who are critical of the content of the stages described by Erikson and other personality development researchers point to some obvious ways in which those life-stages do not apply to women or to men from other cultures (Hassan and Bar-Yam 1987). For example, Erikson's stage of generativity, concern for providing something for the next generation, is supposed to occur in the late forties or fifties, that is, at an age after most women have completed their childrearing.

While these criticisms are severe and cannot be discounted, some researchers, minimalizing the emphasis on stages, have found the idea of Erikson's life-tasks useful. For example, McAdams (1985) argues that the life-task of establishing one's identity, which Erikson fits into early adulthood, is one that may be of central interest at that age but could be returned to at other times in the life-course. The facilitator of the guided autobiography group is familiar with these issues, so she sometimes needs to point out the problems with the topics and trigger questions, but, nevertheless, they form a useful basis for exploring most of the key areas of the life-course.

Empowerment Through Writing

Each week the women will each write two pages on the set topic guided by trigger questions and then read their work to the group for future discussion. Writing is an important part of the process because it requires the women to focus on only the most significant aspects of the topic, it gives them control over their revelations, and it gives their thoughts the status allotted to the written over the spoken word. The sharing and discussion are equally important because the women then see their lives through the eyes of others. There is a gradual progression as the topics become more confronting and trust grows within the group as personal details are revealed and respected. One woman protects herself by limiting her stories to humorous reminiscences, but she is confronted by the stories of others. Gradually she comes to accept her own agency for her past actions that she would prefer to forget or at least deny responsibility for.

Agency

The possibility of the exercise of human agency is an essential part of life-course approaches. Agency here refers to the way in which people can and often do make choices and act on those choices. Agency is always in a certain degree. Noone is ever entirely unconstrained but nor are we entirely helpless victims of our social context. Certainly there is some empirical support for the importance of deliberate choice in determining the life-course. For example, in Hakim's (1991) longitudinal study of young women who were 14-24 years old in the mid 1960s, 25 percent planned to work when they were 35. When followed up 10–20 years later it was found that 82 percent of those who planned to work were in fact working. However, the results for women who did not choose a career were that, due to financial necessity, only 30 percent were at home with children when they were 35,thus illustrating the limitations of explaining life-course purely in terms of individual preferences.

One factor in understanding why some choices seem to have greater power in influencing the life-course than others is the extent to which a choice is owned as a deliberate decision. It appears that many exercises of agency are not understood in terms of choice by the actors. I do not think that I could say that I chose to become a wife and a mother. It was more just a taken-for-granted part of growing up. I suspect that only plans to move into unusual roles are seen as choices. For example, in Brannen's (1987) longitudinal study of 188 women who intended to return to full-time work and 60 who intended to stay home, those returning saw the decision as theirs. Those staying at home did not see their actions as constituting a decision.

Further, in life-course analyzes, the issue of agency is not restricted to a question of did she choose or was she forced, but rather to seek an understanding of the pressures and constraints on choice. For example, Silverstone and Ward (1980) found that women committed to work and family usually have three options: give up work until children are older, work part-time, or work full-time and give up much of the care of the children to relatives or paid carers. The choice between these three options often depended on particular local conditions such as the availability of part-time work.

The concept of life situation (Stewart and Malley 1989; or life space, Richards and Larson 1989) seems to me to be an interesting way of looking at agency. It has been used by life-course researchers to describe differences in the pressures and constraints experienced by different groups of women while still allowing for agency within a particular situation. For example, women in the particular life situation of having children but not being employed were found by Stewart and Malley (1989) to be in a situation in which it was difficult to exercise agency, and those in the life situation of being single mothers often lacked opportunities for both agency and social connection. They were "at risk." The idea of being at risk is an important concept. Stewart and Malley (1989) did not find that all the single mothers they interviewed suffered from a lack of agency or a lack of social connectedness, nor did they expect to. After all, women vary in their need for agency and social connectedness, and also we can be ingenious in finding ways for those needs to be met. Nevertheless, the constraints of being a single parent do noticeably restrict our opportunities.

The concept of life situations, each with certain risks and opportunities, avoids, at one extreme, deterministic approaches that would see the women's thoughts and behaviors as a product of her social situation and, therefore, deny our agency. The other extreme is individualism which either suggests that the social context is largely irrelevant since people are so different from one another that making a satisfactory life is just a matter of taste, or else suggests that social context is simply the outcome of personality (e.g. motherly people become mothers).

Like the academic life-course researchers, the women in the guided autobiography group are prompted by the facilitator to explore the social conditions that allowed for the choices, or lack of choices, that shaped their lives. Through that exploration they realize that accepting agency for past actions does not mean accepting blame. Decisions made in another time in another life space seemed reasonable then, even if they are subsequently regretted. Accepting our agency, however, means not having to make the same mistakes again.

Individual Time, Family Time and Historical Time

The women are surprised that, despite their apparent diversity, they still share common experiences, the experiences of being women in our society. They also notice significant differences between the experiences of the youngest and the oldest. Even ten years can make a substantial difference. The facilitator talks about the sociopolitical changes that have occurred in the last fifty years and encourages the women to see their lives in their historical perspective.

Life-courses need to be understood in terms of historical time, and some of the significant contributions to the study of life-course have been from historians. Hareven (1982) contributed the idea that a life-course can be understood in terms of the intersection of individual time, family time, and historical time. Individual time describes how old and in what state of health was a woman when a given event occurred. Family time identifies her stage in the cycle of family life. Historical time identifies the economic, social, and political conditions pertaining to her world beyond herself and her kin.

To appreciate some of the significance of this contribution, it needs to be understood that the life-course approach arose from family lifecycle research, which was very restrictive in that it equates family with household and cycle with typified stages (in particular, stages of parenthood rather than other roles). The life-course approach, on the other hand, is more concerned with linking the individual with the historical and takes individual variation in the life-course into account (Branner 1987). With Hareven's emphasis on family time, as well as individual and historical time, life-course research subsumes the concerns of family lifecycle researchers.

Using these notions, Hareven demonstrates the way that changes in the twentieth century have created more severe divisions in the life-course than existed during the last century. There was far more variability in the ages at which people left home, started work, married, finished childrearing, and retired than there is now. These contrasts remind us that our current expectations of the life-course are by no means the only way that lives could be organized and prompt us to explore a diversity of life-courses.

Mason's (1987) research provides an illustration of the way an understanding of the intersection of individual time, family time, and historical time changes the interpretation of everyday observations. Mason investigated retired couples' negotiation of domestic chores. The immediate evidence was that women maintained control in the domestic sphere by allowing their husbands to help with the household chores but not giving them full control, by teasing their husbands about their inadequate work, and by nagging their husbands to assist them. At the level of this everyday interaction, therefore, it appears that there is a power reversal when men retire.

Mason, however, investigated the issue further and showed that the reverse is in fact the case. The husbands did not feel threatened by the nagging and often share jokes about it, thus suggesting that the matter of domestic chores is really a trivial one. The women also contributed to that perception with comments to the effect that there is really so little to do that it is not a problem for them to do it. In contrast, when husbands tried to take responsibility for the housework, rather than just helping, it was described by the women as interference or taking over and generally experienced as threatening.

This contrast reflects the power difference. Attempts at assertion by the less powerful person are amusing while attempts at assertion by the more powerful person are threatening. For a wider perspective, Mason asked about aspects of the women's lives beyond the home and found that the women's lives were more limited because most of the men could drive while most of the women could not. Also, the women felt obliged to justify or curtail their activities such as visits to friends so as not to leave their husbands alone.

Mason explains the husbands' greater power partly in terms of historical time. This cohort of women were part of the postwar return to the workforce, but their work was never taken seriously and was often part-time and interrupted for family needs. Certainly they did not acquire savings in their own right or superannuation. In addition, their pensions were joint ones with their husbands and, as they became older, they had less access to the workforce, so they were far more financially dependent on their husbands than they had been previously.

Another reason why the women were less powerful is their position in family time. Although, in theory, the women could have tried to negotiate a larger say in household finances or refused to be responsible for the husband's entertainment, after 25 years of traditional marriage they felt that such a move would be seen as inciting conflict. Mason's research, therefore, illustrates the way in which looking at a broad range of aspects of women's lives, including historical and family time, can have the effect of shifting the interpretation of a set of events, in this example, from one in which the women appear to be totally in control, to an interpretation that reveals that, despite their relative powerlessness, they are able to find ways to maintain some autonomy.

Identity

Identity is another concept that stood out for me as valuable for understanding our life-courses. It shows how women's life-decisions "make sense" in that they reflect our identities (e.g. McAdams 1985; Hornstein 1986; Mann 1988; Spenner and Rosenfeld 1990; O'Neil and Greenberger 1994; Burke and Reitzes 1991). In this case, identity is seen, not just as one stage in personality development (as in Erikson's approach), but as the central organizing concept that makes our lives meaningful. Identity shifts the emphasis from "what women do" to "who we are." It allows for a reciprocal relationship between our selves and our roles, with each influencing the other.

For example, a woman with a strong career identity who takes on the responsibility for the care of a frail parent may define and enact that role very differently from a woman for whom caring is a central part of her identity. Nevertheless, both women will be affected by the acquisition of that role. The identity approach also allows for agency in that as women we can made decisions about the roles we adopt, although those decisions will be constrained by our social context.

While most researchers using the concept of identity have not specifically identified themselves as using a life-course approach, identity and life-course research share common underlying assumptions in that they both allow for personal choice and the influence of the social context. One researcher who has made the specific connection is McAdams (1985), who argues that one's life story is one's identity because it is the life story that gives meaning and coherence. The power of the identity approach is illustrated by Spenner and Rosenfeld's (1990) findings of a clear distinction between the decisions made by women with a career identity from those with a working-for-extra-income identity. Even when in similar life situations to those with career identities, women with income identities were more likely to move out of, and less likely to move into, paid employment. In this conceptualization, identity is like the stabilizer on a ship, which allows for some movement but protects the ship from extreme swings.

Through guided autobiography the women are recreating their identities. Like the producer of a play who comes on stage to take a bow, they bring to the foreground lives that have been in the background. They acknowledge even the ephemeral products of meals, clean shirts, and emotional support. They bring together the diffuse threads of disparate activities and give them an interpretation that creates coherent life-stories in which each woman is the central figure.

Just as the women in the guided autobiography group are bringing together disparate pieces of their lives so too does the life-course researcher. Taking a life-course perspective emphasizes the need to understand women's lives in all of their complexity, which is in contrast to most research, which treats the areas of our lives as though they were separate fields (e.g. women and work; motherhood). Taking up the challenge to try to understand the lived reality of their total interconnectedness is a major contribution of life-course researchers. For this reason, Deem (1990) lists the introduction of life-course studies as one of the main achievements of the 1980s for feminist research.

Conclusion

Through the process of the guided autobiography, the women are empowered. They come to revalue their lives, even those, or perhaps especially those, for whom the major achievement has been survival. By placing their lives in their social context, they come to understand past decisions they regret and, through that understanding, reach acceptance of that past while recognizing their power to devise a different future. So through the life-course approach, whether we use some formal process like a guided autobiography group or other forms of self-reflection, we can recognize the continuity of our life-courses with the possibility of change, despite the restraints of a particular social context, and then claim the right to determine our futures. For the feminist researcher also, the life-course approach opens possibilities: the possibility of engaging with women's capacity for agency while acknowledging the constraints of a particular life situation; the possibility of making salient women as whole people rather than collections of roles or other variables; the possibility of using concepts such as identity, which present women's lives in ways that we ourselves recognize; the possibility of gaining understanding from our history; and the possibility of validating a smorgasbord of powerful storylines for us to choose from.

Chapter Thirteen

The Role of Formal Organizations in the Empowerment of Older Women

Rosemary Leonard

As older women we need our own organizations, not organizations for all women nor organizations for older men and women. Only older women's organizations will foreground the "double wammy of agism and sexism" (Trish Sommers cited in Huckle, 1991) which is our lived experience. Ideally, our organizations can satisfy our personal needs for social connection and empowerment while becoming stronger organizations so they can empower all older women through changes such as influencing the media and government policy. Through them, "older women can be provided with political training in social justice. From the skills developed, they acquire confidence and a new sense of their own rights as individuals" (Onyx, Benton and Bradfield 1992).

Organizations started by older women to further their interests are likely to have aims that reflect both empowerment and social connection; however, they may vary greatly in their emphasis. For some, the social interactions and processes will be more important, while others will focus on tasks and outcomes. Further, they may focus on different types of empowerment. Three levels that can be distinguished are sociopolitical (e.g., political lobbying, protests, media coverage of issues), organizational (e.g., trying to increase funding, membership, and sphere of influence), and the personal empowerment of the members (e.g., through education, encouraging participation, and individual initiatives). While ideally an organization would foster empowerment at each of these levels, in practice each may have a particular focus or even find them incompatible. For example, to strengthen organizational effectiveness, leaders may try to promote cohesion at the expense of individual initiatives. Success on all fronts is no small order, and this chapter identifies some of the ingredients of success as well as the problems and contradictions that can arise. In particular, it examines the development of three organizations of older women—the Older Women's League in the U.S., the Older Women's Network in Australia, and the Growing Old Disgracefully network in the United Kingdom.

The Older Women's Network (OWN)

OWN originated in Sydney as a consequence of a small adult education program directed at low income women within the Combined Pensioners Association. Hence its initial membership was derived from the CPA (O'Beirne 1992). The CPA was a large, hierarchical, highly bureaucratic national lobbying group for people who, due to age or disability, survive on a government pension (It has since expanded to include people with superannuation, and is now the CPSA). Its structure contrasts markedly with the Older Women's network (OWN), its prodigal daughter. Originally each Network was set up independently by older women within a particular geographical area such as Sydney, the Blue Mountains, and St Marys. Regional OWN groups are autonomous and may develop their own objectives, structure, and activities. For example, the aims of the Sydney OWN specify support, friendship, information, skills development, and the promotion of appropriate policies. In contrast, the Blue Mountains' OWN philosophy, while challenging "stereotypical views of aging in the community" (O'Beirne 1992: 4), emphasizes the importance of coming together regularly for sharing and personal growth. A variety of activities are initiated and developed by the women themselves in the OWN groups and are characterized by innovative approaches such as the Sydney OWN theatre group, the St Mary's aqua-aerobics classes, and the Older Women's Festival in the mountains. Monthly meetings and newsletters as well as social activities create a sense of connection and vitality. OWN groups try to avoid hierarchical structures and the role of the coordinator is to attempt to parcel out the work and responsibilities.

In 1993, after several years of independent growth, the Older Women's Network (Australia) was established and incorporated. Set up by several independent OWNs throughout Australia, its objectives (as outlined in its constitution) have a strong activist flavor using the words feminism, agism, sexism, and discrimination. While individuals may apply to be associates, it is intended to be an organization for older women's organizations that accept its aims and rules. Its structure is similar to the CPSA in that it has a national council to which delegates are sent and a national executive who is elected at the annual conference. There are regular general meetings to which the states are entitled to send two delegates each. The establishment of OWN (Australia) has created some debate within the communities concerned. While many believe there are definite benefits to having a national body representing their interests to governments and the public, others are concerned about the potential bureaucratization of OWN and the loss of grassroots energy and representation.

The Growing Old Disgracefully Network

The Network started with courses attractively entitled Growing Old Disgracefully, at a place called the Hen House in Lincolnshire, England. The Hen House is a holiday and study center for women only. The course was not just another retirement seminar but something "totally new to inspire women to challenge the accepted views of growing old in a dynamic way" (The Hen Co-op 1993). The first course, held in 1989, was so successful that many more have been run and local groups of graduates started to organize themselves into the Growing Old Disgracefully Network. A major catalyst for the success of the network has been the publication of the book *Growing Old Disgracefully* in 1993, which was written by six women from the first course. Why a book? First of all it is a bit disgraceful for six old women who have never written before to think they could write a book. But also because they found that the books that did exist in the bookshops and libraries are not at all helpful for older women—clinical books on the pathology of aging, agism in social institutions, or the "I climbed Mt Everest on my 83rd birthday" type of book. (After meeting two women from the Hen Coop in 1994, Jenny Onyx and I went off to the bookshops to check this out. Yes, there they were, usually on the bottom shelf in the basement under women's health.) It is not a "How To" manual because women have had quite enough of the "shoulds" and "oughts." It is a book in which the authors speak in their own words about the experiences of their lives and of growing older with enthusiasm. On the back page was an advertisement: "Do you want to grow old disgracefully in the company of likeminded women?" The response was enormous. Over 2,000 women wrote to the authors, often with detailed personal histories and requests for information. So the authors set to work again on a second book to tackle the most frequently raised issues, such as loneliness and poverty (Hen Co-op 1995). In 1995 the Network became a formal organization with a management committee and held its first annual conference. It has a newsletter advertising courses, holidays, and other disgraceful activities. It contains reports, writings and poems by the women, all in a tone likely to engender further disgracefulness. Growing Old Disgracefully, therefore, is engendering social change not through political lobbying but by inspiring individual women to act in ways that must surely change the popular constructions of older women.

The Older Women's League
    The Older Women's League, founded in 1980 in Oakland, California, was the first older women's political action group in the United States. From the beginning, it was overtly political and had a national scope. It was launched at the White House mini-conference on women and aging and the following year played a significant role in the National White House conference on Aging, at which economic issues, health, discrimination, services, and quality of life were discussed. By 1983, OWL had moved to Washington, DC, and has had a continuing role in lobbying the government on older women's issues. Several factors were important in OWL, reaching such high levels of visibility and influence in a relatively short period of time. It arose from NOW's task force on older women and also the Displaced Homemakers Movement, which focused on the rights and education of women who were impoverished because of divorce or widowhood. Unlike the British and Australian organizations that started with groups of women, the OWL was promoted principally through the activism of Trish Sommers, whose vision and total commitment to the point of personally financing the organization, were essential for its success. Another element in the organization's success was its grass roots support. It grew from 300 in the original group to over 20,000 across the country. Older women were attracted by the social contact and support they received from others but through workshops (e.g., What Kind of an Older Woman Do I Want to Be?) and edu-cational materials (e.g., OWL Organizing Manual 1983) many became politically active for the first time in their lives (Huckle 1991).

Similarities and Differences
    Even from these necessarily brief accounts of these organizations some similarities and differences emerge. Each

organization experienced rapid growth. They held almost instant appeal to large numbers of women in the three countries from which it can be inferred that there was a large unmet need—a need for older women who are often devalued and invisible to find a place where we can be recognized. This social connection appears to be an essential element of a successful group although the three organizations vary in the priority it is given. For example, Trish Sommers was eager for women in OWL to begin political action but gradually realized that social contacts and support were important as well. Her coworker, Laurie Shields, recognized that need and started the *OWL Observer*, a magazine that reported social events and personal accounts as well as political activities. In contrast, Growing Old Disgracefully focuses primarily on social connection and personal growth, and the focus of OWN varies from group to group, some taking a strong political position and others emphasizing personal and social needs. In all three organizations, the publication of a newsletter has an important role in providing connection across groups who are geographically distant.

Another common feature of these organizations is the role of educational workshops. In each case learning is seen within the adult education framework of personal growth rather than the simple transfer of knowledge. Again there are differences in emphasis, with OWL seeing such education mainly as a means to a political end, whereas Growing Old Disgracefully does not have a political focus and OWN has diverse approaches with political and physical education being included as two of many possible approaches to personal growth. It is interesting to contrast the approach to education within older women's organizations to that of the University of the Third Age (U3A), which operates in all three countries as a major source of education for older people. Although U3A's objectives are basically educational, its fourth object, "to help dispel the notion of intellectual decline with age," suggests a challenge to existing stereotypes. In a recent study of OWN and U3A in Sydney, members of U3A focused on the importance of 'food for the mind' and mental exercise out of a fear that, without exercise, their mental capacities would decline. Gaining specific knowledge, let alone using that knowledge for social change, were of lesser importance (Leonard et al. 1994). In contrast are the older women from a women's health center in western Sydney who signed up for a women's fitness class at a gymnasium but ended up rallying against the closure of a domestic violence support service and against French nuclear testing (Leonard and O'Beirne 1995). These were their first political actions. On the surface there are no direct connections between the content of the classes and their political activities. However, there is something rebellious about going to a gym, a place that is usually the domain of the young and fit, and those women seemed to have recognized some of their power for change. This fits within the adult education model for which there does not need to be a direct connection between the content of an educational course and its outcomes. Education is perceived as increasing one's potential for whatever takes your fancy.

A third similarity is one that presents a challenge to all three organizations, that is, the predominance of white, middle-class, educated women in the membership. Each of the three see themselves as open to all older women and would welcome the participation of different groups; however, if they wish to be truly representative then they may need to be proactive in finding out the needs of those groups who are underrepresented at present. There are already some examples of such action —OWL's conference for older black women, but there still seems to be a long way to go.

An area of both similarity and difference is that of the structure of the organization. Structure appears to become more of an issue the longer the organization exists. For the first three years OWL had operated as a collective, with everybody receiving the same low salary. When it moved to Washington, however, more professional women joined the organization and the board decided to markedly increase the salaries of the professionals, thus creating power differences leading to a more hierarchical structure. Led by Trish Sommers, the original workers argued against the change, but they were overruled by the Board. It was a fight and a defeat made all the more painful by the guru status that Trish Sommers had held, in which her decisions were never challenged. It could be argued that OWL had originated as a benign monarchy rather than as a collective.

It was not the first time that the issue of hierarchy had arisen. In the Displaced Homemakers Center, the director had objected to the way every-one had the same salary. "It almost put us out of business . . . I had the title of director but wasn't directing anything . . . I don't like consensus for the actual day to day operation" (Huckle 1991: 197) so there also a hierarchical structure was introduced. As yet it is unclear if OWL's hierarchical structure is creating longer-term problems. Informal channels suggest that some regional groups are disbanding because they no longer feel that they have a say in the initiatives of the central organization.

While debates over structure in OWN have not reached the fierceness of those that occurred in OWL, it is an issue about which members are particularly aware because of OWN's beginnings in the CPA. Within the CPA, women often feel they are left out of the decisionmaking. They hesitate to become too involved because moving into the hierarchy can involve you in unpleasant arguments and distance you from other members (Leonard et al. 1994). So many OWN members are concerned about the more hierarchical structure that has arisen from the development of national OWN and the sending of membership fees to OWN groups in the capital cities that run workshops and produce the newsletter. They are concerned that those involved with political lobbying will lose touch with the issues of ordinary older women.

Hierarchical structure has not become problematic in the Growing Old Disgracefully network. On the contrary, some members are complaining about the lack of central direction, not realizing that they need to take the initiative in developing their own style of disgracefulness (Hen Co-op 1994, personal communication). It is the youngest of the three organizations that leads one to think that it is simply a matter of time before they face that issue.

Over time any power differences that do exist can become entrenched and the disempowered become alienated. However, there are a number of other variables that are relevant. One is size, both in terms of numbers and also in terms of geographical distance. While Growing Old Disgracefully is growing rapidly in numbers the geographical closeness may help to alleviate concerns about a central body losing touch with its members. A more important factor might be the degree to which they engage in political lobbying. It appears to be part of the power of governments that they mold the organizations who seek to influence them (Bordt 1990). A hierarchical structure suits them because they can keep contact with a small number of people and yet maintain the illusion that they are consulting with large sectors of the population. Stability is also seen as desirable by governments. Frequent changes in structure or leadership make the task of consulting and controlling more difficult. At the moment, political lobbying is not part of Growing Old Disgracefully's agenda, and it could be that, away from such influences, structure is less of an issue.

The problems of structure give the impression that there is an irresolvable conflict between having an agenda of political influence and social reform and having an agenda of providing social connection and personal empowerment for members. I believe that is too simple and too defeatist. The power of an organization to influence comes partly from the number and cohesion of its members. Another source of power is the skill with which members can argue the case. Often these skills have been learned within the organization. Further, the arguments that occur within the organization occur because we have learned to speak up, because we have become personally empowered through our organizations.

This argument about the effectiveness of the organization as a whole reflects the tension at the personal level. Within western society there is a readiness to accept the idea that there is a conflict between being personally effective and being sociable or communal. This dichotomy is reflected in a range of psychological theories (see Wiggins 1991, for a review) Usually personal effectiveness is seen as masculine and social connectedness as feminine and women may avoid being too effective for fear of being labelled masculine. Even those researchers who argue women need both dimensions (e.g., Stewart and Malley, 1989) examine them in relation to separate life activities; for example, a person achieving agency through work and social connection through a satisfying relationship. However, a closer study of older women within their organizations (Leonard 1996) illustrated the interconnectedness of the concepts in a number of ways. First, increase in social connectedness was seen as an incentive to agency, that is, working harder for the organization led to firmer friendships. Second, friends can be called on to "give you a shove" to urge you on to greater effectiveness. Third, grouping together can help to solve problems. Fourth, agency in the sense of exercising choice to find some personal space is necessary when social connections have become a burden. These results for the interconnectedness of agency and social connection at the personal level suggest that it will be fruitful to address the way the dimensions interact with one another for the organization as a whole.

The Potential for Empowerment from Our Organizations

There is potential for empowerment at three levels; personal, organizational, and social/political. The achievements that are most often recorded for the public arena are those at the sociopolitical level. Certainly the achievements of OWL and OWN, the two organizations that have participated at that level, have been impressive. More difficult to document is the scope for empowerment at the personal and organizational levels. However, an action research project that we were involved in last year illustrated some important aspects (Leonard et al. 1994). In that project, forty eight women from three organizations of older people (OWN, U3A and CPSA) joined with researchers, using action research principles (Kemmis and McTaggart 1988; Power, Hudson, Leonard, McGee and O'Beirne 1994), to explore the women's roles within their organizations and the possibilities for older women's empowerment.

The women first participated in one of three main workshops and then were invited to the follow-up workshop and later to the review session. The function of the main workshops was to stimulate, structure, and provide space for older women to discuss their thoughts about their organizations and their roles within them. The topics included barriers to achieving greater involvement in the organization and ways to overcome those barriers.

The follow-up workshop was a less structured workshop with more interaction between the academics and the older women. The main content areas were the reporting of any actions or insights that occurred in the interim by the older women; the academics' insights and analyzes of the previous workshops; an exploration of the costs and benefits of participation in organizations; and an exercise in good decisionmaking processes.

The aims of the review session were to report back on the writing-up of the project and a paper that one of the academics had presented; find out more about the change the academics perceived between the follow-up and the earlier workshops; and to reach closure on the project.

One aim of that project was to enhance older women's capacity for participation in decisionmaking. The most important finding here was that the women already had considerable capacity for participation in decisionmaking, which they demonstrated in the workshops. They identified the reasons for their participation as being the organizers interest in hearing from them, the small group discussions, the friendly, supportive atmosphere, or, in a nutshell "It was set up like that." Clearly any problems they have with participation in other forums are more likely to be related to the conditions operating in those forums rather than the women's capacity.

Another aim was to examine barriers to participation at the personal, organizational, and the social/political levels and how to overcome them. In the initial workshops, very few themes emerged at the organizational and the social/political levels; most referred to the personal level (e.g. becoming better at prioritizing or being more confident). That is, women appeared to be holding themselves solely responsible for their level of involvement. By the follow-up workshop, however, there was evidence of change. The twenty women who attended either the follow-up workshop or the review session (or both) expressed their personal autonomy through their behavior at these sessions, their reports of actions elsewhere, and their intentions for future action. At the organizational level there was also some evidence of change. A number of women were now taking a more active role in their organizations. Two others who had been highly involved reconsidered their heavy workloads and decided to reduce them. Also a number of women became critical of their organizations for discouraging participation rather than seeing themselves as inadequate.

The political level finally emerged in the review session when the older women took control of the agenda. It was their initiative to produce a brochure to make the information from the project accessible to a large number of women and to produce a list of women willing to act as spokespersons for older women in public forums and consumer consultations. At the beginning of this project the women were anxious to please and frequently asked us what we wanted and were they doing it right. By the end, the researchers were being told what would be the appropriate outcomes of the research. This change had occurred after only two, one-day workshops, which suggests that older women's participation is not so much a case of their needing to learn new skills but of setting up an environment in which older women are given space and permission to employ their skills.

Conclusion

Our organizations play a crucial role in the agenda for the change to a society that values its older women. From the discussion in this chapter, three factors emerge as important ingredients in their success.

Underlying all others is social connection, that is, identifying and being recognized as older women, which is made all the more important in an age-denying society that makes older women invisible and isolated from each other. It is not to be trivialized as "just socialising" or to be confused with the patronizing approach of "keeping the old dears occupied."

The second factor is an environment that supports participation. Even women who think they have little to offer because they are silenced in many forums were not only able to, but enjoyed, participating in discussions in a supportive environment. Some of the elements of such environments appear to be small rather than large groups, time, and, most importantly, people who want to listen. These requirements are strikingly absent from government consultations, which usually involve large public forums with imposing speakers and the impression that the process is merely a formality rather than a genuine quest for information. Margaret Sargent reported a classic example: a recent state forum on aging, "2000—Your Say" with some workshops of over 50 people and workshop leaders who had the conclusions listed prior to the session.

The third factor seems to be some form of personal empowerment. The exact form seems to be less important than the spirit. It is not an age-fearing spirit that says "I must exercise my body and mind to avoid growing old." It is an age-embracing spirit that says "I am an older woman AND I am going to learn, try out, explore myself and my world, stretch my body and my mind or simply change the world—if I feel like it." Again there is a stark contrast between this requirement and recent government moves to tie funding of community organizations to direct service delivery. Such moves make the organizations extensions of the state system and a means by which services can be provided more cheaply by drawing on a pool of voluntary labor. Such moves are likely to "kill the goose that lays the golden egg." Focusing on services to the needy does nothing to decrease the number of people in need. Allowing women the space to find their own path to empowerment is the only way to decrease dependency and consequent demands for government support.

The problem of how to structure our organizations is likely to remain an issue, especially where we have multiple goals. Perhaps it is important to accept that there is no ideal solution and that an organization needs the flexibility to change structures or to have multiple structures to meet particular demands. What is to be resisted, then, is the inflexibility that comes from the entrenching of one particular form, no matter how desirable that may be to governments.

FACES (2) by Helen Leonard

Chapter Fourteen

Reflections on Death/A Celebration of Aging
Jenny Onyx

While writing this book, Chris, one of our members, died suddenly. She was neither the eldest nor the youngest among us, and her health was apparently in good order. Still, she died, and we were left without a valued friend and colleague. And then Pam had a diagnosis of cancer during the writing of this book. She died as we neared the end of our writing.

The shock of these events left us with several insights. We had been talking about aging for over a year, and never mentioned death. Yet aging only has meaning in the context of death. We cannot write a book of aging, the third age, while ignoring the fourth age of decrepitude and decline that provides the context (Laslett 1995: 14). Furthermore, as Margaret points out, enjoying the opportunities old age offers is not possible until we have individually and collectively come to terms with dying. Paradoxically, a celebration of life, especially the life of old age, needs necessarily to be woven together with reflections of death and dying.

This chapter has been collectively written by some of us in the sense that each has made a contribution to the topic. Much of it was written before Pam's death, and her own reflections are central. It seems particularly appropriate to what we are trying to say that her voice should remain present, even though she is dead. Other contributors are Rosslyn, Rosemary, Sharyn, Margaret, and Noeleen, with a contribution also by Enid Sawley. The chapter is written in the form of a dialogue among us. As editor, I play the role of commentator, linking and weaving the others' reflections together. I begin with my own reflections on Pam's death, reflections that anticipate many of the central themes of the chapter: themes of denial and loss, of connection and celebration. Our reflections are personal ones; we engage with the literature where relevant, but there is little that speaks to our experience. The medical model again fails us. "The attitude and approach of modern medicine confirm that death represents failure; something to be avoided at any cost . . . "(Scrutton 1995). Older women are not well served by the medical model either in dying or in support for bereavement.

This chapter looks at death then, not as a medical issue, nor as a religious issue (where death is seen as a release of the soul from earthly cares). Rather, we are concerned with what death means to us as women growing older and living within our current social context. As feminists and social theorists we have very little to go on beyond our personal experiences and our networking with older women. We draw on these as a rich source of potential understanding in the hope that others may find them useful. [Jenny]

Reflections on Pam's Death

Jenny.   Pam's death was hard. We had been through a lot together as friends and colleagues. We knew about each other's private struggles as we helped each other make sense of mothering, aging, the labor market, injustice. It was she who was adamant about the central but unrecognized importance of women's networks, those myriad invisible, uncounted, uncosted, undervalued connections from woman to woman and from family to family that hold a community together and provide that crucial support in times of crisis. It was her adamance that informed my thinking on social capital.

I knew about her cancer from the beginning, from the time we urged each other to check out those worrying symptoms. I was lucky, she was not. Throughout the following months she struggled to maintain some control and dignity in the face of the medical juggernaut and the inexorable collapse of her body. Her spirit was fierce and unyielding. Her 12 year old daughter needed her. We, her network of friends, supported her as best we could. Each time I went to see her, I took her a beautiful, fragrant apricot rose from my garden.

She would not talk of death; she did not believe in it, at least not its imminence for her. We talked about death in the abstract, but not her death, not the actual dying. Not until the very end when she held my hand tightly and whispered of her fear of the coming abyss. Of course we are afraid, every one of us, as we stand poised on the edge of that abyss. The courage is in acknowledging the fear and moving forward to meet it. Even then, she smiled as she saw women dancing through the breeze blown leaves of the gum tree outside. I felt privileged to be so close to Pam, to share some of her journey, to witness her courage. She died well.

The funeral was brief and unsatisfying. The family and the professionals took over. It was very tastefully done, with flowers and fine words, tributes to her achievements. But I did not feel a part of it. Pam meant many things to many people. Understandably, the focus was on her husband and daughter. We her friends expressed our concern for their well being. They suffered the ordeal with restraint and dignity. But in all that, there was no room for my own grief. I felt offended at the public effort to sanitize Pam's life and death. I wanted to express what Pam's life and death meant for me as her age mate and confidante, yet somehow to do so seemed irresponsible and selfish. Afterall I was not family. It wasn't until several months later that I was invited to join a special memorial evening for her friends that I could reach some sort of closure, to recognize with others the value of our friendships and networks, to acknowledge the loss, to express the grief, to pay tribute to a fine woman.

The Absence of Death

Rosslyn.   We think of death as coming at the end of life, after everything which make up the so-called lifecycle: birth, youth, marriage or taking a partner, children and watching them grow to adulthood and repeat the process. Not that we expect every life to follow this route. But, as a rule, until we are thirty years of age, we cannot conceive of our own mortality. Thirty is "over the hill," beyond comprehension. Death even more so . . .

In the so-called developed industrialized countries, it is easy to ignore death (Becker 1973). For the majority, we are protected from encounters with the death of an infant or child as happened more frequently in our own rural past. The death of youth, especially young men caught up in the violence of the cult of masculinity, is remarked upon but little is done to change it, and we tolerate it while avoiding its reality if we can. Although few of them spend much of their lives there, older people die in separated places like hospitals and nursing homes. Most of us can feel secure that we will not have to deal with the immediate and physical presence of death in our homes and communities. A linear view of the old idea of a life-cycle becomes acceptable in this context . . .

Jenny.   I only ever once saw a dead person. It was while working at a mental asylum as a university student; the nurses showed me an old woman, propped up against the pillows in bed, dead. She had already been made up. She looked calm, pretty almost, but like a made up doll. She did not seem real.

Pam.   For many years I have felt uneasy about the relative absence of experiences of death in my life. My parents are still alive, in their mid-to-late eighties, my in-laws too, in their late seventies. I have worked for much of the last nine years with older (including very old) women, yet few of them have died. My grandparents on one side died before I was born. On the other side, my mother's parents were geographically and emotionally remote, and their deaths occurred when I was deep in my self-centered early twenties and no longer living at home. I didn't even have a sense of whether or how my mother grieved for them. I know of the death of remarkably few of the hundreds of people I've met and been friends with in my 54 years of living. Several deaths have been shocking, but at a remove, like the 38 year old husband of a close friend who died of cancer, leaving her with three children; or the 20 year old daughter of a friend who died in a car accident. But the grief at these deaths was more for my friends' loss than my own.

Even when my brother died of cancer nine years ago, my grief was more for my parents. I had loved him a long time ago when I was a child and he was a young man ten years older. I had gradually distanced myself from him emotionally as he seemed bent on self-destruction via booze. I had one 'real' conversation with him between his cancer diagnosis and his death, but everyone except me was wanting to deny that his death was imminent, so it didn't help me much to sort out my own emotions, mostly guilt for _not_ accepting what I saw as a fake optimism.

Rosemary. Very few mothers are given the choice of life or death for their children. Of course many of us have moments of fury when we are capable of really harming them but that's not the same as having a surgeon ask in all seriousness whether he should operate on your new born baby. He thought that the child was probably "worth saving" and was disappointed that he could not talk to my husband because mothers are not usually able to make considered decisions (Why ask the fathers when it's the mothers who have to do all the work?). I decided, as I think most women would, "If he will die without the operation then there is no choice—you operate." It was not a decision in the cool rational sense of the word. I had not really contemplated death let alone come to terms with it. It was another denial of death in a death denying society. But I'm not sure if an acceptance of death as a part of life would have changed my mind; after all, he had lain on my stomach and looked at me and I loved him. So my son lives and I do most of the daily grind of caring, most of which is caused by intellectual problems which were not predicted by the surgeon.

Sharyn: "Cut tragically short" is the cry of newspaper headlines when a young life is lost. The age matters in this most personal and yet most universally human of experiences. How we link age and death! Yet maybe if we did a statistical analysis of all the deaths in this century we might find that being young is a health hazard. My father died at the age of 25 like many of his comrades. War does not honor youth or age for whoever is/was in the line of fire took the bullet or in the plane that crashed or the gas oven when the gas was turned on. Poverty and starvation do not discriminate between young and old either! Yet we continue to link age and death and so resist the experience of aging . . . my mother resists her aging, not willing to accept her increasing frailty, waiting still to get better . . .

The Pervasive Presence of Death

Sharyn is reflecting on the strange contradiction of death that is simultaneously denied and yet pervasively present through much of life. Both she and Pam reflect on the way in which a death long ago, before their own birth, haunted their own growing. [Jenny]

Sharyn.

> "They shall not grow old
>   As we that are left grow old
>   Age shall not weary them
>   Nor the years condemn
>   At the going down of the sun
>   And in the mornings
>   We shall remember them"

Death is the strangest thing! I feel like I have lived in its shadow for most of my life. Not because I was seriously ill, but because I lived with this poem being enacted in my family life. My eldest brother's father died during *the war* (World War II) that cast the shadow of death and tragedy over the 1950s, that brought such dramatic changes to people's lives at the personal and political levels. Jim's photo in his uniform sat gloriously perfect on my brother's cupboard as my father and my mother aged and wearied!

Without his death I would not have been born—someone, or even two, may have been born with similarities to me, but the "me" I am/became could never have existed without his death brought on by *the war*. Yet his death was a tragedy in my mother's life that she only recently dealt with. When I told her that my father had died, thirty years later, she said "oh no, not again!" More recently when my partner and I brought photos of Jim's war grave to show her, my mother's hand shook and she had to have a smoke before she could look at them.

Pam   I was starting off with that puzzle, the sense of the *absence* of experience with death, at the same time as being aware that it is in fact a pervasive *presence* throughout my life . . . My other brother died before I was born. That was my parents' first child.

My entire life was pervaded with a sense of grief about this child who died aged six. But he wasn't real, he was a mythical kind of person. There was a photograph, one of those large framed photographs of him and my other brother. There were two children who were two years apart and he was the eldest. I've lived my life with a sense, much of the time, of death not touching me particularly because there are no close people who died in the conventional sense.

But of course there is this *absent* person that I never knew, whose death hovered over my whole childhood, and still does . . . It is still an unresolved grief for my mother, I think it's frozen grief, that has permeated all her relationships with other people, with her other children including me . . . It seemed with me that it was very hard for her to allow herself to connect enough, because she might lose me. And I can understand that . . .

Rosslyn.   Women in developing countries, as in our own rural past, are not able to forget death. They live death—death of babies at birth or in infancy and children from malnutrition; of partners from accidents in the course of their work and of the members of their families who survive to old age in their households and communities. Their own potential death in child-birth, as a risk in abortion in the absence of safe, reliable contra-ception, and from malnutrition because of the demands of childbearing, nursing, and traditions which dictate that they eat last and what is left, is an ever present possibility.

Death Connects the Living

Part of the problem for us in developed industrialized countries is not so much the denial of death as the denial of bereavement (Scrutton 1995), the "frozen grief" that Pam talks about. Grief that is not expressed, loss that goes unacknowledged, holds us in a paralyzed state. For all of us, death is more central to our lives and relationships than we readily admit. Pam and Sharyn were both talking about the pervasiveness of the effects of others' deaths through their own growing-up. How death affects the relationships of those still living depends on how the loss is dealt with. Sometimes there is a sense of the silent and forbidden void made bitter by the enforced, frozen silence. Sometimes there is a deeply satisfying and positive sense of connection across the generations, made poignant by the death of a relative. Funerals and other public social events play an important symbolic and social role in the shared acknowledgment of loss and the connectedness of those living and dead (Scrutton 1995).

Pam. The two deaths which I *have* felt connected with were both of aunts, my father's older sisters, who had been important to me at different life stages. One, Oonah, came to live with us during World War II before I was two years old. My father was in New Guinea, my mother working night shift in the post office. Oonah took me with her to the kindergarten where she was a (probably unpaid) worker. Recently released from her destiny of caring for her father, as the only unmarried daughter, Oonah lavished her 45 years of spinster's love on me, provoking the rest of my family to angry remarks about how I was "spoilt" by the toys and cakes in times of war-rationing and scarcity. She was my first, perhaps only, attachment figure, and her departure from our household when the war ended and I was aged four, left me distraught. Although she visited us periodically through the balance of my childhood, I grew to share the adult family's judgement of her imperfections and lost contact with her for 20 years.

In my late 30s circumstances washed her up after several strokes, in a nursing home only a mile from where I lived. For the next year or so I visited her regularly, often simply sitting quietly with her as she dozed. She appeared completely accepting of being bedridden, and of the proximity of death, and would muse about who she would meet in heaven (her mother mostly) and whether they would still look the same as when she had last seen them. She was happy about dying whenever God was ready.

Eventually she had another stroke and never regained consciousness. I sat and held her hand for an hour or so as her breath rasped shockingly. I wept only a little then as I said goodbye. It was time for her to die and I didn't want to hold her there suffering. But at the funeral, somehow the strong singing voices of the old who packed the church connected me to the hurt four year old, and I sobbed as the distraught child had done when she left me the first time.

And now I am confronting my own rather more immediate possibility of dying. It has to do with a sense that the meaning of death is to do with the meaning of one's life. And the meaning of their life in relationship to you; we need to have some sense of what that is and how it is important. It's probably also connected with what Kay (a mutual friend, now dead) is saying "there are no dying people; there are only living people." And that's it, the sense of who they were in their lives, and in your life, and the meaning it gives for you.

Enid. The very week I was thinking about this, wondering just how I would tell you about my mother, my daughter came to me and wanted to know more about my mother's death. This has added another dimension to the story, showing the links that exist between a mother, her daughter, and granddaughter.

When my mother died I was a young married woman with two preschool children, living in a large country town. In August Mum was rushed to the city for an emergency operation and diagnosed as having terminal cancer. She died the following March, having spent most of that period of time in hospital. We were a very close family and I was an only child. During those months we shuttled backwards and forwards between our home town and the city, spending as much time as possible with Mum. The specialist had said we were not to tell her she had cancer.

My aunts and uncles gathered to give us their love and support. One or other would often look after my children to enable Mum and me to spend time together. Mum and I had long discussions about many things, how she felt, but not once did she mention death. There was no doubt in my mind that she knew she was dying. I felt that she was trying to protect me and the family by not talking about her impending death, always she talked about the future, and what we might do when she came home, as if she was trying to give us hope. I played the game too, feeling I was helping her in some way. I felt great sadness and loss when she died, but it was a relief to see her at peace after all the suffering.

Now, all these years later, my daughter, who is 35 years of age, had the need to talk about my mother, her grandmother. She told me that when Nanna died she felt abandoned, somebody who surrounded her with love was suddenly missing from her life, and now she wanted to know more about her grandmother's life and her death. Over the years we have often talked about Mum, but this time she wanted to know it all, as much as I could tell her. We talked for several hours, my daughter and I, we reviewed my mother's life, we shed tears together, we laughed, and we shared a lot of love. This was not only about my mother's death, it was also a celebration of her life and love of a mother, her daughter, and her granddaughter.

Generativity and Connection

One side of death concerns the impact that the death of others has on the still living. The other side of death concerns the impact that the knowledge of our own imminent death has on our personal well-being. This is the hard part, yet paradoxically the most central issue for a joyous old age.

The intergenerational connections that Enid talks about seem to provide consolation both to the bereaved and to the dying. For example, an American study (Alexander, Rubinstein, Goodman, and Luborsky 1991) found that for older women, notions of generativity were central to a sense of well-being. Whether they were childless or not, older women expressed the importance of passing on something of value to the next generation (Erikson 1980). This may be a material transmission or a purely cultural one as in the teaching and nurturing of significant others; but it was invariably expressed through the connection with specific and significant others. The depth of this individual and personal connection was made particularly poignant by those older women whose children had died, leaving no possibility of continuity. For us perhaps, there are also these two important aspects to generativity. One is the sense that we have achieved something worthwhile in this life, something to pass on to the next generation. The other is the sense that we are deeply connected to significant other persons who will remember us. [Jenny]

Pam.   Well I certainly have that sense that people live on in the memories of others. That is neither comforting or discomforting. I don't find that problematic except to the extent that I haven't done as much as I wanted to do. It would be better not to die now because of that . . . Maybe we have to hold the paradox simultaneously that every life has some effect and in another sense that there are many lives which no one will recognize. Will mine be one that's recognized as having value? and by whom and does it matter? Will the people that I care about, care? . . . What does it mean to have experienced some sort of fame? Many people never have any recognition of that kind, external to a very private world.

Margaret. I did some research back in the sixties on older people's depression and their attitudes towards dying. Quite a few seemed to be facing the prospect of death with contentment and without feeling depressed. Their preparedness was associated with feeling satisfied with whatever they had achieved in life and to a lesser degree with regular visiting by their children. Achievement and appreciation seem to make it easier to die happily. I think what makes it harder to die for women who still have young children is the sense that the achievement will not be complete.

The Knowledge of Death Enhances the Experience of Life

As we reach into the third age of our lives we are all acutely aware of time running out. As more and more of our parents' generation die, and indeed those of our own, we become increasingly aware that we are next in line, next to face the abyss of the dark unknown. That awareness brings a terror that needs to be faced (Friedan 1994). But it also brings with it an enhanced sense of pleasure for all the small joys of life, a sense of freedom from petty and unimportant pressures, and a sense of urgency, to use our time wisely, to experience fully, an opportunity for adventure. [Jenny]

Pam. Instead of thinking about death as an abstract thing that will happen at some point in the future, it becomes part of your everyday. It's actually a living part of each of your experiences. It's not just about saying "well this might be the last time I do this." Rather it is that you are living in that moment in a different kind of way . When you are old, or have a strong sense of dying being close, its not only that there's a time limit on how much revisioning you can do but there's an intensity about getting it right, doing it *now* in a way that is satisfying.

This is not about being judgmental or self-critical. In fact, it is about cutting through the crap. It's about trying to let go of irrelevant judgments. There is a whole intensity of processing, of fully engaging *now* rather than somewhere down the track. It's really important that you focus all your energy on doing that now. And you may still get it "wrong," whatever that might mean. But that's not your main concern. It is the engagement that is important, not whether what you're doing is going to be judged by others right or wrong.

I had a dream that I was dancing. The judgment of others was there as I started to dance. I felt indescribably wonderful, the way I was moving, it was very joyous and free. Some judgmental part came in and said "this is not very interesting dancing; its a bit banal." And that judgmental part just floated past because I didn't care. I just kept on dancing because it didn't matter what that judgment was. I was aware of it and it was irrelevant.

Jenny.   I'd like to hold on to a sense that in facing death, you are never more real. That is the ultimate reality, the "cutting the crap." It entails not just rejecting other people's judgement but moving far beyond to where it's totally irrelevant, so that you are most fully you and real. That can only be achieved right at the point of closest engagement with death. The potential for growth and the ultimate reconciliation with the universe is also about becoming more fully real.

I think that in this space of heightened awareness we are able to not only engage more deeply with life, but also speak out more clearly. This is what Audre Lorde was also expressing.

> In becoming forcibly and essentially aware of my mortality, and of what I wished and wanted for my life, however short it might be, priorities and omissions became strongly etched in a merciless light, and what I most regretted were my silences. Of what had I ever been afraid? to question or to speak as I believed could have meant pain, or death. But we all hurt in so many different ways, all the time, and pain will either change, or end. Death, on the other hand, is the final silence. And that might be coming quickly now, without regard for whether I had ever spoken what needed to be said, or had only betrayed myself into small silences, while I planned someday to speak, or waited for someone else's words. And I began to recognize a source of power within myself that comes from the knowledge that while it is most desirable not to be afraid, learning to put fear into a perspective gave me great strength. (Lorde 1980: 20)

Sharyn.   At the moment I am finding it difficult to celebrate aging. I am too conscious of the limitations it brings, physical and emotional, of the losses it brings: my mother's failing health and sense of self is confronting me with it! And it is also in my own life that I am feeling it—my own sense of aging and its limitations . . .The workplace emphasizes youth and the technology of the future—I feel exhausted by it. Sometimes I look around and think, "oh, another year has gone; where did it go?"

At the same time I am conscious of my growing confidence and sense of satisfaction and joy in my life. I want to speak up more and be in the world to the best of my ability, and I believe I have things to contribute. It has taken some time to get here, and I don't want to give it up just because I am middle-aged. I see in my life women who are aging strongly and "gracefully": full of life and energy and grace! There are two women in my life at the moment whom I admire immensely—one is ten years older than me and the other is in her 70s. They are both yogis and remain focused on life and living! One is a committed feminist and grows stronger every day. They are pleasures to be with. They are not unusual either; I spend time with women who are full of life and energy. I saw my mother grow and change as life demanded it and gave her the opportunities. I hope that I will continue to grow and change and become stronger in my being as I continue to age.

Margaret. Being able to celebrate aging rests on an acknowledgment of the process of dying and imminent death. Only after this acknowledgment can older women feel how precious the remaining years are, to be enjoyed and celebrated without anxiety for the future.

The Celebration of the Life of an Unknown Older Woman

She was born at the turn of the present century and in the first year of the federation of six British colonies into the Commonwealth of Australia. Her mother was Australian-born. Her origins were British. Her father was a Prussian-born immigrant farmer, coming to Australia as a youth before the formation of the German state. She was her father's eighth surviving child and her mother's first. Her twin step-brother and sister were just two years old when she was born. She was to have a further four siblings over the next 13 years.

When I was born she had passed her fortieth birthday. She was my "maiden aunt." A goitre operation and early menopause, an active life spent working outdoors in a sub-tropical climate and a general disdain for fashion and cosmetics meant she always seemed to me to be "old." There was something ageless and constant about her as the years went by. Her activity and indomitable spirit meant that she was almost as active at 90 as she had been at 40—mentally, physically, and socially.

She was educated at business college and briefly worked in clerical-secretarial work. But she gave up her paid work to assist her mother caring for her aging father, an intellectually disabled older step-sister, and manage a household of adult siblings, none of whom married until their late twenties. There was a constant procession of relatives and family staying for varying periods within their family home. She milked the cow, tended the fowls, and raised chickens as well as looking after the large vegetable and flower gardens. She helped her mother with cooking and preserving the fruit from the many trees and those cases of produce her father bought at the city markets. She killed, plucked, and dressed poultry for the table. She finished and established the underground air-raid shelter in World War II. When the family purchased a car, she learned to drive and chauffeured her parents—and later her nieces too. She gave permission for the Caesarean section operation to save her youngest sister's life while her husband was away on active military service and then held the child who was not expected to live to her breast because her sister was too weak to hold her own child.

During the war, she was asked if she could do more for the war effort. So she took in laundry for the U.S. servicemen camped on the land where her family used to keep their cow. She went back to work and cleaned, washed, and ironed for a number of other households nearby. When she needed more income for her own support in the 1950s and 1960s, she took on office cleaning as well. By then she was alone, having cared for her mother until she was 90.

When my aunt was 70 and still going to work one day a week, she was hit by a car while using a pedestrian crossing and fractured her hip. With the help of my mother, she determined to refute the claims of those who argued she would never walk again. She couldn't climb trees to prune them anymore. Nor could she mow her lawns. She was forced to give up her job. But she walked. Until she was 90 years of age, twice a week she climbed one of the steepest hills in Brisbane to make sandwiches for the breakfasts delivered to the homeless people who lived in the city parks. At 90 she started to "wear out." Within the year she had died.

True to the stereotype, my spinster aunt never approved of men. But she was not an active feminist like her mother. Her life was, perhaps, more devoted to others and with greater cost than that of most mothers. Eventually she inherited the family home. When she died she left half her small estate to be shared by her three sisters and the other half to her three nieces. Her two nephews had benefited from their father's estate more than their mother. My aunt was, after all, a closet feminist. [Rosslyn]

We Have Much to Celebrate!

Finally, we can recognize that we do indeed have much to celebrate, if we allow ourselves. To get to this point, we have had to acknowledge the losses and oppressions that we face. And we have to reach that point of freedom and confidence where we can defy conventional expectations about who we are. Like that wonderful collective, the "Hen Co-op," we are learning the joys of "growing older disgracefully" (The Hen Co-op 1993). We also recognize that our many years of life experiences creates a wealth of skill and knowledge that enriches those around us. We have a valuable contribution to make. Our celebration carries with it a further recognition of what yet needs to be done to make the joys of aging accessible to all. We realize that we have created an agenda for future political and social change and a determination to act!

The closing contributions of this book are rightly reserved for our two senior members. Margaret is 70 with very poor eyesight, yet she summarizes neatly the many causes we have for celebration in our daily living. We close with a poem written by Noeleen, a feisty woman indeed, who writes a universal yet personal statement of triumph. [Jenny]

Margaret.   There is no way we can enjoy aging until we have faced up to dying. But after that, we may find that life is more valuable and worth living than it was before. Then we can celebrate aging in the here and now, with joy and fun and lightness of being.

Older women are now released from many of the social pressures put on younger women—for example, pressures to marry, cook, and clean for a family, act submissively, be feminine. Nowadays we can mostly choose whether or not to do these things. Indeed many of the roles which have been prescribed for women, and the responsibilities which go with them, do not apply to the older generation. For example, we no longer have to behave in the expected ways as mothers, wives, employees, and so on. Furthermore, in our older years we are not expected to be beautiful, so we can wear what we like (such as baggy trousers), and need not always be well groomed, smart, and uncomfortable. We need not any longer make efforts to appear young and desirable, but can look and act the way we really feel. We have to embrace the freedom this gives us and discover ways of using it for the benefit of ourselves and other older women.

We mostly still have health and energy, which previous generations lacked in their old age. We have discovered for ourselves that the ideology that all older women are sick, in decline, and close to death does not accord with the facts. We know that the period of disability just before death is growing shorter. We may come to feel that many of the changes as we age are not due to some little understood process; they seem to relate more to our personal experiences and environment in our earlier years.

We recognize that there are various ways of enhancing the last third of our lives, and we have explored some of these ways in this book. We know that maintaining and creating social and family networks is associated with well being (Wenger 1982). We understand the importance of maintaining activity. We value continued sexual activity. There are already many opportunities for continuous education and training, such as those provided by the University of the Third Age (Swindell 1993). Lifelong learning is a familiar concept to older people. And through the work of older people's organizations it is gradually becoming accepted by governments, educationists and the rest of society that opportunities for participation in all kinds of education and training must increasingly be made available to older people (Consultative Committee on Aging 1995).

There are many avenues to self-development, sheer enjoyment, and the celebration of our new freedom. At our age, for those not caught in poverty traps, we have leisure for these and peer companions to share them with. It is important to find ways of maintaining an individual sense of control over our lives, for it is associated with retaining our right and capacity to make choices (Rodin 1989).

In our role as consumers, we ourselves must persuade governments to consult with us on how to implement interventions which will enhance our quality of life. Continued independence can be supported even under conditions of increasing frailty and need for services. Policy must anticipate and plan for our potential health crises and housing needs and promote the empowerment of older women. We older women have a major part to play in expanding the understanding and clarifying the values concerning aging that are held by service providers and other professional people.

In the past, gerontologists have noted the "political acquiescence" of older people and have little expectation of political activism (Walker 1995). In the case of older women, their expectations might be in error. For there is a new culture of aging that is developing. Perhaps this is because we are having some success in changing our negative image in society, and because of the increasing proportion of older people in the population and a growing recognition of their contribution. Our diversity in terms of age, race, health, and economic status is becoming recognized. Nevertheless, agism, sexism, and racism still abound, and we are determined to find effective ways of combating these.

There are now peer organizations in which we can engage in activities to influence government and other organizations and improve the conditions of our lives. There exist good examples of interventions specifically designed to enhance the quality of aging. The fact that older people are increasingly being expected to take responsibility for planning for their own old age must open channels of action by older women to engage in improving their own future (Day 1995). This move will, however, require breaking away from the present phallocentric approach to policy and research. We need a feminist approach to aging, and we need more exploration of what constitutes feminist aging and how we can engage in it (Gibson 1995; Watson 1995). We need to move away from the positions of victim, dependent, burdensome. Governments have to be persuaded of our skills and capacities. Only when we value ourselves highly can we celebrate aging.

The good thing about women's experience of oppression is that it has made us what we are today: feisty, independent, active, and empowered. Age also has brought additional experience of oppression. We have, however, a growing knowledge of how to overcome oppression and achieve empowerment. Therefore, we can both acknowledge and embrace that experience, and we can celebrate our status as older women. This is what feminist aging is! Let us celebrate aging!

Ode to the Older Woman
(an affirmation- a celebration)

Noeleen O'Beirne

I'm alive—yes, alive
for I have known what it is
To be a woman and survive,
For-
    I am a warrior-woman, a lioness,
A blazer of trails
A builder of bridges and a mender of them too,
A champion of the many—not the few.
    I encompass the earth, I touch the sky
And plummet to earth,
Phoenix-like I rise from the ashes of my dreams
    Once more to fly and fly and fly.
    I am quite literally the stuff
Humanity is made of.
I am a nurturer giving birth
Not only to my kind, but thru' the fertility of my mind
to concepts unconfined by societal expectations.
    I am a welder of bonds, strong and enduring
Of motherhood, sisterhood, nationhood.
A donor of life-force, endowed with experience
Adorned with wisdom and love.
I am a place of refuge, a dove
I countenance no killing of another's daughter
Or a son—my children everyone.
    I am the music of the universe, from generation to
generation
You'll hear my lilting song.
I am the white crane dancing with extended wings
Dancing to silent music.
The snow leopard, alone, aloof in lofty solitude,
The dolphin frolicking in turquoise waves.
    I am a chameleon—wife, mother, worker,
Artist, dancer, teacher,
The gentle moon illuminating
The darkness of ignorance and hate.
I am a page well-written
My history finely etched
Upon the parchment of my face.
    So, survive I have and gloriously, not in defeat.
Sing out! sing out! in celebration of our sisterhood
We'll meet the challenge life still has in store
With valour, for
Each of us is WOMAN—ageless and unique.

First published in *Womanspeak*, September/October 1991.

References

Adams, R. 1989. Conceptual and methodological issues in studying friendship of older adults. *Older adult friendship: Structure and process*, edited by In R. Adams and R. Blieszner Newbury Park: Sage.

Administration On Aging. 1996. *Population and Housing Patterns Among Older Americans*. National Aging Information Center: Washington D.C.

Age Concern England. 1997. *Older people in the United Kingdom*. London: (htttp://194.152.67.67/stats/full.htm).

Alexander, B., Rubinstein, R., Goodman, M., and Luborsky, M. 1991 Generativity in cultural context: The self, death and immortality as experienced by older American women. *Aging and Society* 11. 417–42.

AARP (American Association of Retired Persons). 1993. Update on the Older Worker: 1992, *Data Digest*, Number 7.

Anike, L., and Ariel, L. 1987 *Older women: Ready or not*. Bexley: Authors.

Arber, S., and Ginn, J. 1990. The meaning of informal care: Gender and the contributions of elderly people. *Aging and Society* 10; 429–54.

———. eds. 1995. *Connecting Gender and Aging: A Sociological Approach*. Buckingham: Open University Press.

———. 1995. Choice and constraint in the retirement of older married women. In *Connection Gender and Aging: A Sociological Approach*, edited by S. Arber and J. Ginn Buckingham: Open University Press.

Arber, S. 1995 Political economy implications of policy and planning for older people, and current gerontology research in the UK. *Proceedings of the National Rural Conference on Aging: Re-writing the Future*. Albury, NSW: Charles Sturt University.

Armstrong, D. 1993. From clinical gaze to regime of total health. In (1993) Beattie, A., Gott, M., Jones, *Health and Wellbeing: A Reader*, edited by L. and Siddell, M. London: Macmillan/The Open University.

Australian Bureau of Statistics. 1981. *Estimated resident population by age and sex*. Cat. No 3201, Canberra.

———. 1986. *Voluntary community work*. Cat. No. 4403.1, NSW.

———. 1988. *Community and voluntary work*. Cat. No. 4402.4. SA.

———. 1990. *1989–1990 National health survey lifestyle and health Australia*. Cat. No. 4366, Canberra.

———. 1993. *Women in Australia*. Cat. No. 4113, Canberra.

———. 1994. *Women's health*. Cat. No. 4365, Canberra.

———. 1995. a. *Australian social trends*. cat. No. 4102, Canberra.

———. 1995. b. *The labor force australia*. Cat. No. 6203, Canberra.

———. 1995. c. *Voluntary work*. Cat. No. 4441.0, Canberra.

———. 1996. d. *Employee earnings and hours. Australia, May 1995*, Cat. No. 6306, Canberra.

Australian Institute of Health and Welfare 1994. *Australian welfare 1993*. AGPS, Canberra.

Bachrach, M. and Baratz, P. S. 1962 The two faces of power. *American Political Science Review* 56. 94–52.

Balbo, L. 1992. Crazy quilts: Rethinking the welfare state debate from a woman's point of view In *Women and the State: The Shifting Boundaries of Public and Private,* edited by A. S. Sassoon. London: Routledge.

Baldock, C. (1983. Volunteer work as work: Some theoretical considerations. In *Women, Social Welfare and the State in Australia,* edited by C.V. Baldock and B. Cass Sydney, Allen and Unwin.

——. 1990. *Volunteers in welfare.* Sydney: Allen and Unwin.

Bartlett, H. 1993. *Nursing homes for elderly people—Questions of quality and policy.* Zurich: Harwood Academic Publishers.

Beattie, A. 1993. The changing boundaries of health. In *Health and Wellbeing: A Reader,* edited by Beattie, A., Gott, M., Jones, L. & Siddell, M. London: Macmillan/The Open University.

Becker, E. 1973. *The denial of death.* New York: Free Press.

Beechey, V. 1982. The sexual division of labor and the labor process: a critical assessment of Braverman. In (ed), *The Degradation of Work? Skill, deskilling and the Labor Process,* edited by S. Wood. London: Hutchinson.

Bernard, M. and Meade, K. eds. 1993. *Women Come of Age.* London: Edward Arnold.

Billis, D., and Harris, M. 1992. Taking the strain of change: UK voluntary agencies enter the post-Thatcher period. *Nonprofit and Voluntary Sector Quarterley, 21, 3:* 211-225.

Bird, E., and West, J. 1987. Interrupted lives: A Study of women returners. In *Women and the Lifecycle,* edited P. Allandt, T. Keil, A. Brymann, and B. Bytheway. London: MacMillan.

Birren, J. E., and Deutchman, D. E. 1991. *Guiding Autobiography Groups for Older Adults: Exploring the fabric of life* Baltimore: John Hopkins University Press.

Bleier, R., and Bleier, R. 1996. *Feminist approaches to science,* Sydney: Pergamon.

Bluestone, B., and Stevenson, M. H. 1981, Industrial transformation and the evolution of dual Labor markets: The case of retail trade in the United States. In *The Dynamics of Labor Market Segmentation,* edited by   F. Wilkinson London: Academic Press.

Bordt, R. 1990 How alternative ideas become institutions: The case of the feminist collectives. *PONPO Working Paper,* 159. New Haven: Yale University.

Borowski, A., and Hugo, G. 1997 Demographic Trends and Policy Implications, In *Aging and Social Policy in Australia,* edited by A. Borowski, S. Encel and E. Ozanne. Melbourne: Cambridge University Press.

Boyages, J. 1993. *Breast Health Newsletter.* Western Breast Screening Unit, Sydney. June, p.1.

Brannen, J. 1987. The resumption of employment after childbirth: A turning-point within a life-course perspective. In *Women in the Lifecycle: Transitions and Turning Points,* edited by P. Allandt, T. Keil, A. Brymann, and B. Bytheway. Basingstoke: Macmillan Press.

Bricker-Jenkins, M. 1994 Feminist practice and breast cancer: The patriarchy has claimed my right breast . . . . In *Women's Health and Social Work: Feminist Perspectives,* edited by   M. M. Olson. New York, The Haworth Press.

Brody, E. M. 1990. *Women in the middle: Their parent-care years.* New York: Springer.

Broom, D. 1989. A Feeling for the enterprise. *Australian Feminist Studies* 9: 123–32.

——. 1989. Masculine medicine, feminine illness: Gender and health. In *Sociology of Health and Illness,* edited by   G. M. Lupton, and J. Najman, Melbourne: Macmillan..

------. 1991. *Damned if we do: Contradictions in women's health care.* Sydney: Allen and Unwin.

Brown, C. 1995. Handing back power to elderly people in residential institutions. *Social Alternatives* 14, 2: 22–3.

Bryson, L. 1994. Women, paid work and social policy. In *Australian Women: Contemporary Feminist Thought*, edited by N. Grieve and A. Burns Melbourne: Oxford University Press.

Burden, D., and Gottleib, N. 1989. *The Women Client.* New York: Tavistock.

Burke, P. J., and Reitzes, D. C. 1991. An identity theory approach to commitment. *Social Psychology Quarterley* 54: 239–51.

Burton, C. 1991. *The Promise and the Price* Sydney: Allen and Unwin.

Butler, J. 1990. *Gender trouble.* New York: Routledge.

Butler, R. 1980. Agism: A foreword. *Journal of Social Issues* 36, 2: 8–11.

Cartwright, C., and Steinberg, M. 1995. Decision-making in terminal care: Older people seek more involvement. *Social Alternatives* 14, 2: 7–10.

Casimir, Jenny. 1994. Family ties on mother and son. *Sydney Morning Herald: The Guide*; February: 7–13.

Castles, I. 1994. *How Australians use their time.* Australian Bureau of Statistics, Cat. No. 4153.0.

Chappell, N., and Badger, M. 1989. Social isolation and well-being. *The Journal of Gerontology* rr, 5: 169–176.

Chetley, A. 1995. Pill pushers, drug dealers. *The New Internationalist* 272: 22–23.

Clare, R., and Tulpule, A. 1994 *Australia's aging society*, EPAC Background Paper No. 37, Economic Planning Advisory Council, Canberra.

Clough, R. 1981. *Old age homes.* London: George Allen and Unwin.

Cockburn, C. 1991. *In the way of women: Men's resistance to sex equality in organizations.* London: Macmillan.

Coffman, T. L. 1981. Relocation and survival of institutionalized aged: A re-examination of the evidence. *The Gerontologist* 21, 5: 483–500.

Cohen, L. 1992. No aging in India: The uses of gerontology. *Culture, Medicine and Psychiatry*, 16, 2: 123–61.

Cole, T. R. 1992. *The journey of life: A cultural history of aging in America.* Cambridge: Cambridge University Press.

Coleman, J. S. 1988. The creation and destruction of social capital: Implications for the law. *Journal of Law, Ethics and Public Policy* 3: 375–405.

------. 1990. *The foundations of social theory.* Cambridge: Harvard University Press.

Coleman, L., and Watson, S. 1987. *Women over sixty: A study of the housing, economic and social circumstances of older women.* Canberra: Australian Institute of Urban Studies.

Colliere, M. 1986. Invisible Care and Invisible Women as Health Care Providers. *International Journal of Nursing Studies* 23, 2: 95–112

Connidis, I. 1986. The relationship of work history to self-definition of employment status among older women. *Work and Occupations* 13, 3: 348–58.

Conran, S. 1975. *Superwoman: Everywoman's book of household management.* Penguin Books: Harmondsworth.

Coombs, R. 1991. Marital status and personal well-being: A literature review. *Family Relations* 40: 97–102.

Corliss, M., and Lawson, D. 1995. Caring for the elderly in the acute care sector: The competent nurse of the future. In (eds) *Issues in Australian nursing*, edited by G. Gray, and R. Pratt. 5, Melbourne: Churchill Livingstone.

Cotterill, P. 1992. But for freedom you see, not to be a baby minder: Women's attitudes to grandmother care. *Sociology* 26, 4: 603–618.

Crompton, L., Hantrais & Walters, P 1990. Gender Relations and Employment'. *British Journal of Sociology* 41, 3: 329–49.

Dalley, G. 1993. Familist ideology and possessive individualism. In (eds) *Health and Wellbeing: A reader*, edited by A. Beattie, M. Gott, L. Jones, and M. Siddell. London: Macmillan/The Open University.

Daly, J. 1994. Women's Voices: Problems and pleasures of menopause. In *Menopause: The Alternative Way*, edited by C. Black Australian Women's Research Center, Monograph Series No.1, Geelong: Deakin University.

Davies, C. ed. 1980. *Re-Writing Nursing History*. London: Croom Helm.

Davis, A., and George, J. 1988 *States of health: Health and illness in Australia*. Sydney: Harper & Row.

Davison, B., Kendig, H., Merrill, V., and Stephens, F. 1994. *It's My Place: Older People Talk about their Homes*. Canberra: AGPS.

Day, A. 1991. *Remarkable survivors: Insights into successful aging among women*, Washington, DC: The Urban Institute Press.

------. 1995. Is there an older people's point of view? *International sociological Association Intercongress Meeting.* Melbourne.

Day, A. T. 1986. Changes in caregiving across generations: Perceptions of people aged over 75 years and over. In *Aging and families: A support networks perspective*, edited by H. Kendig, Sydney, Allen and Unwin.

Deem, R. 1990. Gender, work and leisure in the eighties: Looking backwards, looking forwards. *Work, Employment & Society*, Special Issue: 103–23.

Department of Health, Housing, Local Government and Community Services. 1993. *Annual Report*, Canberra: AGPS.

Depner, C., and Ingersoll, B. Employment status and social status: The experience of the mature woman. In *Women's Retirement: Policy Implications of recent Research*, edited by M. Szinovacz. Beverly Hill: Sage.

De Vaus, D. 1996. Children's responsibilities to elderly parents, presented at *5th Australian Family Research Conference*, Brisbane, Unpublished.

Dingwall, R. and Robinson, K. M. 1993. Policing the family? Health visiting and the public surveillance of private behavior. In (eds) *Health And Wellbeing: A reader*, edited by A. Beattie, M. Gott, L. Jones, and M. Siddell. London: Macmillan/The Open University.

Donnison, D. V., and Ungerson, C. 1982. *Housing Policy*. Harmondsworth: Penguin.

Edgar, D. 1990. Dead neighbourhoods have no volunteers. *Impact*, 20, 5: 13.

Edwards, H. 1995. Communication predicaments of older health care consumers: What can "we" do about it? *Social Alternatives* 14, 2: 33–36.

Ehrenreich, B., and English, D. 1979. *For her own good: 150 years of the experts' advice to women*. London: Pluto Press.

Ehrenreich, B., and English, D. 1973. *Witches, Midwives and Nurses*. London: Writers and Readers Co-op.

Ehrlich, F. 1981. Health and illness. In (ed) *Towards an Older Australia: Readings in Social Gerontology*, edited by A. L. Howe, St. Lucia: University of Queensland Press.

Elwood, J. M., Cox, B., and Richardson, A. K. 1992. *The effectiveness of breast screening by mammography in younger women*. Hugh Adam Cancer Epidemiology Unit and the Department of Health, New Zealand. 30th November.

Encel, S. 1997. Work in later life. *Aging and Social Policy in Australia*, edited by in A. Borowski, S. Encel, E. Ozanne. Melbourne: Cambridge University Press. 137–55.

Encel, S. and Studencki, H. 1997. *Gendered agism: Job search experiences of older women*. Sydney: Department for Women/NSW Committee on Aging.

Epstein, C. F. 1970. *Woman's place: Options and limits in professional careers*. Berkeley: University of California Press.

Erdner, R., and Guy, R. 1990. Career Identification and Women's Attitudes Toward Retirement. *International Journal of Aging and Human Development* 30, 2: 129–39.

Estes, C. L. 1991. The new political economy of aging: Introduction and critique. In *Critical perspectives on aging: The political and moral economy of growing old*, edited by M. Minkler, and C. L. Estes. New York: Baywood Publishing Company.

Evers, H. 1985. The frail elderly women: emergent questions in aging and women's health. In *Women, Health and Healing: Towards a New Perspective*, edited by E. Lewin and V. Oleson. NY/London: Tavistock.

Falk, G., and Falk, U. 1980. Sexuality and the Aged. *Nursing Outlook* Jan: 51–55.

Faucett, J., Ellis, V., Underwood, P., Naqvi, A., and Wilson, D. 1990. The effect of Orem's self-care model on nursing care in a nursing home setting. *Journal of Advanced Nursing* 15: 659–66.

Featherstone, M. 1993. The mask of aging and the postmodern lifecourse. In *The Body: Social Process and Cultural Theory*. 4th ed. edited by M. Featherstone, M. Hepworth and B. Turner. London: Sage Publications.

Fee, E., 1983. Women's Nature and Scientific Objectivity. In *Woman's Nature: Rationalizations of Inequality*, edited by M. Lowe, and R. Hubard. New York: Pergamon.

Fennell, G., Phillipson, C. and Evers, H. 1988. *The Sociology of Old Age*. Milton Keynes, Open University Press.

Ferguson , I. 1995. Carers at work. *Social Alternatives* 14, 2: 37–39.

Feuerbach, E., and Erdwins, C. 1994. Women's retirement: The influence of work history. *Journal of Women and Aging*. 6, 3: 69–85.

Field, J., and Hedges, B. 1985. *A National Survey of Volunteering*, London, Social and Community Research.

Finch, J. 1983. *Married to the Job: Wives incorporation into men's work*. London: Allen and Unwin.

Fine, M. 1984. Directions in sociology—Institutional accommodation for aged persons. Presented at *Care of the elderly—Current issues and future prospects—Proceedings of the 19th annual conference of the Australian Association of Gerontology*, edited C. Sydney. Australian Association of Gerontology: 40–44.

Fitzgerald, Ingrid 1997. *Never too late to learn: A Report on older people and lifelong learning*. Sydney. NSW Committee on Aging.

Flynn, T. 1993. Foucault by and the eclipse of vision. In *Modernity and the Hegemony of Vision*, edited by D. M. Levin. Berkeley, Uniiversity of California Press.

Forsyth, Ann 1992. *Changing places: Case studies of innovations in housing for older people*. Canberra: Department of Health, Housing.

Foucault, M. 1973. *Birth of the clinic: An archaelogy of medical perception*. London: Tavistock.

——. 1976. *Birth of the Clinic*. A Sheridan, trans. London: Tavistock Publications.

——. 1979. *Discipline and punish: The birth of the prison*. A. Sheridan, trans. New York: Vintage Books.

——. 1980. *Power/Knowledge*. by Colin Gordon, trans. Brighton, Harvester Press.

——. 1986. *The care of the self*, R. Hurley, trans. London, Penguin.

——. 1991. The ethic of care as a practice of freedom. In *The Final Foucault*. 2d ed., edited by J. Bernauer and D. Rasmussen. Cambridge, MA. The MIT Press.

Fox, J. 1977. Effects of retirement and former work life on women's adaptation in old age. *Journal of Gerontology* 32: 196–202.

Fox, N. 1993. *Postmodernism, sociology and health*, Buckingham: Open University Press.

Foy, S., and Mitchell, M. 1991. Factors contributing to learned helplessness in the institutionalized aged: a literature review. *Physical and Occupational Therapy in Geriatrics* 9, 2: 1–23.

Francis, D. 1991. Friends from the workplace. In *Growing Old in America*, edited by B. Hess and E. Markson. New Brusnwick: Transaction.

Frank, A. W. 1993. For a sociology of the body: An analytical review. In *The Body: Social Process and Cultural Theory*, 4th ed. edited by M. Featherstone, M. Hepworth and B.S. Turner London. Sage Publications.

Freire, P. 1972. *Pedagogy of the oppressed*. Harmondsworth: Penguin Books.

French, V. 1995. Let's stop perpetuating the myths of aging. *Social Alternatives* 14, 2: 5–6.

Friedan, B. 1993. *The fountain of age*. London: Vintage.

———. 1993. *The Fountain of Age*. New York: Random House.

Fromm, D. 1991. *Collaborative communities: A new concept of housing with shared services*. San Rafael, CA: Ecumenical Association for Housing.

Fuller, D. 1995. Challenging agism through our speech. *Nursing Times* May: 29–31.

Fuller, L., and Smith V. 1991. Consumer' reports: Management by customers in a changing economy'. *Work Employment and Society* 5, 1: 1–16.

Galler, R. 1993. The myth of the perfect body. In *Health and Wellbeing: A Reader*, edited by A. Beattie, M. Gott, L. Jones, and M. Siddell, London, Macmillan/The Open University.

Gallop Organisation. 1986. *American Volunteer*: Washington DC: Independent Sector.

Gergen, M. 1990. Finished at 40; Women's development within the patriarchy. *Psychology of Women Quarterly* 14: 471–93.

Gibson, C. 1995. Representations of aging in children's fiction. *Proceedings of The National Rural Conference on Aging: Re-writing the Future* Albury, NSW. Gerontology Studies, Charles Sturt University.

Gibson, D. 1983. Health Status of Older People. In *Health, Welfare and Family in Later Life*, edited by H. Kendig et al. Canberra, ANU.

———. 1995. Broken down by age and sex: The problem of "older women" redefined. Melbourne: International Sociological Association Intercongress Meeting.

Gilligan, C. 1982. *In a different voice. psychological theory and women's development*. Cambridge: Harvard University Press.

Ginn, J., and Arber, S. 1993. Pension penalties: The gendered division of occupational welfare. *Work Employment & Society* 7, 1: 47–70.

Goffman, E. 1968. *Asylums*: Harmondsworth: Penguin Books.

Gonski, H. 1994. *Grand parenting: A new challenge*. Sydney: Milner.

Gore, J. 1992. What can we do for you! What can "we" do for "you"? Struggling over empowerment an critical and feminist pedagogy. In *Feminisms and Critical Pedagogy*, edited by C. Luke and J. Gore. New York: Routledge.

Graham, H. 1983. Caring: A labor of love. In *A Labor of love: Women, work and caring*, edited by J. Finch, and D. Groves. London: Routledge & Kegan Paul.

Gray, G., and Pratt, R. 1995. Introduction: Making a difference through clinical practice. In *Issues in Australian Nursing* 5, edited by G. Gray, and R. Pratt. Melbourne: Churchill Livingstone.

Graycar, A. ed. 1982. Age Care—Whose Responsibility? Social Welfare Research Center Report No. 20, March. Sydney. University of New South Wales.

Greer, G. 1970. *The Female Eunuch*. London: MacGibbon & Kee.

———. 1991. *Aging and the menopause*. London: Hamish Hamilton.

Guillory, J.A. 1994. Breast Cancer: A serious threat to elderly women'. *Journal of Women & Aging* 6, 1/2: 151–163.

Gurney, C., and Means, R. 1993. The meaning of home in later life. In *Aging, Independence and the Life Coruse*, edited by S. Arber and M. Evandrou. London: Kingsley.

Hailstones, A., and Sadler, P. 1993. *Abuse of older people in their homes—Final report and recommendations of the NSW Task Force on abuse of older people.* Sydney: Office on Aging.

Hakim, C. 1991. Grateful slaves and self-made women: Fact and fantasy in women's work orientations. *European Sociological Review* 7, 2: 101–121.

Hareven, T. K. 1982. The life course and aging in historical perspective. In *Aging and Life Course Transitions,* edited by T. K. Hareven, and K. J. Adams. New York: Guilford.

Harwood, E. 1995. The longevity spiral: How old is old? *Social Alternatives* 14, 2: 24–27.

Hassan, A. B., and Bar-Yam, M. 1987. Interpersonal development across the life span: Communion and its interaction with agency in psychological development. *Contributions to Human Development* 18: 102–28.

Hatch, L. 1990. Effects of work and family on women's later-life resources. *Research on Aging* 12, 3: 311–38.

Hayes, C., and Parker, M. 1993. Overview of the literature on pre-retirement planning for women. *Journal of Women and Aging,* 4, 4: 1–18.

Hayward, M., Grady, W. and McLaughlin, S. 1988. The retirement process among older women in the United States. *Research on Aging* 10, 3: 358–82.

Helson R., and Picano, J. 1990. Is the traditional role bad for women? *Journal of Personality and Social Psychology* 59: 311–20.

Hen Co-op 1993. *Growing Old Disgracefully.* London, Judy Piatkus.

———. 1995. *Disgracefully yours.* London. Judy Piatkus.

Hewison, A. 1995. The power of language in a ward for the care of older people. *Nursing Times,* May: 32–33.

Hilary Commission. 1990. *Life in New Zealand.* LINZ.

Hobbs, F., and Damon, B. 1996. *65+ in the United States,* Bureau of the Census, U.S. Department of Commerce.

Hockey, J., and James, A. 1993. *Growing up and growing old; Aging and dependency in the life course.* London: Sage Publications.

Hocking, S. 1994. Counting the cost of aging society. *Courier Mail* 4/2/94.

Hodgkinson, V. and Weitzman, M. 1990. *Giving and volunteering in the United States: Findings from a National Survey.* Washington D.C.: Independent Sector

Hollenshead, C. 1982. Older women at work. *Educational Horizons* 60, 4: 137–46, 195–96.

Homburg, D. 1991. Pills and older people. *Refractory Girl,* 39: 19–21.

Hooyman, N. and Kiyak, H. 1993. Cognitive changes with aging. In *Social Gerontology,* Boston: Allyn and Bacon.

Hornstein, G. A. 1986. The structuring of identity among midlife women as a function of their degree of involvement in employment. *Journal of Personality,* 54 3: 551–75.

Howe, A. L. 1992. *Housing for older Australians: Affordability, adjustments and care.* Canberra. National Housing Strategy.

Huckle, P. 1991. *Trish Sommers, activist, and the founding of the older women's league.* Knoxville: University of Tennessee Press.

Hudson, R. 1990. Volunteers or paid workers?' *Impact,* May.

Ironmonger, D. 1994. Household Industries. In *The Changing Structure of Australian Industry,* edited by K. Sawyer and J. Ross. Sydney: McGraw-Hill.

Jamieson, D., and Webber, M. 1991. Flexibility and part-time employment in retailing. *Labor and Industry* 4, 1: 55–70.

Jewson, R. 1982. After retirement: An exploratory study of the professional woman. In *Women's Retirement: Policy Implications of Recent Research,* edited by M. Szinovacz. Beverly Hills: Sage.

Johnson, L. 1993. *The modern girl.* St Leonards: Allen and Unwin.

Johnson, P., and Falkingham, J. 1992. *Aging and Economic Welfare,.* London: Sage.

Jones, C. 1985. *Patterns of social policy: an introduction to comparative analysis*. London: Tavistock.

Jones, J. 1994. Embodied Meaning: Menopause and the change of life. In *Women's Health and Social Work: Feminist Perspectives*, edited by M. M. Olson (ed). New York: The Haworth Press.

Kalish, D., and Williams, L. 1983. Discrimination in the labor force at older ages. *Australian Journal on Aging* 2, 2: 8–16.

Katz, C. and Monk, J. 1993. Where in the world are women? In *Full Circles: Geographies of Women Over the Life Course*, edited by C. Katz and J. Monk. New York, Routledge. 1–26.

Kassner, E. 1992. Falling through the safety net: Missed opportunities for Americas' elderly poor. Washington D.C.: American Association of Retired Persons.

Kelly. B. 1995. Ethnicity and aging in rural areas. *Proceedings of The National Rural Conference on Aging: Re-writing the Future*. Albury, NSW: Gerontology Studies, Charles Sturt University.

Kemmis, S., and McTaggart, R. 1988. *The action research reader*, 3rd ed. Geelong: Deakin University Press.

Kendig, H. ed. 1986. *Aging and families*. Sydney: Allen and Unwin.

------. (1989) *Directions on Aging in New South Wales:* Sydney: Office on Aging.

------. 1984. a. Aging, families and social change. In *Aging and families: A Support Networks Perspective*, edited by   H. Kendig. Sydney: Allen and Unwin.

------. 1984. Perspectives on aging and families. In *Aging and families: A support networks perspective*, edited by H. Kendig. (ed) Sydney: Allen & Unwin.

------. 1990. Aging and housing policies. In *Grey Policy*, edited by H. Kendig and J. McCallum. Sydney: Allen and Unwin.

Kendig, H., and McCallum, J. 1986. *Greying Australia: Future impacts of population ageing*. Canberra: Migration Committee, National Population Council.

Keohane, N., Rosaldo, M., and Gelpi, B. eds 1985. *Feminist Theory: A Critique of Ideology*. New York: Harvester.

Kerlikowske, K., Grady, D., Barclay, J., Sickles, E. A., Eaton, A., and Ernster, V. 1993. Positive Predictive Value of Screening Mammography by Age and Family History of Breast Cancer. JAMA, November 24th, 270, 20: 2444–50.

Kinnear, D., and Graycar, A. 1984. Aging and Family Dependence. *Australian Journal of Social* Issues 19, 1: 13–24.

Kitzinger, J. 1990. Audience understanding of AIDS media messages: A discussion of methods. *Sociology of Health and Illness* 12, 3: 320–35.

Kjervik, D. 1986. A conceptualization of women's stress. In *Women in Health and Illness*, edited by D. Kjervik and   I. Martinson. Philadelphia: W. B. Saunders Co.

Knapman, C., and Waite, H. 1995. Dementia care: Time to ask new questions. *Social Alternatives* 14, 2: 41–43.

Langer, E. J., and Rodin, J. 1976. The effects of choice and enhanced personal responsibility for the aged: A field experiment in an institutional setting. *Journal of Personality and Social Psychology* 34, 2: 191–98.

Lash, S. 1993. Genealogy and the body: Foucault/Deleuze Nietzsche. In *The Body: Social Process And Cultural Theory*, 4th ed. edited by M. Featherstone, M. Hepworth, and   B.S. Turner. London: Sage Publications Ltd.

Lawson, O. 1990. *The first voice of Australian feminism: Excerpts from Louisa Lawson's The Dawn 1888-1895*. Brookvale: NSW: Simon & Schuster.

Laslett, P. 1995. The third age and the disappearance of old age. In *Preparation for Aging*, edited by E. Heikkinen, J. Kuusinen and I. Ruoppila. London: Plenum Press.

Lazarowich, N. M. 1990. A review of the Victoria, Australia Granny Flat Program. *The Gerontologist* 30, 2: 177–77.

Learman, L. A., Avorn, J., Everitt, D. E., and Rosenthal, R. 1996. Pygmalion in the nursing home—The effects of caregiver expectations on patient outcomes. *Journal of the American Geriatrics Society* 38, 7: 797–803.

Legge, V., and Cant, R. 1995. A lonely old age? *Social Alternatives* 14, 2: 44–7.

Leonard, R. 1996. Formal organizations of older women as context for the development of agency and communion. *Journal of Women & Aging*.

Leonard, R., and O'Beirne, N. 1995. *Older Women's Health and Fitness Project: An Evaluation of the Pilot Study*, sponsored by WILMA women's health, Dept. of Sport, Recreation and Racing, Student Representative Council, University of Western Sydney, Macarthur. Unpublished.

Leonard, R., O'Beirne, N., Power, A., McGee, S. and DeMole, J. 1994. Older Women: Consultation, participation and empowerment. *Women's Research Center, Working Papers in Women's Studies*, No 15, University of Western Sydney.

Levinson, D. J., Darrow, C. N., Levinson, M. H., and McKee, B. 1978. *The Seasons of a Man's Life*. New York: Knopf.

Liffman, M. 1978. *Power for the poor: the family center project: An experiment in self help*. Sydney: Allen and Unwin.

Limerick, B. and Heyward E. 1992. *Purists, wowsers, do-gooders and ultruists*, Working Paper No 9, Program in non profit corporations, QUT, Brisbane.

Limerick, D. 1994. Australian Federation of University Women Seminar, Brisbane, September.

Lind, J. 1995. Life Situation as a factor explaining retirement. In *Preparation for Aging*, edited by E. Heikkinen, J. Kuusinen and I. Ruoppila. New York: Plenum Press.

Logue, J. 1995 Living With Breast Cancer. In *THE Key Center for Women's Health*, in Society World Health Organization Collaborating Center for Women's Health, The University of Melbourne, January, pp. 3–5.

Loroe, A. 1980. *The Cancer Journals*. San Francisco: Spinsters Ink.

Lupton, D. 1992. The establishment of mass mammographic screening programs; In Whose Interests? *Australian Journal of Social Issues* 27, 2: 112–24.

------. 1994. *Medicine as culture: illness, disease and the body in western society*. London: Sage.

Lynn, P., & Smith, J. D. 1991. *The 1991 National Survey of Voluntary Activity in the UK*. York: Joseph Rowntree Foundation.

Madden, R. 1995. *Women's Health*, Cat. No. 4365.0. Canberra. Australian Bureau of Statistics.

Mann, P. 1988. Personal identity matters. *Social Theory and Practice*, 14, 3: 285–317.

Martin, J., and Roberts, C. 1984. *Women and employment A lifetime perspective*. Report of the 1980 DE/OPCS women and employment survey, London.

Mason, J. 1987. A bed of roses? Women, marriage and inequality in later life. In *Women in the Lifecycle: Transitions and Turning Point*. edited by P. Allandt, T. Keil, A. Brymann, and B. Bytheway. Basingstoke: Macmillan Press.

------. 1990. Reconstructing the public and the private. In *Home and Family; Creating the Domestic Sphere*, edited by G. Allan and G. Crow. London: MacMillan.

Mathews, A. and Brown, K. 1987. Retirement as a critical life event. *Research on Aging* 9, 4: 548–71.

Mathews, S. H. 1979. *The social world of old women*, Beverly Hills/London: Sage.

Matthews, J. 1992. *Good and mad women*, 5th ed. Sydney: Allen and Unwin.

McAdams, D. P. 1985. *Power, intimacy, and the life story*. Homewood, II: The Dorsey Press.

McCallum, J. 1982. Perspectives on the transition from work to retirement. *Australian Journal on Aging* 1: 1.

------. 1984. Retirement and widowhood transitions. In *Aging and families: A support networks perspective*, edited by H. Kendig. Sydney: Allen and Unwin.

McDonald, B., and C. Rich, 1984. *Look me in the eye: old women, aging and agism.* London: The Women's Press.

McHoul, A., and Grace, W. 1993. *A Foucault primer: Discourse, power and the subject.* Melbourne: Melbourne University Press.

McKinnon, C. 1985. Feminism, Marxism, method and the state: An agenda for theory. In *Feminist Theory: A Critique of Ideology*, edited by N. Keohane, M. Rosaldo, and B. Gelpi. New York: Harvester.

McLellan, B. 1992. *Overcoming anxiety.* Sydney: Allen and Unwin.

Meddaugh, D. I. 1990. Reactance—Understanding aggressive behavior in long-term care. *Journal of Psychosocial Nursing* 28, 4: 28–33.

Mentes, J. C., and Ferrario, J. 1989. Calming aggressive reactions—a preventive program. *Journal of Gerontological Nursing* 15, 2: 22–7.

Metcalf-Kendall, W. 1995. Aged wedlock. *Social Alternatives* 14, 2: 20–1.

Minichiello, M. V. 1984. Social processes in entering nursing homes. In *Aging and families: A support networks perspective*, edited by H. Kendig. Sydney: Allen and Unwin.

Minichiello, V., Alexander, L. and Jones, D. 1992. *Gerontology: A multidisciplinary approach.* New York: Prentice Hall.

Misson, A. 1990. Women: Will they be forever volunteers? *Impact*, 20, 5: 15.

Morgan, D. 1994. Looking outwards from our organization. AFUW Seminar, Brisbane, September.

Morgan, L. 1991. Economic security of older women: Issues and trends for the future. In *Growing Old in America*, edited by B. Hess and E. Markson. New Brunswick: Transaction.

Moyal, A. 1989. Women and the Telephone in Australia. *Report to Telecom*, CIRCIT.

Mullender, A., and Ward, D. 1991. *Self-directed groupwork: Users taking action for empowerment.* London: Whiting and Birch.

Nay, R. 1993. *Benevolent oppression: Lived experience of nursing home life.* School of Sociology, Sydney, University of New South Wales.

------. 1996. Nursing home entry: Meaning making by relatives. *Australian Journal on Aging* 15, 3: 123–26.

------. 1997. Relatives experiences of nursing home life: Characterized by tension. *Australian Journal on Aging* 16, 1: 24–9.

Nay, R., Barrett, C., and Gorman, D. 1997. Sexuality in Aged Care. In *Nursing Elderly People: Issues and Innovations for the 21st Century*, edited by R. Nay, and S. Garratt. Sydney: MacLennan Petty.

Newton, E. 1979. *This bed my center.* Melbourne: McPhee Gribble.

Ngaanyatjarra Pitjantjatjara Yankunytjatjara Women's Council Aboriginal Corporation. 1995. *They might haave to drag me like a bullock: The Tjilpi Pampa Tjutaku Project*, Alice Springs, Ngaanyatjarra Pitjaantjatjara Yankuntjatjara Women's Council Aboriginal Corporation and Commonwealth Department of Human Services and Health.

Noble, J. 1991. *Volunteering*, Adelaide, Volunteer Center, SA.

NSW Council on the Aging. 1987. *Towards Better Retirement Housing Design*, Sydney.

Nuccio, K. 1989. The double standard of aging and older women's employment. *Journal of Women and Aging* 1, 1: 317–38.

Office of Local Government, Department of Immigration, Local Government and Ethnic Affairs. 1991. *Local Housing Action: An Overview and Guide to Good Practices*, Canberra.

O'Beirne, N. 1993. Women and Aging. In *Proceedings of the Women and Psychology Conference* (MA Students), Women's Research Center Working Papers in Women's Studies, University of Western Sydney.

O'Neil, R., and Greenberger, E. 1994. Patterns of commitment to work and parenting: Implications for role strain. *Journal of Marriage and the Family* 56: 101–12.

Older Women's League 1993. *Room for improvement: the lack of affordable, adaptable and accessible housing for middle and older women*. Washington: Older Women's League.

Older Women's Network. 1994. *Well being for and by older women*. Sydney: Older Women's Network, Inc.

------. 1992. *Older women, feminism and health*, Report of the conference held in Sydney, 3–4th July.

Onyx, J. A. 1996. *Why women do not plan for their retirement*. Sydney, Association of Superannuation Funds of Australia.

Onyx, J. 1998. Issues affecting women's retirement planning. *Australian Journal of Social Issues* (in press).

Onyx J., and Bullen 1998. Measuring social capital. *School of Management Working Papers*, No. 3, Sydney, University of Technology, Sydney.

Onyx, J., and Benton, P. 1996. Retirement: A problematic concept for older women. *Women and Aging* 8, 2: 19–34.

Onyx, J., Benton, P., and Bradfield, J. 1992. Community development and government response. *Community Development Journal* 27, 2: 166–74

Palmer, G. R., and Short, S. D. 1989. *Health care and public policy: an Australian analysis*. Melbourne: Macmillan.

Parliament of the Commonwealth of Australia. 1995. *Report on the management and treatment of breast cancer*, House of Representatives Standing Committee on Community Affairs, February.

Parsons, T. 1949. Age and sex in the social structure of the United States. In *Essays in Sociological Theory, Pure and Applied*, edited by T. Parsons. Glencoe: II. Free Press.

Pateman, C. 1983. Feminist critiques of the public/private dichotomy. In *Public and Private in Social Life*, edited by S. Benn and G. Gaus. London: Croom Helm

Paul, P. 1995. Healthy wealthy and why? *Social Alternatives* 14, 2: 28–32.

Peace, S. 1993. The living environments of older women. In *Women Come of Age*, edited by M. Bernard and K. Meade. London: Arnold.

Pearson, A., Nay, R., Taylor, B., Tucker, C., Angus, J., Griffiths, V., and Ruler, A. 1996 *Relatives' experience of nursing-home entry: Meanings, practice and discourse—Interim Report*. Adelaide: The University of Adelaide.

Peele, S. 1989. *Diseasing of America: Addiction treatment out of control*. Boston: Houghton Mifflin Company.

Penhale, B., and Kingston, P. 1995. Recognizing and dealing with the abuse of older people. *Nursing Times* 91, 42: 27–8.

Pettman, J. 1996. *Worlding women: A feminist international politics*. Sydney: Allen andUnwin.

Petrou, M. F., and Obenchain, J. V. 1987. Reducing incidents of illness posttransfer. *Geriatric Nursing* 264–66.

Philipson, C. 1982. *Capitalism and the construction of old age,*. London: Macmillan.

Phillips, A., and Taylor, B. 1980. Sex and skill: Notes towards a feminist economics. *Feminist Review* 6: 79–88.

Piercy, M. 1976. *Woman on the edge of time*. London: Women's Press.

Pilgrim, D., and Rogers, A. 1993. *A sociology of mental health and illness*. Buckingham: Open University Press.

Porcino, J. 1991. *Living longer, living better: Adventures in community housing for those in the second half of life*. New York: Continuum.

Porter, E. 1991. *Women and moral identity*. Sydney: Allen and Unwin.

Power, A., and Bevington, L. 1995. *Creating older women: Discourses on gender and aging in the Health and Community sectors*. Sydney: University of Western Sydney.

Power, A., De Mole, J., Leonard, R., McGee, S., and O'Beirne, N. 1994. *Research and empowerment: Developing theory and practice in a collaborative project with older women*. Sydney: University of Western Sydney.

Power, A., Hudson, J., Leonard, R., McGee, S., and O'Beirne, N. 1994. Empowerment through research: Tilting at Windmills? Australian Association of Social Research, Research and the Quality of Life Conference, University of Tasmania, Launceston, January.

Price-Bonham, S., and Johnson, C. 1982. Attitudes toward retirement: A comparison of professional and nonprofessional married women. In *Women's retirement: Policy implications of recent research*, edited by M. Szinovacz. Beverly Hills: Sage.

Pulling, J. 1987. *The caring trap*. London: Fontana Paperbacks.

Putnam, R. D. 1993. *Making democracy work: Civic traditions in modern Italy*. New Jersey: Princeton University Press.

-------. 1994. *Bowling alone: Democracy in America at the end of the Twentieth Century*. Nobel Symposium, Democracy's Victory and Crisis. Uppsula, Sweden, August.

Reed, R. 1995. Social Policy for older women is not working. In *Social Policy and the Challenges of Social Change: Proceedings of the National Social Policy Conference Sydney, 5-7 July 1995*, Volume 2, Sydney, edited by P. Saunders and S. Shaver. The University of New South Wales, pp. 167–81.

-------. 1996. *The Invisibility of older women workers: Women aged 55 and over in retailing*. Canberra: Australian Government Publishing Service.

-------. 1997. Older women workers: A challenge to unions. In *Proceedings of the 5th Women and Labor Conference, Sydney 29 September to 1 October 1995*, edited by M. Oppenheiner and M. Murray. Sydney, Macquarie University, pp. 581–91.

Reekie, G. 1993. *Temptations: Sex, selling and the department store*. Sydney: Allen and Unwin.

Regner, V., Hamilton, J., and Yatabe, S. 1991. *Best practices in assisted living: Innovations in design, management and Financing*. Los Angeles: National Eldercare Institute on Housing and Supportive Services, University of Southern California.

Reinhartz, S. 1992. *Feminist methods in social research*. New York: Oxford Univ. Press.

Richards, M. H., and Larson, R. 1989. The life space and socialization of the self: Sex differences in the young adolescent. *Journal of Youth and Adolescence* 18, 6: 617–26.

Roberts, H. 1981. ed. *Doing feminist research*. London: Routledge and Kegan Paul.

Roberts, S. 1983. Oppressed Group Behavior: implications for nursing. *Advances in Nursing Science* July,: 21–30.

Robertson, I. 1989. *Society: A brief introduction*, New York: Worth.

Rodin, J., and Langer, E. 1980. Aging labels: The decline of control and the fall of self-esteem. *Journal of Social Issues* 36, 2: 12–29.

Rodin, J. 1989. Sense of control: Potentials for intervention. *Annals of the American Academy of Political and Social Science* 503: 29–42.

Rose, H. 1986. Beyond masculinist realities: A feminist epistemology for the sciences. In R. Bleier, op cit: 57–66.

Rose, H., and Bruce, E. 1995. Mutual care but differential self-esteem: Caring between older couples. In *Connecting Gender & Aging: A Sociological Approach*, edited by S. Arber and J. Ginn. Buckingham: Open University Press.

Rosenman, L., and Winocur, S. 1990. Australian women and income security for old age: A cohort study. *Journal of Cross-Cultural Gerontology* 5: 277–91.

Rosenman, L., and Warburton, J. 1997. Retirement incomes and Women. In *Aging and Social Policy in Australia,* edited by A. Borowski, S. Encel and E. Ozanne. Melbourne: Cambridge University Press.

Rossiter, C. 1984. Family care of elderly people: Policy Issues. SWRC Report No. 50, Sydney, University of NSW, December.

Rowland, D. 1991. *Aging in Australia.* Melbourne: Longman Cheshire.

Rowland, D. T. 1984. Family structure. *Aging and families: A support networks perspective,* edited by In H. Kendig. Sydney: Allen and Unwin.

Rubenstein, G. 1994. *Foxspell.* Victoria: Hyland House Publishing Pty Ltd.

Rubery, J. 1988. *Women and recession.* London: Routledge and Kegan Paul.

Rubin, L. 1982. Sex and Sexuality: Women at midlife. In *Women's Sexual Experience: Explorations of the Dark Continent,* edited by M. Kirkpatrick. New York: Plenum Press.

Rule, J. 1987. *The memory board.* London: Pandora Press.

Runciman 1992. *Factors affecting job tenure in the Australian retail industry.* Canberra: unpublished Ph.D. Thesis, Australian National University.

Russell, C. 1981. *The aging experience.* Sydney: George Allen and Unwin.

Russell, C. 1987. Aging as a feminist issue. *Women's Studies International* Forum 10, 2: 125–31.

Russell, C., and Schofield, T. (1986) *Where it hurts: Sociolgy of health for health workers,* Sydney, Allen and Unwin.

Russell, C., and Schofield, T. 1995. Aged care, research and policy making: What role for older consumers. *Social Alternatives* 14, 2: 48–51.

Ryan, E., and Prendergast, H. 1982 "Unions are for Women Too!." In *Power, Conflict and Control in Australian Trade Unions,* edited by K. Cole. Melbourne: Pelican.

Saggers, S., and Gray, D. 1991. Policy and practice in Aboriginal health. In *The Health of Aboriginal Australians,* edited by J. Reid and P. Trompf. Sydney: Harcourt Brace Javonovich.

Saltman, D. 1991. *Women and health: An introduction to issues.* Sydney: Harcourt Brace Jovanovich.

Sarason, I. G., and Sarason, B. R. 1984. Life changes, moderators of stress and health. *Handbook of psychology and health,* edited by In A. Baum, S. E. Taylor and J. E. Singer (eds). New Jersey: Lawrence Erlbaum Associates.

Sargent, M. 1994. *Older women free at last.* Sydney: Older Women's Network.

——. 1994. Consumer Consultation: Extending housing options for older people. *Papers on Housing Choice for Older People: A Consultation.* Sydney: NSW Consultative Committee on Aging

Sargent, M. 1996. Empowering options in housing and design for older people. *Proceedings of National Conference on Housing and Aging Society,* Canberra, Department of Transport and Regional Development.

Sargent, M., Nilan P., and Winter, G. 1997. *The new sociology for Australians.* 4th ed. Melbourne: Longman Cheshire.

Sax, S. 1993. *Aging and public policy in Australia.* Sydney: Allen and Unwin.

Schmidt, M. G. 1990. *Negotiating a good old age—Challenges of residential living in later life.* San Francisco: Jossey-Bass.

Scrutton, S. 1995. *Bereavement and grief: Supporting older people through loss.* London: Arnold Press.

Seccombe, K., and Lee G. 1986. Gender differences in retirement satisfaction and its antecedents. *Research on Aging* 8, 3: 426–40.

Seligman, M.E.P. 1975. *Helplessness on depression, development and death.* San Francisco: W. H. Freeman and Company.

Sheard, J. 1986. *The politics of volunteering.* London: Advance.

Short, S. D., and Sharman, E. 1989. The nursing struggle in Australia. In *Sociology of health and illness*, edited by G. M. Lupton, & J. Najman. Melbourne: Macmillan.

———. 1990. *Feminist reconstructions of health-care and their relevance for nursing in Australia*. Women's health studies discussion papers and research reports, No.2, Cumberland College of Health Sciences, Lidcombe, The University of Sydney.

Short, S. D., Sharman, E., and Speedy, S. 1993. *Sociology for nurses: An Australian introduction*. Melbourne: Macmillan Education Australia.

Silverstone, R., and Ward, A. 1980. *Careers of professional women*. London: CroomHelm

Singer, L. 1993. *Erotic welfare: Sexual theory and politics in the age of epidemic*. New York: Routledge.

Smart, C. 1991. Penetrating women's bodies: The problem of law and medical technology. In *Gender, Power and Sexuality*, edited by P. Abbott & C. Wallace. London: MacMillan.

Smith, D. 1994. How the phone puts us through the wringer. *Sydney Morning Herald*, May 30, 11.

Social Policy Directorate NSW and Australian Bureau of Statistics. 1995. *Older people in New South Wales: A profile*. Sydney: Office on Aging.

Sontag, S. 1978. The Double Standard of Aging. In *An Aging Population*, edited by V. Carver, and P. Liddiard. London: Hodder and Stoughton in association with Open University Press.

Spender, D. 1983. *Feminist thoughts: Three centuries of women's intellectual traditions*. London: Women's Press.

Spenner, K. I., and Rosenfeld, R. A. 1990. Women, work and Identities. *Social Science Research* 19: 266–99.

Stanley, L., and Wise, S. 1983. *Breaking out*. London: Routledge and Kegan Paul.

Statistics Canada 1997. *A portrait of seniors in Canada*, 89-519-XPE. Statistics Canada.

Staples, L. H. 1990. Powerful Ideas about Empowerment. *Administration in Social Work*. 14, 2: 29–42.

Starkman, E. M. 1993. *Learning to sit in the silence: A journal of caretaking*. Watsonville: Papier-Mache Press.

Stella, R., and Tulpule, A. 1994. *Australia's Aging Society*. Canberra: Economic Planning Advisory Council.

Stewart, A. J., and Malley, J. E. 1989. Case studies of agency and communion in women's lives. In *Representations: Social constructions of gender*, edited by R. K. Urger. Amityville, NY: Baywood Publishing.

Suls, J., and Mullen, B. 1981. Life change and psychological distress: The role of perceived control and desirability. *Journal of Applied Social Psychology* 11, 5: 379–89.

Swain, C., and Harrison, J. 1979. The Nursing Home As Total Institution. *Australian Journal of Social Issues* 14, 4: 274–83.

Sweet, M. 1994. A Cancer in the System. *Sydney Morning Herald*, 19/9/94.

———. 1994. Heart disease—women lose out. *Sydney Morning Herald*, 10/9/94.

Swindell, R. 1993. The University of the third age in Australia: a model for successful aging. *Aging and Society* 13: 2.

———. 1995. Intellectual change in later life: Why bother? *Social Alternatives* 14, 2: 15–19.

Sybylla, R. 1990. Old plans, new specifications: A political reading of the medical discourse on menopause. *Australian Feminist Studies* 12, Summer, pp. 95–107.

Szinovacz, M., and Washo, C. 1992. Gender differences in exposure to life events and adaptation to retirement. *Journal of Gerontology* 47, 4: 191–96.

Thone, R. R. 1992. *Women and aging: Celebrating ourselves*. New York: Harrington Park Press.

Tong, R. 1989. *Feminist thought: A comprehensive introduction*. Sydney: Unwin Hyman.

Townsend P. 1981. The structured dependency of the elderly: A creation of social policy in the twentieth century. *Aging and Society* 1: 5–28.

United Nations 1996 *The aging of the world's population: Preparing for the International Year of Older Persons in 1999* New York: United Nations Department of Public Information DPI/1858/AGE.

Urban Design Task Force 1994 *Urban design in Australia: Report by the Prime Minister's Urban Design Task Force*. Canberra: Australian Government Publishing Service.

Villekoop-Baldock, C. 1990. *Volunteers in Welfare*. Sydney: Allen and Unwin.

Voges, W., and Pongratz, H. 1988. Retirement and the lifestyles of older women. *Aging and Society* 8: 63–84.

Wajcman, J. 1992. *Feminism confronts technology*. Sydney: Allen and Unwin.

Walkem, B. 1995. Quality care for the hospitalised elderly: Can nurses actualize this goal? In *Issues in Australian nursing*, edited by G. Gray and R. Pratt. Melbourne: Churchill Livingstone.

Walker, A. 1983. Care for elderly people: A conflict between women and the state. In *A Labor of Love: Women, Work and Caring*, edited by J. Finch and D. Groves. London: Routledge and Kegan Paul.

------. 1995. From acquiescence to dissent? A political sociology of Aging in the UK. Melbourne: International Sociological Association Intercongress Meeting.

Walker, B. 1988. *The Crone*. San Francisco: Harper and Row.

Walker, J. 1989. Labor market structure in the community services sector and the development of community care. *National Economic Review* 11: 102–14.

Warburton, J., Rosenman, L., and Winour, S. 1995. The Meaning of Retirement. *Social Alternatives* 14: 2.

Ward, D., and Mullender, A. 1991. Empowerment and oppression: An indissoluble pairing for contemporary social work. *Critical Social Policy* 32: 21–30.

Waring, M. 1988. *Counting for nothing: What men value and what women are worth*. Wellington: Allen and Unwin.

Watson, E. A., and Mears, J. n.d *Women in the middle: Care givers with a double burden of care*. Sydney: Faculty of Arts and Social Sciences, University of Western Sydney, Macarthur.

Watson, S. 1986. *Housing and homelessness: A feminist perspective*. London: Routledge and Kegan Paul.

------. 1988. *Accommodating inequality: Gender and housing*, Sydney: Allen and Unwin.

------. 1995. Reclaiming social policy. In *Transitions: New Australian Feminisms*, edited by B. Caine and R. Pringle. Sydney: Allen and Unwin.

Watt, A., and Rodmell, S. 1993. Community involvement in health promotion: Progress or panacea? In M. *Health and Wellbeing: A reader*, edited by A. Beattie, M. Gott, L. Jones, and M. Siddell. London: Macmillan/The Open University.

Waxler, N. E. 1981. Social labelling and other patterns of social communication—The social labelling perspective on illness and medical practice. In *The Relevance of Social Science for Medicine - Culture, Illness and Healing 1*, edited by L. Eisenberg and A. Kleinman. Holland: D. Reidel Publishing.

Wearing, B. 1990. Beyond the ideology of motherhood: Leisure as resistance. *Australia and New Zealand Journal of Sociology* 26, 1: 36–58.

Weedon, C. 1987. *Feminist practice and poststructuralist Theory*. Oxford: Blackwell.

Wenger, G. 1982. Aging in rural communities: Family contacts and community integration. *Aging and Society* 2, 2: 211–29.

Wicks, D. 1995. Nurses and doctors and discourses of healing. *The Australian and New Zealand Journal of Sociology* 31, 2: 122–39.

Wieneke, C., and Arrowsmith, R. 1993. *When I'm 65 ... or 70 or 75 ... Women and the abolition of retirement age.* Hawkesbury: University of Western Sydney,

Wieneke, C., Power, A., Bevington, L. and Rankins-Smith, D. 1994. *Separate lives: Older women, connectedness and well-being.* Hawkesbury: University of Western Sydney.

Wiggins, J. S. 1991. Agency and communion as conceptual coordinates for the understanding and measurement of interpersonal behavior. In *Thinking Clearly about Psychology,* 2, edited by W. M. Grove and D. Cicchetti. Minneapolis: University of Minneapolis Press.

Wilkinson, S., and Kitzinger, C. 1993. 'Whose breast is it anyway? A feminist consideration of advice and "Treatment" for Breast Cancer. *Women's Studies International Forum* 16, 3: 229–38.

Williams, B. 1975. *Kevin's Grandma.* Illustrated by K. Chorao. New York: E. P. Dutton and Co. Ltd.

Willis, E. 1989. *Medical dominance, the division of labor in Australian health.* 2nd ed. Sydney: Allen and Unwin.

Wilson, D. 1995. Continuing Employment. *Positive Aging: Recognition and Reward, Two Day Seminar, 6-7 July, 1995,* Sydney, Australian Federation of University Women Inc., pp. 51–63.

Wolf, N. 1991. *The Beauty Myth.* London: Vintage.

Wolfe, D., and Kolb, D. 1980. Beyond specialization: The quest for integration in midcareer. In *Work, Family and the Career,* edited by C. Derr. New York: Praeger.

Yeandle, S. 1984. Women's working lives: Patterns and strategies. London: Tavistock.

Young, M., and Schuller. T. 1991. Life after work: The Arrival of the ageless society. London: Harper and Collins.

Index

hostels, 187
housing, 35–37, 59, 157, 177–193, *see also*
        home, living in own; nursing
        homes
    as a human right, 185–186, 192
    cooperatives, 189–190
    government policy, 141–143,
        182–184, 190–193
    rental, 188, 191
    social class divisions, 182–183
Housing Options for Older Women
        (HOOW), 189–190
Housing Options for Women, 187
human agency, *see* agency
human rights, 185–186, 192
human sciences, 127, 133–135

I

identity, 12–13, 111–113, 152–153, *see*
        also images of older women;
        self-esteem
    and breast cancer, 122
    and community, 158, 162
    in nursing homes, 144–145, 147,
        152–153
    life-courses, 199, 204–205
illnesses, *see* disease (illnesses)
images of older women, 7–8, 12–19,
        110–111, 171, 175, *see also*
        labels
    and medicalization, 129
    and sexuality, 153
    good nursing home resident, 147
    Growing Old Disgracefully, 210
income, 26–32, *see also* paid work ;
        retirement income
    and trade unions, 75
    gender wage gap, 28, 64
    versus meaningful work, 90–91
independence, 178–181, *see also*
        dependence; home, living in
        own
    and connections, 163–164
    housing options, 150, 186, 189, 191
    Separate Lives project, 159–170
indigenous women, 11, 24–25, 71
individual time, 161–162, 202–204

individuality, *see* identity
infantalizing processes, 70
institutional settings, *see* nursing homes
interpersonal relationships, *see*
        friendship; marriage
isolation, 158–160, 164–166, 168–171

K

kinship networks, *see* family
knowledge, 41, 44–45, 126–127
    and feminist theory, 54–55

L

labels, 2–3, 145, 171, 175–176, *see also*
        images of older women
labor force participation, *see* paid work
        (employment)
"learned helplessness", 145
learning, *see* education
lesbian feminists, 89
liberal feminism, 50–51
life experience, *see also* experiential
        analysis
    and knowledge of death, 228–234
    life course approach, 105, 195–205
living independently, *see* home, living
        in own; independence
loneliness, 163, 165–166
longevity, 23, 169–170

M

males, 24, 151, *see also* gender
mammographic screening program,
        109–110, 114–122
marginalization, 18–19
    and housing, 177–180, 185–186
marriage, 164–165, 168–169
    retirement income, 72–73, 103–104
masculinity, *see* males
Mature Workers Advisory Committee
        Strategic Plan, 74
media images of older women, 7–8,
        12–16, 18, 175
medical dominance, 42–45, 125, 128
medical model, 42–43, 58–59, 127–133
    and death, 45, 220

ERUPTIONS
New Thinking across the Disciplines

Erica McWilliam
General Editor

This is a series of red-hot women's writing after the "isms." It focuses on new cultural assemblages that are emerging from the de-formation, breakout, ebullience, and discomfort of postmodern feminism. The series brings together a post-foundational generation of women's writing that, while still respectful of the idea of situated knowledge, does not rely on neat disciplinary distinctions and stable political coalitions. This writing transcends some of the more awkward textual performances of a first generation of "feminism-meets-postmodernism" scholarship. It has come to terms with its own body of knowledge as shifty, inflammatory, and ungovernable.

The aim of the series is to make this cutting edge thinking more readily available to undergraduate and postgraduate students, researchers and new academics, and professional bodies and practitioners. Thus, we seek contributions from writers whose unruly scholastic projects are expressed in texts that are accessible and seductive to a wider academic readership.

Proposals and/or manuscripts are invited from the domains of: "post" humanities, human movement studies, sexualities, media studies, literary criticism, information technologies, history of ideas, performing arts, gay and lesbian studies, cultural studies, post-colonial studies, pedagogics, social psychology, and the philosophy of science. We are particularly interested in publishing research and scholarship with international appeal from Australia, New Zealand, and the United Kingdom.

For further information about the series and for the submission of manuscripts, please contact:

Erica McWilliam
Faculty of Education
Queensland University of Technology
Victoria Park Rd., Kelvin Grove Q 4059
Australia